COLLABORATIVE
AUTOETHNOGRAPHY

DEVELOPING QUALITATIVE INQUIRY

Series Editor: Janice Morse
University of Utah

Books in the new **Developing Qualitative Inquiry** series, written by leaders in qualitative inquiry, will address important topics in qualitative methods. Targeted to a broad multidisciplinary readership, the books are intended for mid-level/advanced researchers and advanced students. The series will forward the field of qualitative inquiry by describing new methods or developing particular aspects of established methods.

Series Editorial Board

H. Russell Bernard, Kathy Charmaz, D. Jean Clandinin, Juliet Corbin, Carmen de la Cuesta, John Engel, Sue E. Estroff, Jane Gilgun, Jeffrey C. Johnson, Carl Mitcham, Katja Mruck, Judith Preissle, Jean J. Schensul, Sally Thorne, John van Maanen, Max van Manen

Volumes in this Series:

1. *Autoethnography as Method*, Heewon Chang
2. *Interpretive Description*, Sally Thorne
3. *Developing Grounded Theory: The Second Generation*, Janice M. Morse, Phyllis Noerager Stern, Juliet Corbin, Barbara Bowers, Kathy Charmaz, and Adele E. Clarke
4. *Mixed Method Design: Principles and Procedures*, Janice M. Morse and Linda Niehaus
5. *Playbuilding as Qualitative Research: A Participatory Arts-based Approach*, Joe Norris
6. *Poetry as Method: Reporting Research Through Verse*, Sandra L. Faulkner
7. *Duoethnography: Dialogic Methods for Social, Health, and Educational Research*, Joe Norris, Richard D. Sawyer, and Darren E. Lund, editors
8. *Collaborative Autoethnography*, Heewon Chang, Faith Wambura Ngunjiri, and Kathy-Ann C. Hernandez

COLLABORATIVE AUTOETHNOGRAPHY

Heewon Chang
Faith Wambura Ngunjiri
Kathy-Ann C. Hernandez

Walnut Creek, California

LEFT COAST PRESS, INC.
1630 North Main Street, #400
Walnut Creek, CA 94596
http://www.LCoastPress.com

ISBN 978-1-59874-555-9 hardback
ISBN 978-1-59874-556-6 paperback
ISBN 978-1-61132-781-6 institutional eBook
ISBN 978-1-61132-680-2 consumer eBook

Library of Congress Cataloging-in-Publication Data:

Chang, Heewon, 1959-
Collaborative autoethnography / Heewon Chang, Faith Wambura Ngunjiri, Kathy-Ann C. Hernandez.
    p. cm.— (Developing qualitative inquiry vol.8)
  Includes bibliographical references and index.
  ISBN 978-1-59874-555-9 (hardback : alk. paper) — ISBN 978-1-59874-556-6 (pbk. : alk. paper) — ISBN 978-1-61132-781-6 (institutional eBook) — ISBN 978-1-61132-680-2 (consumer eBook)
  1. Ethnology—Authorship. 2. Ethnology—Research. 3. Ethnology—Methodology.
  I. Ngunjiri, Faith Wambura, 1973- II. Hernandez, Kathy-Ann C., 1968- III. Title.
  GN307.7.C43 2012
  305.8'00723—dc23
                    2012024594

Printed in the United States of America
♾™ The paper used in this publication meets the minimum requirements of American National Standard for Information Sciences—Permanence of Paper for Printed Library Materials, ANSI/NISO Z39.48–1992.

Contents

List of Illustrations   7

Preface   11

Chapter 1. What Is Collaborative Autoethnography?   17
            Autoethnography   18
            Autoethnography and Collaborative Autoethnography   21
            Collaborative Autoethnography   23
            Benefits of Collaborative Autoethnography   25
            Challenges of Collaborative Autoethnography   30
            Conclusion   35

Chapter 2. Typology of Collaborative Autoethnography   37
            The Size of Research Teams   37
            The Extent of Collaboration   40
            Modes of Collaboration   43
            Methodological Variations of Collaborative   46
            Autoethnography
            Conclusion   52

Chapter 3. Getting Ready for Collaborative Autoethnography   55
            Forming a Research Team   55
            Deciding on a Research Focus   62
            Selecting a Collaboration Model   67
            Defining Roles and Setting Boundaries   69
            Conclusion   71

Chapter 4. Data Collection   73
            Collection of Diverse Data   73
            Personal Memory and Archival Data   75
            Self-Observational Data   77
            Self-Reflective and Self-Analytical Data   78
            Conversational and Interactive Data   86
            Data Collection Strategies   87
            Conclusion   93

Chapter 5. Data Analysis and Interpretation   95
            Data Organization and Management   95
            Logistical Considerations for Data Analysis   98
            and Interpretation

Data Analysis   101
To Use CAQDAS or Not, That Is the Question   109
Data Interpretation   110
Conclusion   113

Chapter 6.   Collaborative Autoethnographic Writing   115
The Writing Challenge   115
The Collaborative Writing Paradigm   117
Pre-Collaborative Autoethnography Writing   118
Collaborative Autoethnography Writing   123
Post-Collaborative Autoethnography Writing   131
Conclusion   134

Chapter 7.   Applications of Collaborative Autoethnography   137
Practice in the Classroom   137
Building Community   142
Research as Activism   145
Tool for Critical Work   146
Professional Development   147
Conclusion   148

Epilogue: Our Approach   151
The Beginnings   151
Planning Our Data Collection   152
Collaborative Autoethnography Writing   153
In Retrospect   157

Notes   159

References   161

Appendix A   Writing Prompts Used for Individualized   171
Data Collection

Appendix B   Article: "Exemplifying Collaborative   175
Autoethnographic Practice via Shared Stories of
Mothering" by Geist-Martin et al.

Index   189

About the Authors   199

Illustrations

Figures

Figure 1-1   Autoethnography continuum   19
Figure 1-2   Common dimensions of AA/CAE   22
Figure 1-3   The iterative process of collaborative   24
              autoethnography
Figure 4-1   An example of a culturegram   80
Figure 4-2   Symbols used for a kinsgram (Chang, 2008, p. 83)   81
Figure 4-3   An example of a kinsgram (Chang, 2008, p. 84)   82
Figure 4-4   An example of a sociogram   83
Figure 4-5   A constellation of social relationships   84
Figure 4-6   A Venn diagram of our similarities and differences   85
Figure 4-7   The sequential model of data collection   91
Figure 5-1   Micro-coding example   105
Figure 5-2   Relationships among codes, categories, and themes   106

Tables

Table 2-1   Comparison among various collaborative   47
              autoethnographic approaches
Table 4-1   Autoethnographic data types   74
Table 6-1   CAE supporting member tasks and responsibilities   122
Table 6-2   Prominent typologies of collaborative   125
              autoethnography writing

To
Each of Our Husbands
Klaus, Chas, and Mark
Our Collaborators in Life

Preface

Collaborative autoethnography. Sounds like an oxymoron, don't you think? Autoethnography is the study of self, writing about individual experiences of life within the context of family, work, schooling, and society and interpreting the meanings of the experiences. Collaboration entails doing so with others. How could an exploration of self be done collaboratively? Indeed, collaborative autoethnography (CAE) is engaging in the study of self, collectively; it is a process and product of an ensemble performance, not a solo act. In the last three or four years of presenting conference workshops on CAE as a research approach, participants have asked us many questions. "Can autoethnography [the study focusing on self] be done collaboratively?" "How much collaboration is needed?" "How much should I share?" "What are my ethical obligations to sharing personal incidents that involve others?" "How does one effectively deal with the issue of several voices in the research process?"

In this book, we share our perspective on the collaborative approach, using our experience as well as a review of published CAE books and articles to answer these and many other questions. Our goal is to articulate the current state of CAE as a research method, to offer a scaffold for supporting researchers who are interested in using CAE, and to address some of the legitimate challenges and opportunities inherent in this approach. There have been many participants in our workshops who showed genuine interest in CAE as a research method and as a way to engage in action research; their interest and feedback was the impetus for writing this book.

In 2009, Heewon, who had published *Autoethnography as Method* (2008), invited Faith and Kathy-Ann to join her in designing a CAE project. During our initial meeting, we realized that our starting point for such a project ought to be our shared experience as immigrants, women, and *minoritized* faculty in the U.S. academy. Thus began the project on "exploiting the margins," where we explored navigational strategies that had enabled us to be successful in the academy in the midst of discovering new identities as minorities and "women of color" in the United States.

Our project soon grew beyond our initial imagination, to involve not only collecting, analyzing, and interpreting autoethnographic data on our own experiences, but also to design a grant that would have enabled us to expand our CAE to women of color in other institutions, conference presentations of our collaborative project, and eventually many collaborative/autoethnography workshops in conferences as diverse as the International Leadership Association, the Pennsylvania Teacher Educators Association, the International Congress of Qualitative Inquiry, and the American Anthropological Association. We also expanded our collaborative efforts to include coediting a special issue on "Autoethnography as Method" for the *Journal of Research Practice* (Vol. 6, Issue 1), writing individual autoethnographies for a book on *Spirituality in Higher Education* that Heewon coedited, and article manuscripts on CAE method and on our exploiting the margins study.

We have, therefore, benefited tremendously, growing in our individual and collective productivity in the academy. We have also grown in our understanding of theoretical perspectives because we are an interdisciplinary team: anthropology of education (Heewon), leadership studies (Faith), and educational psychology (Kathy-Ann). As we indicate in the epilogue to this book where we provide in-depth details of our process, we have also grown as friends and continue to support each other in the academy where Heewon is a full professor with tenure, Kathy-Ann is an associate professor with tenure, and Faith is the junior professor of the team—an assistant professor who is not yet tenured. We are definitely sisters in the academy. But we have not done this all by ourselves as a research team; others have also been involved (yes, even implicated) in our journeys thus far, and we acknowledge them later in this preface. But first, let us give you a succinct introduction to the contents of the book (or e-book) you hold in your hands.

The book consists of seven chapters and an epilogue: two conceptual chapters and five methodological chapters. In Chapter 1, we introduce CAE as a qualitative research method that is both autoethnographic and collaborative. We also explicate the benefits of employing CAE such as power sharing, learning from one another, and efficiency in engaging in qualitative data collection. Finally, we explore the limitations inherent in a collaborative project

In Chapter 2, we explain the broad categorizations of CAE designs depending on the size of research teams (in pairs or with three or more members), the extent of collaboration (full or partial), and the modes of collaboration (sequential or concurrent). A variety of CAE models are also introduced, including autoethnographic conversations, CAE, community AE, duoethnography, and performative CAE.

In Chapter 3, we provide the practical guide of how to engage in a CAE project. In this chapter, we discuss logistic considerations for forming a team and deciding on a focus, then choosing the design, and applying ethical principles.

In Chapter 4, we provide detailed explanations about personal memory and archival data; self-observational, self-reflective, and self-analytical data; and conversational and interactive data. We also introduce different collection strategies such as sequential and concurrent collaboration models as well as individual and group collection strategies.

Chapter 5 focuses on data analysis and interpretation. Beginning with data organization and management techniques, we introduce various strategies for individual and collective analysis and interpretation of data. With a brief explanation of computer-assisted qualitative data analysis software, we offer our perspectives on the use of such a tool.

In Chapter 6, we try to make the process of collaborative writing more transparent. First, we discuss some of the persistent challenges in turning research into publishable pieces, challenges from which we ourselves are not immune, as well as the opportunities and challenges that occur when this is done as part of a CAE team. We then break down the writing process into three phases: (1) pre-CAE writing; (2) CAE writing; and (3) post-CAE writing.

In Chapter 7, we argue that research is inherently communal; CAE engenders the practice of community and collaborative learning. We summarize the uses and benefits of CAE as research method. We begin with CAE as used in the classroom and then demonstrate its use as activism research, in empowering co-researchers, and for professional development.

We end with an epilogue, where we go into details on our own process of CAE as a research approach. In the appendices, we provide one published CAE article that explained both the process the authors engaged in to collect, analyze, and interpret data and the process of writing their article for publication. It involves collaboration among faculty and graduate students at different stages of their academic careers (Geist-Martin et al., 2010). We also chose this article for pragmatic reasons: It was published in an open-access journal (*Journal of Research Practice*) freely available for use/reprinting. With the authors' blessings, we offer to you the pleasure of reading it. We would have wanted to provide an exemplar article written from the more evocative end of the spectrum but were not able to gain permission in time.

As mentioned previously, our journeys have involved and implicated others along the way. We begin by acknowledging those who have supported us as a team.

First, we want to express our deep gratitude to Dr. Mitch Allen, publisher of Left Coast Press, Inc., who has sustained his interest in our work and has encouraged us to spur on for more than two years. Without his firm commitment to our work, demand of accountability, and indefatigable patience, this project would not have seen the light of day. Thank you, Mitch, for having faith (pun intended) in us and in this book.

Dr. Janice Morse, the series editor of Developing Qualitative Inquiry, deserves our sincere acknowledgment. Dr. Morse, who has herself written many books, has a deep appreciation of the competing demands authors face when they try to put a book together in the midst of teaching and service obligations. Thank you for your grace, encouragement, and constructive criticism.

Dr. Linda Stine, our friend and copyeditor of the *International Journal of Multicultural Education* (www.ijme-journal.org), read our final manuscript thoroughly and provided quick turn around; thank you for your willing service to the cause! Your keen eyes caught many typos, awkward sentences, and incorrigible constructions; whatever mistakes remain are our responsibility alone.

We also want to thank Dr. David Greenhalgh, director of the Ph.D. program in Organizational Leadership at Eastern University, for his professional and financial support and encouragement that have resulted in our conference presentations and professional engagements. Thank you, David, for your willingness to be counter-cultural and for providing much needed support for our conference participation; your understanding of the need for doctoral faculty to be productive researchers has helped us achieve our individual, collective, and departmental goals.

Several others have also helped us sharpen our manuscript through reading and checking references. We want to acknowledge Dr. Harry Wolcott, Emeritus professor of anthropology at the University of Oregon, for his careful reading of the manuscript for valuable comments; Mrs. Maggie Madimbo and Mrs. Kay Nussbaum, doctoral students at Eastern University, for their thorough reference checking and thoughtful comments. Next, we want to express our profound gratitude to our families and friends whose support was imperative in this process: it took three villages to raise this one book.

I (Heewon) want to acknowledge my parents for their continuous inspiration. My father, Chin-Ho Chang, retired as educational sociologist from a professorial position in Korea 25 years ago and still writes and publishes books at the age of 90. My mother, Eui-Sook Cho, also retired as an education professor 24 years ago, keeps up with my father in her daily spiritual reading, and is still writing at the age of 89. I am humbled by their intellectual and spiritual energy. I am greatly indebted to both of them for my intellectual curiosity, spiritual reflection, innovation, and collaboration. I also want to thank my husband Klaus, daughter Hannah, and son Peter. Our stimulating (sometimes heated) conversations, provoking questions, calming encouragement, and nourishing music (solo or in ensemble) have sustained me throughout this long process.

I (Faith) want to acknowledge my best friend and partner Charles Henry Nowlin, III (aka Chas Munene Nowlin) for his patience, love, and understanding. My Munene, you were always responsive to my needs, ensuring I ate healthy meals and went to the gym (well, sometimes) in the midst of very busy writing periods. In spite of being a graduate student with a busy schedule, too, you were so accommodating. You woke me up to attend our Quaker meeting for worship so I would be nourished spiritually; you took me to the theater and concerts to ensure I had some semblance of work-life balance. Thank you, Chas. You are the best. I also acknowledge the faculty who faithfully participated in my Faculty Learning Community meetings, thus enhancing our collective productivity and ensuring accountability. I acknowledge my students and dissertation advisees who inspire me to keep learning and keep writing; I am so glad to have been a facilitator of your developing scholarly identity. Finally, I thank God, through whom all things are possible; I can do all things (write, publish, teach, advise dissertations, and have work-life balance) through Christ who strengthens me.

As Heewon and Faith have shared, no one gets through academic writing alone, we stand on the shoulders of others who support us through the ups and downs of giving life to our ideas in the form of words. I (Kathy-Ann) am indebted to my coauthors for inviting me to come along on this journey. It has been a great learning experience. I stand on the shoulders of my father, Peter Hernandez (deceased), who early in life instilled in me a love of learning and an appreciation for books. What a rich legacy! I am also grateful for the encouragement of the first writing mentor I ever had, my elementary schoolteacher, Anderson Antoine, who believed that I had it in me to write books someday. To my soul-mate and best friend, Mark Avery, I say thank you for your unwavering confidence in my abilities and for bringing me hot tea at 1 a.m. during some of those almost all-nighters; our faith is the source of all our accomplishments. Finally, I acknowledge my daughters, Alyssa and Amya, whose existence is a constant reminder to me to step away from my work and take time out for precious "life moments."

We have equally contributed to the making of this book, therefore we equally share responsibilities for the content and presentation. We hope that, like us, you will come to appreciate CAE as a rich addition to the field of social inquiry. We are excited to share it with you.

March 2012
Philadelphia, Pennsylvania
Heewon, Faith, and Kathy-Ann

CHAPTER 1

What Is Collaborative Autoethnography?

Collaborative autoethnography (CAE) is a qualitative research method that is simultaneously collaborative, autobiographical, and ethnographic. Putting these three terms together in one definition may appear to be oxymoronic. Ethnography, for example, is the study of a cultural group; therefore, pairing it with autobiography, the study of self, seems contradictory. Despite the seeming inconsistency, some qualitative researchers have succeeded in joining these two conceptual opposites to create a research method called autoethnography (AE). To this relatively recent approach to qualitative inquiry, we are adding another dimension—collaboration.

The notion of collaboration requiring group interaction seems directly at odds with that of a study of self. How can a study of self be done collaboratively? To answer this question, we ask you to imagine a group of researchers pooling their stories to find some commonalities and differences and then wrestling with these stories to discover the meanings of the stories in relation to their sociocultural contexts. The obvious follow-up questions are: If anyone intends to study self, why does he or she want to do it in the company of others? What are the benefits of exploring self in community rather than in solitude? These are the very questions we hope you will ask. Moreover, we hope you ask another question: How does one actually conduct a collaborative autoethnographic study?

In this chapter, we discuss how a study of self can be conducted in the company of others and how a study of individuals can be a catalyst to understanding group culture. We begin by explaining what AE is and then how it relates to CAE. We then discuss CAE as a social science research method and explain how the method preserves the unique strengths of self-reflexivity associated with autobiography, cultural interpretation associated with ethnography, and multi-subjectivity associated with collaboration.

AUTOETHNOGRAPHY

AE is a qualitative research method that focuses on self as a study subject but transcends a mere narration of personal history. Chang (2008, 2011) defines AE as a research method that enables researchers to use data from their own life stories as situated in sociocultural contexts in order to gain an understanding of society through the unique lens of self. This definition highlights two vital aspects of AE also noted by other AE scholars: (1) the use of autobiographic data; and (2) cultural interpretation of the connectivity between self and others (Anderson, 2006; Bochner & Ellis, 2002; Denzin, 1997; Ellis, 2004; Reed-Danahay, 1997). Researchers who embark on autoethnographic research methods have agreed on the importance of "data on the self" as relevant in social inquiry. By taking the liberty of "outing" their own experiences as the subject of exploration, autoethnographers reject "claims to objectivity" and value "subjectivity and researcher-participant intersubjectivity" (Foster, McAllister, & O'Brien, 2006, p. 47). Namely, they occupy dual roles of researchers and participants in their study. This approach to research challenges the hegemony of objectivity or the artificial distancing of self from one's research subjects. Instead, autoethnographers place value on being able to analyze self, their innermost thoughts, and personal information, topics that usually lie beyond the reach of other research methods.

How researchers interject their stories into the research process varies in autoethnographic research. Ellis and Bochner (2000) articulated the interplay among three components—auto, ethno, and graphy—in AE research: "Autoethnographers vary in their emphasis on the research process (*graphy*), on culture (*ethno*), and on self (*auto*)" such that "different exemplars of AE fall at different places along the continuum of each of these three axes" (p. 740). We translate their thinking into a continuum anchoring on two ends, one emphasizing autobiography and the other ethnography (see Figure 1-1). On the autobiographic end, researchers are likely to put more emphasis on self (auto) narration (graphy); on the ethnographic end, researchers focus more on the cultural interpretation (ethno) of self (auto). The continuum of AE research allows researchers of various disciplines to self-select their positionality in telling their interpretive stories. What researchers bring to this method of inquiry is an approach to research that will ultimately reflect their level of comfort with emotive self-disclosure and personal orientation in conducting research.

Attention to self is indeed a unique feature of this method of inquiry. However, AE must be distinguished from autobiography, which focuses on personal stories. Autoethnographers use personal stories as windows to the world, through which they *interpret* how their selves are

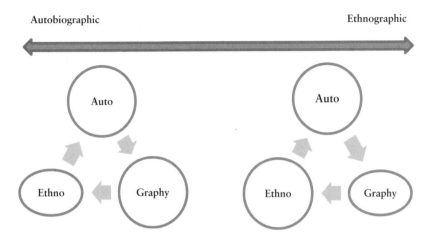

Figure 1-1 Autoethnography continuum.

connected to their sociocultural contexts and how the contexts give meanings to their experiences and perspectives. Intentional and systematic consideration of various autobiographical data give rise to autoethnographic interpretation that transcends mere narration of their past to help researchers reach explanations of the sociocultural phenomena connected to the personal. They tell stories to *explain* how they respond to their environments in certain ways and how their sociocultural contexts have shaped their perspectives, behaviors, and decisions. The sociocultural interpretation of self-society connectivity sets this inquiry method apart from other self-narratives such as autobiography and memoir. With this distinctive goal, autoethnographers explore their own experiences to construct interpretive narration (presented most frequently as evocative stories) or narrative interpretation (presented more often in academic discourse).

Ellis and Bochner, pioneers of autoethnographic work, lean more toward "interpretive narration" (Ellis, 2004, 2009; Ellis & Bochner, 2000). Their approach to AE has been linked to the adjective "evocative" (Ellis, 1997) or "heartfelt" (Ellis, 1999) AE. The focus is on challenging researchers to embrace an approach to writing that favors emotional self-reflexivity as a rich data source. Many followers of this orientation have produced evocative autoethnographies, focusing on personal matters traditionally shunned by social scientists: for example, abortion (Ellis & Bochner, 1992), teen pregnancy (Muncey, 2005), death and grief (Ellis, 1995; Wyatt, 2008), mother-daughter relations in the midst of illness (Ellis, 1996), childhood with a psychotic parent (Foster, McAllister, & O'Brien, 2005), childhood with a "mentally retarded" mother (Ronai, 1996), motherhood with a schizophrenic child (Schneider, 2005), sexual abuse (Fox, 1996), domestic violence (Olson, 2004), bulimia (Tillmann-Healy, 1996), brain injury (Smith, 2005), illness (Ettorre, 2005; Kelley & Betsalel, 2004; Neville-Jan, 2003), pregnancy as a gay couple (Atkins, 2008), and a spiritual journey as an academic (Abigail, 2011; Poplin, 2011).

Anderson (2006), however, was concerned that a narrow focus on "evocative or emotional ethnography may have the unintended consequence" of stymieing the development of this emerging practice (p. 374). Unlike the evocative approach to AE, which can be based solely on the experience of the researcher, Anderson insisted that analytical AE must involve data from others. His advocacy of involving others in autoethnographic studies has not been received favorably by solo autoethnographers (although his suggestion does inform the work of some collaborative autoethnographers). However, his plea for an analytical approach to autoethnographic interpretation is well aligned with the orientation of "narrative interpretation" (the ethnographic end in the continuum). Others (Chang, 2008; Reed-Danahay, 1997) advocate an AE akin to more conventional ethnography, grounded on ethnographic data collection, analysis, and interpretation. This approach has been used for studies of both personal and professional topics. Many examples of analytical autoethnographies have been published. On the topic of the work-life-family balance, Cohen, Duberley, and Musson (2009), Galman (2011), and Geist-Martin et al. (2010)[1] stand out. Regarding professional responsibilities in the academy, we can point to works on teaching practices (Duarte, 2007; Hernandez, 2011; Romo, 2004), research agenda (Ngunjiri, 2011), and the role of an administrator (Walford, 2008). These are only a fraction of the autoethnographies written in academic discourse.

We do not argue that one style of expression is superior to the other or that both styles cannot be mixed. The ultimate goal of self-inquiry may differ, depending on philosophical orientations specific to one's discipline. Whereas those schooled in qualitative social phenomena, as Anderson (2006) described, may adopt more analytic paradigms, others may choose to share the specificity of their experiences in more evocative discourse. All examples we have provided so far have adopted the medium of prose. AE can also be presented in more creative and performative mediums such as poetry (Ricci, 2003) or drama scripts (Cann & DeMeulenaere, 2010; McMillan & Price, 2010; Pelias, 2002). Although means of expression may differ depending on researchers' personal and professional preferences, Vryan (2006) argues that all kinds of AE engage cultural analysis: "[T]here are many ways analysis via self-study may be accomplished, and the term analytic autoethnography should be applicable to all such possibilities" (p. 406). We agree that it is this embrace of cultural interpretation that distinguishes autoethnography from other autobiographic or self-narrative writings.

The use of self as a window to society gives a particular vantage point to autoethnographers compared to other social scientists because autoethnographic researchers can tap into their most personal thoughts and experiences that are not readily opened to others. In addition, with intimate understanding of their personal data from the beginning, they can significantly reduce the time needed to piece together fragmented data before entering into a holistic interpretation. Despite these benefits, AE has limitations. Since researchers are dealing with self-data all too familiar to themselves, they could be easily influenced by their own presumptions about personal experiences without the benefit of fresh perspectives from others who could question their presumptions. In addition to the danger of self-perpetuating perspectives, a study of one's self lacks the possibility of demonstrating researcher accountability during the research process because the researcher is also the participant. CAE attempts to overcome the limitations of potentially self-absorbing AE while preserving the wealth of personal data inherent in autoethnographic research.

AUTOETHNOGRAPHY AND COLLABORATIVE AUTOETHNOGRAPHY

AE was popularized as solo work in creative, evocative, and/or analytical AE paradigms within the last two decades. Due to its focus on the researcher self, AE became almost synonymous with the study of a person. However, collaborative projects have branched out of the foundational work of AE. CAE still focuses on self-interrogation but does so collectively and cooperatively within a team of researchers. A variety of labels have appeared in the literature to introduce multi-researcher AE designs, including: duoethnography (Lund & Nabavi, 2008a; Norris, Sawyer, & Lund, 2011; Sawyer & Norris, 2004, 2009), co-ethnography (Ellis & Bochner, 1992), collective AE (Cann & DeMeulenaere, 2010), co/autoethnographic (Coia & Taylor, 2006), CAE (Kalmbach Phillips et al., 2009; Rose, 2008), community autoethnography (Toyosaki et al., 2009), and community-based ethnography (Stringer et al., 1997). These labels grew out of authors' ingenuity in naming their self-refined methodology, not out of any logical typology of methods. Therefore, some differences among these labels may be merely nuanced and others substantive. In the next chapter, we tease out both nuanced and substantive differences to better understand methodological differences within CAE.

CAE is emerging as a pragmatic application of the autoethnographic approach to social inquiry. Before discussing CAE in depth in the following section, we will compare AE and CAE to identify commonalities and obvious differences (see Figure 1-2).

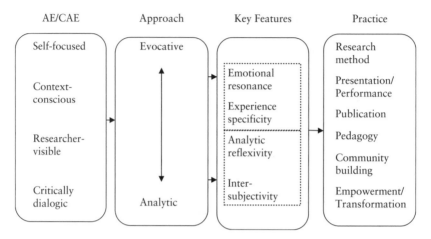

Figure 1-2   Common dimensions of AA/CAE.

Both AE and CAE are qualitative approaches to research that position self-inquiry at center stage. Though opinions differ about the purpose and scope of AE, the points of agreement remain robust. Drawing from the literature, we see both approaches to be self-focused, researcher-visible, context-conscious, and critically dialogic.

Self-Focused

The researcher assumes the dual role of researcher and research partici-pant; his or her views and experiences are under investigation even as he or she leads the investigation. Anderson (2006) calls this dual role "com-plete member researcher" (p. 378). In both AE and CAE, the researcher is simultaneously the instrument and the data source.

Researcher-Visible

Critical self-reflection is a corollary to being self-focused. The researcher turns the lens inward to make personal thoughts and actions visible and transparent to the audience. This is a critical perspective that is offered only by AE. The researcher is uniquely positioned to interrogate self and simultaneously be able to understand the nuances behind responses. Thus, autoethnographers are able to make the inner workings of their mind visible. Moreover, the researcher is free to explore this process in detail, as the focal point and not a subordinate element of research practice (Anderson, 2006; Atkinson, Coffey, & Delamont, 1999).

Context-Conscious

As part of the larger social context, the researcher's experiences and interrogation are presented as they shape and are shaped by specific contexts (Anderson, 2006). Ellis and Bochner (2000) describe the intricacy of studying self in context as follows:

> Back and forth autoethnographers gaze, first through an ethnographic wide angle lens, focusing outward on social and cultural aspects of their personal experience; then, they look inward, exposing a vulnerable self that is moved by and may move through, refract, and resist cultural interpretations. . . . As they zoom backward and forward, inward and outward, distinctions between the personal and cultural become blurred, sometimes beyond distinct recognition. (p. 739)

This continual juxtaposing of self and context is an essential element of autoethnographic work.

Critically Dialogic

The autoethnographic research process allows the researcher to become an active instrument and participant in creating meaning and constructing values (Anderson, 2006; Lapadat, 2009). Because AE enables individuals to occupy both researcher and participant perspectives simultaneously, a rich internal dialogue develops. In CAE, this dialogue is further enriched by each team member's occupation of these dual spaces as well as the dialogue that is created in community. In either scenario, this chameleonic capacity, unique in autoethnographic work, creates a rich space for meaning-making and analysis.

These commonalities are augmented in the teamwork of collaborative autoethnographers. One obvious difference between these two research methods is that autoethnographers interrogate their self-world by themselves and collaborative autoethnographers work together, building on each other's stories, gaining insight from group sharing, and providing various levels of support as they interrogate topics of interest for a common purpose. In the teamwork, researchers increase the sources of data from a single researcher to multiple researcher perspectives.

COLLABORATIVE AUTOETHNOGRAPHY

If AE is about interrogating the self to gain deeper understanding of "society and self," is there room for others in these interrogations? We say, "Yes!" We define CAE as a qualitative research method in which researchers work in community to collect their autobiographical materials and to analyze and interpret their data collectively to gain a meaningful understanding of sociocultural phenomena reflected in their autobiographical data. AE is to a solo performance as CAE is to an ensemble. While the combination of instruments creates a unique musical piece, the success of the composition is dependent on the authentic and unique contribution of each instrument. In CAE, each participant contributes to the collective work in his or her distinct and independent voice. At the same time, the combination of multiple voices to interrogate a social phenomenon creates a unique synergy and harmony that autoethnographers cannot attain in isolation.

In CAE, researchers can alternate between group and solo work. We argue that the combination of individual and group works adds rich texture to the collective work. When the group works together, individual voice is closely examined in community. Others' questioning and probing add unique depth to personal interrogation. The researchers can then retreat to embark on individual meaning-making—practicing their piece. Individual meaning-making is again followed by group meaning-making, which is negotiated among participants. In Figure 1-3, we illustrate this process that we practiced in our own CAE project (Ngunjiri, Hernandez, & Chang, 2010). Each step combining individual and group activities can be repeated for as many iterations as necessary. Also, researchers can return to a previous step to enhance data collection, analysis, or interpretation. Therefore, the research process is more iterative than linear.

Researchers may adopt this research approach to advance combinations of analytic and/or evocative research agendas. We lean more

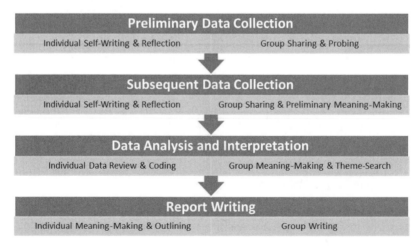

Figure 1-3 The iterative process of collaborative autoethnography.

toward narrative interpretation (analytical) rather than interpretative narration (evocative) of autobiographical data. The former approach is particularly well suited to the epistemological frameworks that guide our collective thinking. However, as stated above, because of the common threads in the practice of AE as method, researchers can find several commonalities between our approach and those advocated by the more evocative orientation. Whereas the debate on the analytical/evocative paradigm has at times been polarizing (see *Journal of Contemporary Ethnography*, Vol. 35, No. 4, 2006), we argue that CAE as an emerging research practice should not be limited to a particular approach or style of representation as long as it holds true to the salient aspects of methodological rigor. Rather, it should yield to the demands of the research community as it is shaped by the pragmatics of social inquiry and lends itself to the understanding of social phenomenon. Therefore, we include all orientations in our discussion.

BENEFITS OF COLLABORATIVE AUTOETHNOGRAPHY

CAE allows researchers to benefit simultaneously from self and collective analysis. The juxtaposition of these two seemingly contradictory frames of reference is useful to the researcher, also the inclusion of multiple voices and perspectives adds rigor to autobiographic interrogation. Several benefits can result from employing a CAE research method. Here we focus on five benefits relating to: (1) collective exploration of researcher subjectivity; (2) power-sharing among researcher-participants; (3) efficiency and enrichment in the research process; (4) deeper learning about self and other; and (5) community building.

Collective Exploration of Researcher Subjectivity

In the traditional paradigm, researchers are assigned to the role of actors and participants to the role of objects of investigation; researchers are expected to keep distance from the researched to maintain their objectivity. From this orientation, therefore, the injection of the researcher into their investigation is considered a capital offense.

However, as more and more researchers recognize the importance and inevitability of researcher subjectivity influencing their research process and product, many of them have crossed the researcher-participant divide by exploring their own subjectivity and interactivity with participants. In her study of race, Pompper (2010) took a retrospective look at how her ethnicity as a Caucasian woman had impacted her research practice to gain a deeper understanding of "self in socio-cultural context [as] both the subject and object of the research enterprise" (p. 1).

Similarly, Maydell (2010) examined how her ethnicity as a Russian immigrant studying identity construction among Russian immigrants in New Zealand was a critical subtext in understanding her own identity construction and a critical lens for viewing and interpreting her findings. Self-reflexivity allowed these researchers to examine the sort of researcher-participant interaction in their work that previously remained unreported or unexamined.

AE takes this paradigm of inquiry one step further: It merges the researcher and the participant. Merging two roles has given autoethnographers a vantage point of considering sociocultural phenomena from perspectives familiar to self as a researcher and participant. In reflecting on our scholarship, we have also found that the crafting of our individual research agendas was implicitly informed by our life stories. Chang (1992), trained as a high school teacher, chose to investigate the adolescents at a U.S. high school. Ngunjiri (2007, 2010), a Kenyan who has a seminary education and church work experience, focused on spiritual leadership among African women. Hernandez (2005, 2006), who grew up on the island of Trinidad and taught there, studied achievement among African Caribbean and African American high school students. Only recently have we allowed our research agendas to be explicitly influenced by our experiences, and we have chosen our common experiences as immigrant faculty of color as the subject of our CAE. CAE offers us a scholarly space to hold up mirrors to each other in communal self-interrogation and to explore our subjectivity in the company of one other.

Power-Sharing among Researcher-Participants

The relationship between researchers and participants in traditional paradigms is unequal. The researcher holds the power to interrogate, analyze, interpret, and represent the perspectives of research participants. This paradigm gets a dramatic make-over in CAE, where researchers are participants in their own studies. When researchers pool their personal stories and autobiographical material for collective examination, all become are subject to collective interrogation. This flipping of dynamics among researcher-participants puts all members of a research team on an even playing field.

Even in cases of collaborative research teams formed with preexisting power differentials, it is noticeable that power among researchers is diffused through collaboration. For example, such a shift has been observed in CAE teams made up of professors and graduate students (Chapman & Sork, 2001; Ellis, Kiesinger, & Tillmann-Healy, 1997; Lapadat et al., 2009). Sharing personal experiences and perspectives on topics of mutual interest made all members equally vulnerable to each other and became a liberating equalizer in their relationships.

Efficiency and Enrichment in the Research Process

What could be more efficient than having a ready-made sample of participants? Team members do not initially need to look further than their own experiences/lives to find rich data sources. Furthermore, since research agendas are often birthed in personal experiences, researchers are in a unique position of being able to collect relevant data effectively and expeditiously. The efficiency of CAE also lies in the team research model. Work involved in well-conceptualized and conducted studies is demanding. A team model enables researchers to pool their resources to achieve their research goals efficiently: They can collect a variety of data from a wider range of sources more quickly than solo researchers.

The team model is beneficial not only at the stage of data collection but also at the stage of data analysis and interpretation. In spite of ample evidence in support of an interdisciplinary approach to the study of social phenomenon, much social science research is painfully discipline-specific. The result is often research that does not bring to bear the theoretical advances of various fields to the study of complex social phenomenon. Through the process of collaboration on research projects, researchers can benefit from the insight of others from disciplines other than their own.

In our case, each of us comes from a different field of social science inquiry. In our collaborative work, we have recognized the value that each member adds to our conceptualization, analysis, and interpretation of data. The presence of other voices from different disciplines has challenged us to interrogate our understanding of what seems to be self-evident interpretations of data. For example, in one of our data collection sessions on the role of women's leadership in the academy, we discussed how women often chose to self-identify first as mothers or wives when introducing themselves in professional settings. We questioned why this was the case. From a leadership perspective, this could be interpreted as a coping mechanism for justifying one's place in a professional space. From a human development perspective, consistent with theories of life-span development, stages of personal development can provide a level of life satisfaction that supersedes career advancement. From an anthropological perspective, this practice could be interpreted as the result of socialization and enculturation into motherhood in the gendered culture. We wrestled with different disciplinary and conceptual frameworks and constructed *multifocal lenses* in our group interpretation sessions (Hernandez, Ngunjiri, & Chang, 2011).

Deeper Learning about Self and Other

Collaborative work has potential to engender a deeper understanding of self and others in the social and cultural context than is possible from a solo analysis. This is because, in the process of dialogically engaging with each other's stories, collaborators interrogate others' experiences intimately and deeply. An example from our project can illustrate how this plays out. In one of our data collection/data analysis conversations, one of us shared a brief comment about her parents' relationship but quickly moved on to another topic. The other team members immediately asked her to go deeper: "Tell us more about that." We were interested in how the perception of her parents' relationship as she was growing up impacted the choices she made about her own relationship with her spouse, especially as she had followed in her parents' footsteps in being part of a household of career academics. Here are some the questions that emerged:

- How did that make you feel about men and women in relationships?
- Did your upbringing impact the choices you made when you were raising your own children?
- Is it likely that your upbringing had something to do with how you became a strong-minded, feminist woman, in spite of the fact that this places you at odds with your culture of origin?

This kind of deep probing by team members was a recurring scenario throughout our collaborative work . . . meaning-making. Some things that might have remained hidden from the individual's view were more apparent to the co-researchers. In the process, not only did the collaborative product turn out better, but the individual stories became richer, uncovering those hidden assumptions and elaborating on previously taken-for-granted events that were perhaps critical incidents impacting our identity formation as women, wives, mothers, professors, and leaders. This kind of collaborative meaning-making requires that each team member be willing to be vulnerable and open with co-researchers in order to enable the deeper analysis and interrogation that enriches the final product.

Working collaboratively also offers each researcher the ability to tell her or his story in a way that connects with others. Having two or more co-researchers collectively making meaning of personal stories can enable them to reach a deeper level of analysis, connect the stories to wider issues within the disciplines, link to existing literature, and overall provide the scholarly balance necessary to keep it from being mere navel-gazing.

Community Building

The level of sharing that ensues from a collaborative autoethnographic research process inherently promotes community building among research participants. The use of this methodology easily lends itself to the study of under-researched or sensitive topics that might otherwise be ignored: for example, spiritual integration in university teaching (O'Shea et al., 2011), coalition among female academics in a Hispanic-serving institution (Nuñez, Murakami-Ramalho, & Cuero, 2010), White privilege and racial issues (Toyosaki et al., 2009), and feminist identity (Kalmbach Phillips et al., 2009). Participants who would perhaps benefit significantly from this research approach are often the ones whose stories have been silenced in academic and public circles.

To tell one's life story effectively requires an honest level of sharing among participants. Published collaborative autoethnographies, including the aforementioned studies, represent communities resulting from their time-tested relationships through communal sharing of stories but also mutual probing into their private space. When their stories and interpretation were shared in a public space such as publication, sensitive care had gone into protecting each other's confidentiality as well as that of others who were implicated in these stories (Hernandez & Ngunjiri, 2013). One example is evident in the performative script of Weems et al. (2009), in which their personal experience with racial discrimination in their department is infused into the voices of composite characters.

When sensitive issues are discussed as being experienced collectively (e.g., racial discrimination in the workplace, sexual harassment, and mental health challenges), the individuals who have experienced them can have their identities protected in the group stories—stories that are sometimes told as allegories or with fictional characters. Pearce (2010) noted that telling one's stories of struggles with traumatic life events can be both cathartic and emotionally draining, sometimes opening wounds afresh and raising questions with no answers. Further, in an article reflecting on her struggles to write about her own eating disorder, Chatham-Carpenter (2010) observed the need first to "do thyself no harm" as the autoethnographers. We argue that working within a team offers autoethnographers grappling with such traumatic issues and events an opportunity to enjoy the catharsis of sharing their stories, while at the same time also getting the help they need from the co-researchers, such as when and how to protect themselves, how to tell the stories authentically yet without unnecessarily placing themselves at risk. Furthermore, the team can offer the individual researcher the accountability necessary—when to place brakes on the storytelling in order to cry together or seek help.

CHALLENGES OF COLLABORATIVE AUTOETHNOGRAPHY

While CAE seems to be the answer to some of the persistent challenges that face researchers, it is not without its share of challenges. We discuss a few of those challenges below: (1) vulnerability and trustworthiness; (2) logistical challenges; (3) interdependency of research efforts; (4) the other side of multivocality; (5) team effort; and (6) ethics and confidentiality.

Vulnerability and Trustworthiness

Research relies on the honest responses of participants. In CAE, the quality of the data quickly deteriorates if participants are not willing to be transparent with each other. This can limit the extent to which the team can explore issues deeply and honestly. While CAE does promote community building, that building is predicated on some initial trust and goodwill among participants. When trust is not fully established, participants may be tempted to affirm each other too quickly and reach a consensus, which can compromise the trustworthiness of data. However, this challenge often works itself out, since individuals who share common interests and ideas often organically gravitate toward each other with an implicit understanding of trust and vulnerability. Given the intimate nature of group sharing, it is often also possible that researchers work together or share similar contexts and are already privy to some aspect of each other's vulnerabilities.

When researchers want to attempt CAE with individuals outside their social network, it may be necessary to embark on some form of community building prior to actual data collection. Since trustworthiness among participants is essential to accurate data collection, researchers interested in embarking on CAE should weigh the members' level of comfort with group sharing when forming CAE teams. We discuss this in detail in Chapter 3.

Logistical Challenges

CAE requires frequent contact and communication. Many CAE efforts have come from researchers who share some type of social context and benefit from this kind of proximity. We are aware of only a few studies that involved a part or a whole research team collaborating from distant locations (Geist-Martin et al., 2010; Toyosaki et al., 2009). Insufficient examples are perhaps indicative of logistical challenges, among others.

We have been fortunate in that we work at the same institution, which affords us great flexibility in the frequency and length of our meetings. Whereas we have at times met using web-conferencing and e-mail, we value the richness of face-to-face communication. In CAE, deep probing and interrogating benefit from reading and understanding nonverbal communication—intonations, pauses, grimaces, gestures, smiles, and sighs. As the team of researchers builds community, the level of sharing intrudes in everyday communication and can become rich data for further analysis. In one of our projects in which we continue to interrogate the experiences of women of color in higher education, we have had some of our most profound insights in unplanned moments of sharing—working on committees, chit-chatting over a celebratory birthday luncheon for Heewon, planning Faith's wedding, and visiting Kathy-Ann in the hospital after the birth of her second child. These moments of sharing would not have been possible had we not been so close to each other. Where such proximity is not possible for the team, however, researchers can creatively strategize how best to utilize technology to achieve similar results.

Interdependency of Research Efforts

Like other methods of ethnography, data collection continues until a point of saturation is reached where no new information surfaces. In 2009, we began working on the aforementioned project on the experiences of women of color in higher education. Since our work is dependent on each other and not on us as individuals, we have had to stop-start to accommodate schedule changes and life challenges—marriage, the birth of a child, a move to a new house, and demands of our individual research agendas. This can be a problem for academicians used to having autonomy over their own schedules and publishing agendas.

In an effort to deal with this challenge, we view our collaboration as another arm of our research agenda, so that our efforts at publications are not stymied by the vagaries of life and we are not held hostage to our co-researchers' agendas. As important to us as the research collaboration is, it is equally important to preserve the community and not harbor feelings of resentment about each other by accepting the challenge as an inevitable aspect of collaborative work. At the same time, we have tried to set clear expectations as to deadlines and commitments, with the understanding that we are accountable to each other.

The Other Side of Multivocality

We view one of the strengths of CAE as the critical perspective that is offered when multiple voices are part of the research process. Moreover, as Anderson (2006) observed about AE, each of us is "a more analytical and self-conscious participant in the conversation than is the typical group member, who may seldom take a particularly abstract or introspective orientation to the conversation and activities" (p. 382). As each researcher is involved in the collection, analysis, and interpretation of the research data, the potential for being unduly influenced by the voices of one or more assertive team members is a persistent challenge.

How does one distinguish between consensus building and coercion? Can dominant voices in a group silence other voices? Or, rather than being a belligerent exception to a group position, will a member acquiesce and give up his or her convictions? This is a real challenge that we have grappled with in our work. The strategy for dealing with it is not new to other attempts at collaborative efforts and adds to the rigor of qualitative inquiry (see Geist-Martin et al. [2010], who discuss this struggle in their own work). As we continue to advocate for trustworthiness and authenticity in the field (Creswell, 2012; Hansen et al., 2007), it is imperative that researchers discuss and write about the challenge of representing multiple voices and open up their processes to scrutiny (Anfara, Brown, & Mangione, 2002; Denzin & Lincoln, 2000). This is part of our ethical responsibility as social science researchers. Moreover, representing multiple voices and discussing the challenges involved enhances the methodological rigor.

Team Effort

While team effort can be a more efficient way for completing a complex task, it is also fraught with several opportunities that can slow down the process. Consensus building or multi-dimensional consideration of interpretive possibilities can be slow and tedious. Moreover, there is much negotiating that must take place in crafting a cohesive report from varied experiences. At the same time, decisions have to be made about what remains in the final report, which voices are highlighted, and which voices become part of the prose that carries the piece (see Geist-Martin et al., 2010). Some members may feel that their voices have been stifled in the construction and presentation of the story. Unlike the traditional research participant, each researcher/participant has a stake in wanting her or his perspective to be heard as equally as other perspectives. However, trying to present disparate data makes for a lengthy and sometimes disjointed research report. In Chapter 5, we discuss how researchers can work together effectively to analyze data, and in Chapter 6 we provide strategies that can be utilized to ensure that the final report represents the team effort.

Whereas each project may have a unique orientation based on the level of collaboration among members, it is important that each team delineates clearly how members will work together early in the research process including team roles (Lapadat, Mothus, & Fisher, 2005) and authorship (Paulus, Woodside, & Ziegler, 2010). We will discuss these issues further in Chapter 3. In all of our projects to date, we have been guided by the principle that the final project should reflect a team effort. This product is the result of ongoing negotiation and group meaning-making. In keeping with the tenets of social constructivism, therefore, the final product is reflective not only of the research process of designing, collecting, analyzing, and interpreting data, but also of the group process of meaning-making inherent in the collaborative analysis, interpretation, and writing up of the final product. This aspect of CAE continues to be a challenge that we readily embrace.

Ethics and Confidentiality

Like any research involving human subjects, CAE adheres to the standard of protecting privacy and confidentiality of research participants. Protection of privacy needs to be addressed at three levels: (1) involuntary participants; (2) co-researchers; and (3) autoethnographers themselves.

The first group, involuntary participants, may be treated unfairly in autoethnographic studies. Since researchers' lives are connected to others, it is inevitable that others are implicated in our stories, often unknowingly (Ellis, 2007). Tolich (2010) has critiqued the way that autoethnographers implicate others in their stories without obtaining informed consent. In particular, he references a few prominent works. For example, Ellis (1996), in "Maternal Connections," related experiences of taking care of her mother with great detail, thus exposing her elderly mother to public scrutiny. In "Chronicling an Academic Depression," Jago (2002) discusses poignantly her struggle with depression, but also implicates 23 other individuals and relationships. In both instances, these authors sought consent after the fact, a practice that Tolich (2010) describes as "problematic and potentially coercive, placing undue obligation on research 'subjects' to volunteer" (p. 1600). What guidelines should autoethnographers follow in protecting the rights of subjects in research on self that invariably involves others? Should AE and CAE be subject to institutional review board (IRB) reviews as other fields of social inquiry? Currently, there are no definitive answers to these questions.

In 2005, the International Congress of Qualitative Inquiry created a *Position Statement on Qualitative Research and IRBs* to address the nuances of qualitative methods. The sixth standard requires that qualitative researchers "respect participants' autonomy and voluntary nature of participating, and document the informed consent processes that are foundational to qualitative inquiry" (p. 1). However, the application of this principle to autoethnographic work is still evolving. In telling our stories, we need to be sensitive to these concerns and intentional in implementing strategies to protect the rights of those implicated in our stories. Scholars have provided useful guidelines for researchers to follow in determining how best to protect others in AE and CAE (Ellis, 2007; Tolich, 2010; Hernandez & Ngunjiri, 2013).

The second group, co-researchers, also deserves protection. Since data are collected for the collaborative research effort, ownership of data can become a problematic issue after the study is completed. For example, if a sub-group or individual on the research team intends to reutilize the collective data pool for further analysis or writing, this can create conflict in the team. To avoid unintended conflict and breach of confidentiality, it is wise at the onset to have an agreement as to who can access the collected data after the completion of research and how ownership of data should be credited. Additionally, in researcher teams where there are preexisting relationships that have power differentials, such as collaborations between professors and students, it is important for team members to create rules that will guide data collection and sharing. For example, in her CAE with two of her students (Ellis et al., 1997), Ellis (2007) later reveals that she told them "not reveal anything to me they might regret later because they might be concerned about how I, their professor, saw them" (p. 20). Protection of co-researchers is important in CAE.

Finally, autoethnographers themselves must make important decisions about how much to disclose about their personal lives. What they reveal can have serious implications for how they are viewed in their social contexts, in their professional relationships, and how they come to view themselves. In documenting her experiences as a Black woman at a predominantly White institution William-White (2011) experienced such negative repercussions from her departmental colleagues that she likened it to a public "beheading" (Brown & William-White, 2010). Jago's (2002) candid confession about her struggle with depression had the potential to affect how she was perceived in the academy. As Ellis (2007) noted in reflecting on the published account (Ellis & Bochner, 1992) of her experience with abortion, "You become the stories you write. . . . No matter that we might feel differently now than then and see ourselves as changed from the characters presented in the story, this portrayal of ourselves is edified in print" (p. 23).

Researchers need to be cautious of how and what they reveal in their autoethnographies for public scrutiny. Chatham-Carpenter (2010) warns autoethnographers to be wise about what they disclose and how they present themselves in their stories. Drawing from her own experiences writing about her struggles with bulimia, she shared some strategies for protecting oneself from the unintended harm of public disclosure. Tillmann (2009) would probably agree with Catham-Carpenter based on the lesson learned from her autoethnographic writing about the eating disorder. Ethical concerns are critical in CAE. We will address these issues in later chapters (e.g., Chapter 3) as they may arise during the research process.

CONCLUSION

AE and CAE offer movement away from the view of the researcher as separate from the research process to the specific, sometimes evocative or analytical, and often untold aspect of research from the perspective/s of researcher/s. In AE, the researcher opts to take this journey alone. In CAE, researchers journey together as co-participants in the research process. Whereas in the past researchers wanting to interrogate how self is omnipresent in the research process have often had to do so in separate "confessional tales" (Van Maanen, 1988), the stories behind our intimate connection with our work can now find voice through AE and CAE.

As an evolving paradigm, we expect that CAE will continue to be redefined to meet the complex needs of research practitioners. This is perhaps the litmus test for the viability of a research methodology. Is it malleable to the needs of a diverse research community and practice while remaining steadfast to the foundational tenets of effective research practice? Given the diverse fields of origin of this approach to inquiry (social science and humanities), these foundational tenets will no doubt vary as they reflect the philosophical approaches to research practice within various disciplines.

Our experience with AE suggests that it has this property of research malleability. Respectively, we represent the fields of anthropology (Heewon), leadership studies (Faith), and educational psychology (Kathy-Ann). As we have collaborated on autoethnographic research projects, our alignment with a more evocative or analytical approach to the practice of research design, data collection, interpretation, and analysis of data has invariably reflected the tenets of our disciplines and of our individuality. However, through the collaborative process, we have been challenged to find a comfortable middle ground. We have found CAE to be a valuable approach to investigating social phenomenon of mutual interest and a rigorous and useful addition to the field of qualitative inquiry. Moreover, CAE is more than a research method. We have experienced CAE as a transforming process whereby we have been able to create community, advance scholarship, and become empowered within our social context.

CHAPTER 2

Typology of Collaborative Autoethnography

"Collaboration in qualitative research is ubiquitous. . . . It is therefore somewhat surprising that with a few notable exceptions . . . most qualitative studies have tended not to make explicit . . . the ways in which co-authors worked together," noted Gershon (2009, p. xvii). Collaboration is, obviously, essential in collaborative autoethnography (CAE). Therefore, we attempt to make the ins and outs of collaboration explicit so that researchers may implement this research method fully informed about various options and strategies involved in working together.

Similar to other group research, collaborative autoethnographers adopt a team research model in which a group of researchers conduct research and produce reports together. However, this collaboration model is unique. Instead of studying others outside their research team, collaborative autoethnographers turn their interrogative tools on themselves, generating and utilizing their autobiographical data to understand social phenomena. In an attempt to make explicit how collaborative autoethnographers study themselves individually and collectively, here we discuss different modes of collaboration based on the size of a research team, the extent of collaboration, data collection strategies, and presentation formats. Following the general discussion of collaboration, we explain in detail specific CAE types such as duoethnography, coethnography, collective autoethnography, community autoethnography, and co/autoethnography.

THE SIZE OF RESEARCH TEAMS

CAE engages two or more researchers. We have discovered from the literature that CAE groups have involved as few as two and as many as 11 researchers. Larger research groups involving five or more tend to be rare; most groups involve two to four researchers. Even among smaller-group collaborations, two-person autoethnographies are more common than other models.

Two-Person Autoethnography

Two-person autoethnographies often stem from already existing relationships (Cann & DeMeulenaere, 2010; Ellis & Bochner, 1992; Sawyer & Norris, 2004, 2009; Stephens & Delamont, 2006). Their professional, sometimes personal, rapport becomes a fuel for enriching stories. In many of the two-person autoethnographies, stories are presented in a dialogic format, either fully or partially. Dialogues incorporated in the text are likely to have been constructed and composed based on data collected in their research processes instead of reflecting their actual conversations verbatim. Even creative construction of dialogue does not usually detract readers from gaining realistic insights about the phenomena the researchers explore together.

Duoethnography exemplifies a full dialogue model of CAE between two researchers (Lund & Nabavi, 2008a). This model will be further discussed later in this chapter. The constructed dialogue style has been used in other two-person collaborative autoethnographies fully or partially, although they were not labeled as "duoethnography." For example, Cann and DeMeulenaere (2010) discussed how they bridged two "discordant" communities of basic education (K–12) and higher education by concurrently teaching in these two settings. The dialogue presented in the writing is constructed based on many hours of living-room conversations on the topic and is interspersed in their narrative text. Focusing on their personal passion and ethnographic interest, Stephens and Delamont (2006) also composed a dialogue about *capoeira*, a Brazilian dance and martial art form. Since they used nicknames for themselves, the dialogue has the appearance of creative writing. With close examination, however, readers can easily detect that the dialogues were composed based on their data, not created out of the authors' imagination. Similarly, Subedi and Rhee (2008) used dialogue in their autobiographical reflexivity on research experiences with their respective Asian immigrant communities: Indian, Pakistani, and Filipino for Subedi and Korean for Rhee (p. 1071). Despite seeming similarities, these two studies used dialogues differently: Stephens and Delamont (2006) "constructed" their dialogue in the tradition of duoethnography, whereas Subedi and Rhee (2008) populated the section on research findings mostly with selected verbatim conversations from their data. Chawla and Rawlins (2004) chose yet another way of presenting their dialogue focusing on their doctoral mentor-mentee relationship. Their dialogue reads like a series of correspondences in which one writes a short letter and the other responds, preserving the authenticity of their respective voices.

Not all two-person collaboration results in collaborative autoethnographies in the dialogic format. Ellis and Bochner (1992) presented their abortion story in their co-mingled voices; Waterson and Kukaj (2007) juxtaposed two autobiographical reflections on social violence and war in two separate voices. It is notable that many more two-person autoethnographies have been published in recent years with varying combinations of dialogues and narratives on different topics: for example, a supervisory relationship between a feminist graduate student and a non-feminist professor (Chapman & Sork, 2001), self-transformation as a result of listening to rap music composed by indigenous young people in Canada (Lashua & Fox, 2006), marginalization experienced by a teen mother and a mental health patient (Muncey & Robinson, 2007), mid-life decisions to become professors (Klinker & Todd, 2007), gay body image (Gust & Warren, 2008), workaholism (Boje & Tyler, 2009), and the relationship between a personal tutor and student (Gardner & Lane, 2010).

Three-or-More-Person Autoethnographies

When research teams consist of three or more members, the level of complexity can increase, due to greater logistical challenges and growing demands for negotiation among researchers. Despite the growing complexity inherent in multi-member teamwork, collaborative autoethnographies by multiple researchers have been increasing steadily in recent years. Endowed with research and writing capacities, academics have been taking advantage of this research method and turning self-interrogation tools on themselves and their work environment. The increasing presence of collaboration among female autoethnographers is an interesting phenomenon that deserves the attention of future research.

Seven sets of trios, mostly made up of women and people of color, are presented here as exemplars of the growing trend of CAE among academics. The first group of collaborative autoethnographies was produced by four sets of university faculty. Ngunjiri, Hernandez, and Chang (2010) explored their navigational strategies as female immigrant faculty members of color in a faith-based higher education; Cohen, Duberley, and Musson (2009) presented their critiques of the traditional discourse of work-life balance; Defrancisco, Kuderer, and Chatham-Carpenter (2007) discussed how autoethnography (AE) helped them learn about self as they collaboratively studied women and self-esteem; and Nuñez, Murakami-Ramalho, and Cuero (2010) analyzed their teaching experiences in Hispanic-serving higher education institutions. There are also examples of CAE constructed by doctoral students. Gurvitch, Carson, and Beale (2008), one male and two female authors, explored their dissertation journey focusing on mentoring relationships with their advisors; Murakami-Ramalho, Piert, and Militello (2008), two females and one male, reflected on and analyzed self-identity formation as researchers of color; three "Latina sisters" (Espino, Muñoz, & Kiyama, 2010) discussed the mutual support they provided to each other during their doctoral studies. A team of two doctoral students and their advisor also explored, in a playscript, their struggles surrounding the submission and examination of a jointly written dissertation (Gale, Speedy, & Wyatt, 2010).

Collaboration among more than three researchers is less frequent, according to our literature review. Two teams of four members have published collaborative autoethnographies on race and gender issues respectively. Toyosaki et al. (2009) discussed the meaning and impact of White privilege in their lives; Kalmbach Phillips et al. (2009) focused on their collective journeys of becoming feminist poststructural thinkers, practitioners, and teachers. In a six-member team, O'Shea et al. (2011) engaged in a collaborative discovery of how each author integrated spirituality in their teaching as part of faculty learning community activities and eventually developed their writing into CAE. A study of mothering by Geist-Martin et al. (2010) involved seven researchers. In the case of Hernández et al. (2010), nine senior and junior scholars originally explored their socialization process as scholars in a Spanish university, but only four continued collaboration at the writing stage and appeared in the publication as coauthors. Weems et al. (2009) included 11 members in their research team; seven of then participated in writing up the results for publication.

Collaboration is tighter when a smaller number of researchers are involved. Group coordination and negotiation among members is likely to be simpler in smaller groups than large groups during data collection, analysis, and writing. Blending researcher voices may come easier in smaller groups. In comparison, collaboration within larger groups appears to be looser; Individual voices are preserved more in juxtaposition than blended and integrated in final writings (Geist-Martin et al., 2010; Hernández et al., 2010; O'Shea et al., 2011).

THE EXTENT OF COLLABORATION

Collaboration within a research team can be full or complete if all co-researchers share responsibilities for all aspects of the research process and production. Collaboration can also be done partially, where different co-researchers collaborate on different aspects of the research process. There is no formula as to when and how researchers should share research responsibilities. Each research team makes decisions depending on the unique needs of the team and individual researchers.

This kind of decision making is not always explicit in research reports. It is usually difficult to determine the extent of collaboration by merely reading research reports because most autoethnographies, typically emphasizing evocative narratives, are devoid of the discussion of their research process and procedures. Therefore, unless researchers reveal explicitly their collaboration process in research reports, we can only speculate how fully or partially each researcher might have been engaged in their research process. Based on publications that made their research processes explicit and studies that we have conducted, we discuss how collaboration can be done fully or partially.

Full Collaboration

In the full collaboration model, all members of a research team are engaged in all aspects of the research process from the beginning to the end. Although each member's participation and contribution to the study may vary at different points of the study, full collaboration implies that all are engaged and share responsibilities at all levels until research reporting is completed.

Full collaboration is articulated in many studies in which all participating researchers have agreed on their investigative topic and participated in data collection, analysis and interpretation, and writing reports. Kalmbach Phillips et al.'s (2009) study exemplifies full collaboration. Building on their preexisting collegiality, the four women decided to explore their process of becoming poststructural feminists. They described their collaboration process: "Over a period of ten months, we came together on a regular basis to question, discuss, and map our individual stories as a way of making sense of theories of subjectivity . . . and to study the concept of transitional space" (p. 1456). They elaborate on their data collection and analysis process: "This data included individual researchers' journals written after rereading Ellsworth . . . and returning to other feminist poststructural theorists. . . . We met together six times to discuss our readings and journeys. During our face-to-face meetings, we mapped themes from previous e-mail dialogues" (p. 1458). Their full collaboration resulted in a coauthored article.

Geist-Martin et al. (2010) also articulated steps that seven researchers took to explore the meaning of mothering in relation to their own mothers or children during their full autoethnographic collaboration process:

[W]e utilized "collaborative autoethnographic practice" to illustrate the complexities of mothering by (a) writing sole-authored autoethnographic tales on mothering, (b) sharing these tales in a public forum, (c) discussing collaboratively the heuristic commonalities across these tales, (d) tying those commonalities back to the literature on the topic of mothering, and (e) revisiting the tales for aspects of social critique when we (unwittingly) hegemonically reproduced *cultural scripts* of mothering. (Abstract)

Other full-collaboration studies that describe their research process substantively include Ellis and Bochner (1992) and Toyosaki et al. (2009), discussed elsewhere in this book.

Partial Collaboration

Partial collaboration occurs when researchers contribute to different stages in the process but do not fully engage from the beginning to the end. We have noted different possibilities for partial collaboration in existing publications: (1) although not all researchers add their autobiographical data to the collective pool of data, they contribute to other research steps in the collaborative process; (2) all researchers actively contribute their autobiographical data and participate in other research steps, but some discontinue at the writing stage; and (3) all researchers engage in various research stages prior to writing, but only leading researchers author research reports.

Ellis, Kiesinger, and Tillman-Healy's study (1997) is a good example of the first type of partial collaboration. Although three authors collaborated from the inception of the study, the first author's contribution to the autobiographical data was limited because the second and third authors' lived experiences with bulimia were the focus of the study. The first author contributed to the study with her interpretive lens and research expertise as an autoethnographer. Similarly, Lietz, Langer, and Furman's (2006) study engaged the third author partially. Jewish spirituality is the focus of the study, and the first two authors drew on their lived experiences for their AE. To increase the objectivity of their interpretation, they invited the third author as a research consultant who commented on their interpretations. The study is similar to Ellis, Kiesinger, and Tillman-Healy's (1997) study in that one of the authors did not contribute his autobiographic data to the collective pool of data but rendered his research expertise. One difference between the two studies may be noted—whereas Ellis (Ellis, 2009; Ellis, Kiesinger, and Tillman-Healy, 1997) actively participated in the study from the beginning, Furman (Lietz, Langer, & Furman, 2006) was brought in at the later stage of research—data analysis and interpretation.

Hernández et al. (2010) demonstrate the second type of partial collaboration. Nine researchers initially engaged in the CAE work. They describe their beginning step: "On starting the construction process of the professional autoethnographies the nine members of the research team spent several meetings forming a consensus and defining how to undertake this task" (p. 4). They used the gatherings to establish the common framework for this collaborative work and decided to write their individual stories about their own development as university scholars. They published their individual autoethnographies elsewhere, and four authors of this work decided to converge their narratives as a CAE. Although the four-authored work is a result of full participation of the authors, we put this CAE in the category of partial collaboration because the published work is a representation of the portion of the grand collaborative project. Considering the size of the original collaboration team, it is reasonable to assume that the team of four researchers was more manageable when converging autoethnographic narratives.

The third type of partial collaboration takes place where researchers engage participants in various stages of research but do not share authorship with them. In many ways, social science studies soliciting interviews from human subjects are fundamentally collaborative because participants contribute their knowledge and perspective to each research endeavor in the form of data. In most cases, they remain anonymous or hide behind pseudonyms. We do not argue against measures to protect privacy of research participants but recognize their considerable, though nameless, contribution to social science research as partial partners of collaboration. Although we do not intend to bring to light the whole spectrum of social science critiques, autoethnographers who report on their projects without sharing authorship with their participants need to be mindful of power differentials between researchers and the researched (Lund & Nabavi, 2008a, 2008b; Sawyer & Norris, 2009; Subedi & Rhee, 2008) and the need for researcher-researched reciprocity (Foley, 1997). "Co/Autoethnography" (Coia & Taylor, 2006) illustrates this type of partial collaboration, in which research participants were students in the authors' class, shared their autobiographical narratives, but did not take part in the authorship of the paper. In Rose's study (2008), she single-authored her study although her research participants participated in the autoethnographic exploration with her. To differentiate any social science studies with human subjects from this category of partial autoethnographic collaboration, you need to make sure that authors appropriating other participant stories also contribute to the collaborative autoethnographic process as co-participants.

MODES OF COLLABORATION

Collaboration can differ depending on how researchers collaborate during data collection and analysis stages. Some research teams move along with more concurrent research activities, while others have their members engaged in research activities more sequentially. In concurrent collaboration, researchers usually engage in same tasks at the same time, often independently, and bring the fruit of their individual labor together for discussion and further progress. In sequential collaboration, researchers take turns to contribute to the process, allowing them to build scaffolds together. This modal difference appears clearer during data collection and occasionally in the presentation styles of research reports. In this section, we introduce different examples of collaboration modes and discuss methodological strengths and limitations in both modes.

Concurrent Collaboration

In concurrent collaboration, all researchers engage in engage in the research process steadily, often mixing individual activities with collective activities. Individually, they may collect, review, or reflect on data. Their individual research activities are not likely to take place in one location where everyone is present, although their collaboration is constant and concurrent. The concurrent model would allow researchers to write individually about a selected topic and then share their stories; whether they work individually or collectively, they keep pace with each other at a given time. The process of writing individually and sharing collectively is iterative. Klinker and Todd (2007) described their data collection process as follows:

> For a period of three–four weeks, each of us found the time to review our pasts and write about those peak emotional experiences that had shaped our decision to become professors. Then our conversations with one another about those experiences prompted more insights, more recollections, and we both would again go back to our writings. The memories were there, the emotional residue still a part of who we had become, and it was that experience through the writing that allowed us to see our present from the past. (p. 168)

Similar iterative processes of collaboration are reported by Hernandez, Ngunjiri, and Chang (2011) and Kalmbach Phillips et al. (2009). For both studies, research teams spent a considerable length of time (over a year for the former and 10 months for the latter), undergoing a concurrent iterative process of individual writing and reflection and collective discussion and analysis. Both studies utilized full collaboration, but concurrent collaboration is not synonymous with full participation. For example, Coia and Taylor's (2009) co-autoethnography, explained as the third type of partial collaboration, used a partial concurrent mode of collaboration.

The strength of the concurrent mode is to give researchers space and time for their individual reflection and consideration while collecting autobiographical data. Since their thoughts are formulated without the influence of their co-researchers, when the thoughts are shared, their individual voices can be heard at their full value. Despite the strength, this mode of collaboration poses a risk of allowing each member to think and collect data too independently from each other because each member can operate in a vacuum without feedback until the team meets for conversation. This constant divergence and convergence may enrich their exchanges but could also prolong the research process until they reach a point of reasonable compromise. If members are separated by distance, insufficient interactions may diminish cohesiveness among individual data.

Sequential Collaboration

The sequential model would allow researchers to contribute to the pool of data one person at a time. When collecting autobiographical data, one researcher writes about her or his experience and passes the writing along to the next researcher who then adds her or his account in response to the previous writer before passing it on the the next person. Toyosaki et al. (2009) describe their data collection process like this:

> I (Satoshi) write an autoethnographic piece and share it with my coauthors. If someone finds a theoretical, conceptual, or performative connection to his or her lived experience, then that writer expresses to all coauthors an interest to write next, and does so dialogically to my piece. Then, this coauthor reveals the whole thing—both autoethnographic pieces—to all coauthors. This process goes on. There is no specific order by which the writing turns are organized except the connections we each bring to advance an understanding of whiteness education. Rather than supplying themes to which we write, we champion the emerging connections that we embody through community-autoethnographic writing and reading. Our experiential connections drive our investigation. (p. 60)

This sequential model allows individual's stories to build on one other and expand not only in quantity but also in depth. The model also presents challenges. Since only one researcher can work on data collection at a time, members have to wait for their turns to contribute to the data set. This process can easily stretch the duration of data collection, and the team's success is determined by individual members' accountability.

With an understanding of the procedural distinctiveness and methodological benefits as well as challenges of these models, each team will need to make a decision to find a model that fits their research timeline and collaboration situation. The good news for this decision is that the team does not need to select one or the other. Unlike full or partial collaboration, the selection of the sequential and concurrent model is flexible in that it is possible to combine both models or stick to one kind.

Methodological Variations of Collaborative Autoethnography

As we indicated in Chapter 1, researchers developed different names to describe their collaborative autoethnographic approaches. Among the wide range of terminologies used to describe CAE are the following: autoethnographic conversation (Cohen, Duberley, & Musson, 2009), co/autoethnographic (Coia & Taylor, 2006), co-ethnography (Ellis & Bochner, 1992), CAE (Geist-Martin et al., 2010), collective autoethnography (Cann & DeMeulenaere, 2010), community autoethnography (Toyosaki et al., 2009), community-based ethnography (Stringer et al., 1997), dialogical autoethnography (González et al., 2002), duoethnography (Lund & Nabavi, 2008a; Norris, Sawyer, & Lund, 2011; Sawyer & Norris, 2004, 2009), ethnodrama (Randolph & Weems, 2010), performance CAE (Kalmbach Phillips et al., 2009; Rose, 2008), performative autoethnographic novel (McMillan & Price, 2010), and simply, dialogue (Stephens & Delamont, 2006).

Although some methodological distinctiveness has been shown for each label, naming of different approaches has not followed preexisting ontological (relating to existence), epistemological (relating to knowledge), and methodological (relating to method) logics or typology. It appears that researcher preference and intuition are the basis of the naming practice. Therefore, instead of proposing all approaches as separate research designs of CAE, we here present five approaches for comparison and further explanation. We have selected these five simply because researchers expounded on their research processes. Table 2-1 shows the comparison of the five different approaches by four criteria: research group size, the extent of collaboration, data collection model, and writing style.

Each approach is explained further in the following subsections.

Autoethnographic Conversations

Autoethnographic conversations refer to collaborative autoethnographies in which researchers engage in conversations (face to face or e-mail) on an agreed-on topic with the purpose of gaining a deeper understanding of the topic through a self-other analysis. One such example is by Cohen, Duberley, and Musson (2009), who focused their conversations on work-life balance issues. Falling within the more analytical end of the spectrum, the coauthors viewed AE as "not simply a confessional tale but a provocative weave of story and theory. . . . Through using what we might call collaborative autoethnography, we hope to further develop our understanding of our own and each other's experiences" (p. 233).

Table 2-1 Comparison among various collaborative autoethnographic approaches.

Collaborative Autoethnography Approaches	Example	Group Size of the Example	Extent of Collaboration	Data Collection Model	Writing Style
Autoethnographic conversations	Cohen, Duberley, & Musson (2009)	3	full	concurrent	analytical
Collaborative autoethnography	Geist-Martin et al. (2010)	7	full	concurrent	analytical and narrative
Community autoethnography	Toyosaki et al. (2009)	4	partial	sequential	dialogic and analytical
Duoethnography	Lund & Nabavi (2008a, 2008b)	2	full	concurrent	dialogic
Performance collaborative autoethnography	Kalmbach Phillips et al. (2009)	4	full	concurrent	performative

Taking a critical incident approach, Cohen and colleagues. exchanged e-mails focusing on the dynamics of their work and non-work lives, followed by three face-to-face meetings for in-depth discussions. Each meeting lasted about four hours, typical of autoethnographic meetings as we have experienced. The co-researchers described the process as follows: "One person started off discussing issues particularly pertinent to her at that time and then the other two chipped in, asking questions, making comments, and then talking about their own situations" (p. 233). Such a process evokes "interactive introspection" (p. 233). The iterative process between data collection and data analysis is demonstrated in the following description:

> [T]he meetings were followed by email exchanges among the three of us. These included notes of what had been said and attempts to conceptualize our experiences. Thus our discussions and emails contained both our memories . . . and our attempts to theorize them. (p. 233)

Sometimes collaborative autoethnographies are not labeled as such but include concepts associated with collaborative approaches such as "collaboration," "dialogue," and "iterative." Murakami-Ramalho, Piert, and Militello's (2008) study is aligned with autoethnographic conversations without being labeled that way. The study focuses on experiences of doctoral students of color as they learned to develop identity as researchers. They described their research process involving activities such as the crafting of individual narratives, collaborative analysis of those narratives in a dialogical process, the iterative process of data collection, data analysis, back to further/deeper data collection, and then again analysis. They appear to have adopted an autoethnographic approach from Ellis and Bochner (2000) in their exploration of vulnerability. Their article demonstrates how the dialogical process enables co-researchers to go deeper and also to discover areas of similarities and differences (Chang, 2008; Murakami-Ramalho, Piert, & Militello, 2008).

Collaborative Autoethnography

This approach was named by the coauthors of a recent article in a journal that the three of us coedited, after we encouraged the coauthors to focus their article on reflecting upon their autoethnographic process (Geist-Martin et al., 2010). Geist-Martin and her colleagues focused on the topic of mothering; the project began with the first author's invitation to others to participate in a conference panel on mothering and the mother-child relationship. The co-participants each wrote their own autoethnographic stories of mothering following a more evocative, interpretive, and artistic writing process, thus avoiding constricting academic prose (Ellingson, 2009; Ellis, 1999; Ellis & Bochner, 2000).

After the individual data collection process, the co-researchers engaged in a collaborative discussion of the issues surrounding the phenomenon of mother-child relationship (i.e., data analysis) to co-create a meta-narrative about mothering based on their experiences (Geist-Martin et al., 2010). Their process fits within the concurrent collaboration model because each individual researcher wrote his or her autoethnographic narrative independently but at the same time, then shared those stories in a group discussion that was aimed at analyzing the stories to come up with emerging themes that would create a coherent story about the phenomena. Additionally, they collectively and discursively presented at a conference, then continued to work together toward constructing the reflection paper. Their efforts were collaborative from start to finish, and, though some were senior faculty, some junior faculty, and some graduate students, they all participated as equal co-researchers in the project.

Community Autoethnography

Toyosaki and colleagues (2009) conceptualized "community autoethnography" based on at least three different approaches to AE: the exploration of personal matters inspired by Ronai (1995), community ethnography as advocated by Stringer et al. (1997), and narrative co-construction introduced by Bochner and Ellis (1995). These approaches have shaped three primary characteristics of community AE.

First, reflecting the work of Ronai (1995), which blurred the distinction between the personal and academic, community autoethnography is characterized as an intimate research method that supports self-discovery and self-construction.

Second, infusing Bochner and Ellis's (1995) "intention of studying relationship construction as joint action" (p. 59) and Stringer et al.'s (1997) work on community ethnography, community autoethnography engenders a sense of community among the co-researchers: "It is, in essence, a community building or team-building activity as much as it is an approach to the production of knowledge" (Stringer et al., 1997, cited in Toyosaki et al., 2009, p. 58). As such, Toyosaki and colleagues intended community autoethnography to be a relationship-making activity in which researchers co-construct each other's realities.

Third, adopting Ellis, Kiesinger, and Tillman-Healy's (1997) interactive interviewing, CAE focuses on a set topic and creates a safe conversational environment for discussing intimate details about the topic; in the case of Toyosaki and colleagues, it relates to their experiences with whiteness. It allows for growing intimacy and probing deeper into one another's thoughts and feelings.

In terms of procedures, community autoethnography falls within what we are calling sequential CAE. The process of data collection begins with one researcher writing his or her experience and sharing it with co-researchers. "If someone finds a theoretical, conceptual or performative connection to his or her lived experience, then that writer expresses to all coauthors an interest to write next" (Toyosaki et al., 2009, p. 60). That next writer then writes dialogically to the first piece, and then sends his or her piece as well as that of the first writer to all coauthors, and the process repeats itself, each time involving writing in connection or response to previous autoethnographic pieces. Themes emerge through that dialogic process of back-and-forth writing process as opposed to being provided a priori. This research team involved four researchers. For this sequential process to work effectively, it is conceivable that at least three members compose a community autoethnography team.

Duoethnography

Duoethnography exemplifies a full dialogue model between two researchers. Sawyer and Norris (2009) define duoethnography as an approach in which:

> [T]wo or more researchers work in tandem to dialogically critique and question the meanings they give to issues and constructs. Examining personal artifacts, stories, memories, compositions, texts and critical incidents, duoethnographers excavate the temporal, social, cultural and geographical cartography of their lives, making explicit their assumptions and perspectives. (p. 127)

This method was conceived by Sawyer and Norris (2004, 2009) and has expanded into Norris, Sawyer, and Lund's (2011) book, *Duoethnography: Dialogic Methods for Social, Health, and Educational Research.* Duoethnography is a relatively new qualitative research approach, which they described as borrowing from two traditions: storytelling, as with other autoethnographic methods, and Pinar's concept of *currere,* which means a curriculum of daily/personal life to produce a dialogic research process (Norris et al., 2011; Sawyer & Norris, 2004). By having two or more co-researchers, the dialogue in duoethnography produces multivocal texts that are dependent on a relationship of trust and a willingness to speak into each other's stories. As such, "this provides a necessary rigor to the research, similar to that of a second reader" (Sawyer & Norris, 2009, p. 135).

Tenets of duoethnography are clearly articulated in Sawyer and Norris (2009). These core tenets include: (1) communal and dialogic conversations; (2) the transformation of meaning; (3) a focus on the phenomenon or construct, not the person; (4) the importance of difference; (5) the need to recognize power differentials; and (6) the importance of noting the situatedness of meaning. Researchers are generally fully involved in the process of conducting and constructing duoethnography. Although the dialogic presentation of duoethnography gives an impression of researchers sequentially collecting data, one researcher at a time, the process of data collection seems to resemble the concurrent model of collaboration when researchers engage in synchronous conversations to gather their autobiographical data and construct their dialogues.

Their prominent use of the method was presented in Sawyer and Norris's (2004) article in which they explicated their experiences or "personal curriculum" with sexual orientation. They employed the use of vignettes that demonstrate their experiences with and of homosexuality in their formative years and their later interpretation of those experiences in view of social systems within schools. They "tell their stories to expose the curriculum of the past in the hope that it can positively change the curriculum of the present and the future" (p. 140). Through exposing the reader to the fear, shame, and pain that homosexuals and those perceived by the school community as such experienced, they call for justice in schools as institutions "that promote tolerance, democracy, inclusion and equity" (p. 157).

Lund and Nabavi (2008a, 2008b) engaged in a duoethnographic project that required not only trust and respect but also a recognition of the power differentials sometimes present between the co-researchers. Nabavi was a graduate student, whereas Lund was faculty, although they were in different institutions and met in the context of their antiracism activism. In their case, they entered the project as co-researchers and equal collaborators. To reduce the chance of reifying power differentials, Sawyer and Norris (2009) recommend that researchers "take the time to talk about how they want to work together, covering everything from their roles as they collect data to their participation in the analysis and reporting of findings" (p. 136).

Performance Collaborative Autoethnography

In the literature, we find several examples of collaborative autoethnographies that are performative in nature. Performance autoethnographies are written as reading theater scripts (Cann & DeMeulenaere, 2010; McMillan & Price, 2010), a series of poetry, or performance narratives (Kalmbach Phillips et al., 2009). A trigger for performance CAE could be personal experiences or some social or theoretical concerns that researchers share. Co-researchers collect autoethnographic data individually by writing in their research journals over an agreed-upon period of time. They then meet face to face to dialogue through their individual data in a collaborative meaning-making process. This process may lead to further data and/or which require further individual writing. The dialogues may happen in face-to-face meetings or via other telecommunication medium (e.g., e-mail, phone, or virtual conferences).

From an epistemological perspective, performance autoethnographies "challenge core beliefs about research: on whom it is done, how it is done, who does it, and how it is reported. At their very core, such venues challenge those who believe they are in the locus of control of research" (McMillan & Price, 2010, p. 6). That is, performance autoethnographies shake the core of what is believed to be legitimate knowledge and how that knowledge is transmitted because of their use of literary techniques such as poetry, performative prose, metaphors, and stories, often in evocative language. Performativity, defined as "the writing and rewriting of meanings that continually disrupt the authority of texts," becomes part of the defining characteristics of this method as co-researchers critique the status quo (Finley, 2005, p. 687).

Collaborative performance autoethnographies involve a multiplicity of voices, even though in some cases, the written form may involve finding a common collective voice. They are therapeutic in nature and help uncover deeper meanings due to their dialogic nature (Kalmbach Phillips et al., 2009). They are co-constructed, dialogic, and concerned with making meaning of shared phenomena in a written document or a performance on stage (Ellis, 2004; Kalmbach Phillips et al., 2009).

Performance autoethnographies done collaboratively, then, always involve the writers/performers/researchers and the audience/readers, as the former interacts among themselves while also connecting and resonating with the experiences of the latter. They can, and often do, have a political or institutional activism as part of the end goal (Finley, 2005).

CONCLUSION

As discussed so far, CAE can be completed in many different ways. Namely, researchers adopt different combinations of CAE in terms of the research team size (two-person, medium size, or large group), the extent of collaboration (full or partial), collaboration mode (concurrent or sequential), and presentation style (narrative, analytical, dialogical, or performative). The literature shows that different combinations of various options are manifested in different collaborative autoethnographic designs named in this chapter: autoethnographic conversations, collaborative autoethnography, community autoethnography, duoethnography, and performance collaborative autoethnography. We do not claim this to be an exhaustive list or that each design be mutually exclusive from each other. With this disclaimer, however, we still argue that it is important to be informed of varieties of collaborative autoethnographers and their distinctiveness.

Variations in CAE result from different processes and products of collaboration, yet all collaborative autoethnographies share common elements; they are autobiographic (self-focused and researcher-visible), ethnographic (context-conscious), and interactive (critically dialogic).

CAE is autobiographical in that the individual co-researchers collect their own biographic data about an agreed-on experience or phenomena. CAE is ethnographic because it involves analyzing and interpreting the sociocultural contexts where researchers live, work, or worship and their lived experiences are acted out. Without incorporating analysis of the sociocultural context, the collaborative process results in merely autobiographic narratives. CAE is also interactive. Dialogue is the link that helps extend AE into CAE where two or more co-researchers discuss and deliberate on their collected data. Without dialogue, it would be merely individual autoethnographies put together, as opposed to CAE. Interaction among researchers is integral to the process. The process, from deciding on a topic for the research project, to analyzing data, to incorporating theory, and writing up the finished product. With these three common tenets of CAE in mind (autobiographical, ethnographic, and interactive), we move to the next chapter where we discuss how to begin the process of CAE research.

CHAPTER 3

Getting Ready for Collaborative Autoethnography

Now that you have gained the theoretical and methodological knowledge of collaborative autoethnography (CAE) from Chapters 1 and 2, you may feel encouraged to launch your own project. Despite your excitement about this research method, nagging questions like where to start and how to get going are yet to be answered. Beginning with this chapter, we will provide practical tips to help you begin and complete a CAE project. In this chapter, we discuss five steps to consider when you undertake CAE: (1) forming a research team; (2) deciding on a research focus for your research team; (3) selecting a collaboration model for your team; (4) defining roles and setting boundaries for each participant; and (5) considering ethical principles for the team. You may not always take the steps in the exact order as presented here. Sometimes, some steps may be reversed or merged with others to meet the unique needs of your project. For example, forming a research team and deciding on a research focus can be easily reversed or merged into one step. However, we explain each step in turn for the sake of clarity.

FORMING A RESEARCH TEAM

Conducting scientific research is an arduous, often time-consuming, journey. Like any other journey, it starts with setting a goal. Selecting a destination, planning an itinerary, working out logistics, and obtaining necessary material are all part of an exciting but often anxiety-laden process. Facing intimidating challenges of reaching an unknown destination, the researcher may appreciate having one or more traveling companions. We consider the task of embarking on a CAE project as analogous to taking a journey with fellow travelers. In this chapter, however, we do not intend to paint an overly romantic or optimistic picture about collective research journeys. Instead, we hope to help you set out for the journey with positive but realistic expectations about collaborative self-exploration and self-analysis.

55

For CAE, companions are not just nice-to-haves but are must-haves because the shared autobiographic stories of all travelers become the core of their collaborative data. In addition, the synergistic interaction throughout their joint travel enhances the collective work. They must negotiate their relative positions to each other, resolve different perspectives and disagreements, and complement each other's strengths as researcher, critic, and writer. Therefore, inviting "just right" companions along for the journey will be critical to the success of a CAE project.

Finding "Just Right" Companions

How can you find just right fellow travelers for your CAE project? One approach to forming an effective research team is recruiting close colleagues with whom you have shared collegiality and similar research interests. Waterston and Rylko-Bauer's (2006) study illustrates this approach. When they decided to do an "intimate ethnography" about their parents' similar experiences in concentration camps during the Nazi regime in Poland, they had already worked on other projects and had developed a relationship as friends and colleagues. Although they did not label their study CAE, their collaborative reflections as daughters of violence survivors, combined with an ethnohistorical analysis of their parents' experiences, resemble the efforts that collaborative autoethnographers put forth in their team research. Their pre-formed relationship made it easier for them to be vulnerable about their parents' painful past as a Jewish Polish Holocaust survivor and a Catholic Polish resistor to the Nazi regime respectively.

Many more collaborative autoethnographies exemplify collaboration growing out of preexisting collegial relationships. Here we present only three cases. Our CAE focusing on immigrant faculty experiences in U.S. higher education institutions (Hernandez, Ngunjiri, & Chang, 2011) also grew out of our collegial relationship.[1] As departmental colleagues, we knew each other's professional interests and personal backgrounds. Although our collaborative research ended up bringing out much deeper and broader understanding of each other, our prior knowledge facilitated our collaboration. When your team is formed with colleagues, your topic will be determined by your common interests. In the case of Sawyer and Norris (2004), they have diametrically different lived experiences—Sawyer as a gay man and Norris as a straight man—yet their common interest of exploring sexual orientation and social justice formed the basis of their duoethnography. Cann and DeMeulenaere (2010) built their "collective autoethnography" on a collegial relationship despite their personal differences.

Bridges

One is a Black single mother and the other is a White married father. Yet they are committed to practicing social justice education by teaching at both college and K–12 settings concurrently and playing the role of "transformative intellectual" activists. Through this unlikely relationship, Cann and DeMeulenaere were able to forge an alliance to probe, critique, and enlighten each other on racial and class factors contributing to White privilege and educational injustice.

Although it would be a blessing to have long-term colleagues who are willing to explore their lived experiences together, another approach to forming a research team is more common: seeking out new companions for research purposes. In this approach, the topic to pursue should be the beginning point when seeking just right companions for a research group. For example, Hernández et al. (2010) formed a CAE group with a set goal of exploring how team members constructed their identity as scholars in a Spanish university at a time of institutional changes. Geist-Martin et al. (2010) also did not know each other well when beginning their collaboration; they were drawn to each other when Patricia Geist-Martin sent out a call for collaborators to engage in explicating their experiences with mothering and motherhood.

Whether working with familiar colleagues or strangers, there are both benefits and challenges in these relationships. Collaboration with long-term colleagues may save you time establishing rapport with research companions and, in turn, allow your team to delve into a mutually selected research topic immediately. Negotiation over disagreement or differences may also be easier because you have prior knowledge of your colleagues' perspectives and styles of conflict resolution. However, previous relationships with each other may constrict the possibility of forming new relationships, and familiarity could blind you from gaining new perspectives about each other and your research topic.

In contrast, working with new research partners could help you gain fresh perspectives on the research topic through the eyes of strangers. New questions, insights, and struggles have the potential to bring you to a new level of understanding. Such benefits may accompany challenges in that your team will need to invest time to discover authentic selves behind each other's managed initial images and find ways to avoid miscommunication and resolve conflict.

Sometimes your initial avoidance of tension could lead to a bigger conflict at a later stage. Easterby-Smith and Malina (1999) illustrate such a case. Their study is not autoethnographic; however, their reflective analysis of collaboration between U.K. and Chinese researchers of management sheds light on the potential difficulty that can rise from researchers of different backgrounds. They pointed out that their initial avoidance of discussing different perspectives about research—seeking consensus versus juxtaposing differences—led to difficult negotiation in the later process of data analysis and interpretation. Authors from the United Kingdom attributed the initial avoidance to their counterparts' fear of losing face. Ultimately, they had to face the "demon" head-on and bring the disagreement to the table for discussion and resolution. They concluded that they should have had clarifying discussions earlier in their collaboration. Considering both the benefits and the challenges associated with collaboration with friends or strangers, you will need to decide which direction you will take to form your "just right" team of CAE research.

Including a Sounding Board

Collaborative research teams typically expect all participating members to contribute their autobiographic information to the common pot of data. The collective data become the database for the teams to analyze and interpret to reach collective conclusions. Therefore, collaborative research teams are typically made up of researchers who can and are willing to share their lived experiences with each other.

However, it is possible to include in a research team a member who does not add his or her lived experiences to the collective data set but makes a significant contribution to the collaborative process in different ways (e.g., as a project manager who initiates and/or leads the process, a seasoned autoethnography (AE) researcher assisting data analysis and interpretation, and/or a scholarly writer). Above all, the added member can play an important role as a sounding board, listening to stories or asking probing questions to help others, sometimes caught in their own experiences, connect their stories with those of others. Although this member could be an experienced autoethnographic researcher, we call her or him a non-autoethnographer in relation to the particular research project he or she is involved in, because the non-autoethnographer's autobiographical data is not part of the investigation.

Here are some examples that included non-autoethnographer members. Toyosaki played such a role when he invited his colleagues to participate in a "community autoethnography" with him to explore White privileges (Toyosaki et al., 2009). He is not White but is a scholar of diversity studies who shared the common interest with his colleagues in investigating how Whites discover and counteract their privileges in society. With his scholarly focus and qualitative researcher competence, he was able to lead his co-researchers to complete their collaborative investigation on the topic.

In a "co-constructed autoethnography" (Ellis, 2007, p. 19), Ellis explored the meaning and experience of bulimia with her then students (Ellis, Kiesinger, & Tillmann-Healy, 1997). Ellis claimed that she "did not have an eating disorder" but "shared with [her] coauthors who did concerns about food and bodies that arise from women's immersion in cultural contradictions of thin bodies and abundant consumption" (Ellis, 2007, p. 20). They were engaged in interactive interviews, sharing personal stories, feelings, and perspectives about the issue. One may question the role of Ellis as an autoethnographer because she could not contribute her story of bulimia to their collective pot of data. Yet her insights and understanding, as well as her expertise as an autoethnographic researcher and writer, contributed significantly to the birth of their co-constructed AE.

In Lietz, Langer, and Furman's (2006) study of Jewish spirituality, after two autoethnographers—a male Jew and a female convert Jew—wrote their autobiographical journals on the topic of their Jewish identity and discussed their writings, they invited a third person to assist with their autoethnographic data analysis. Their goal of adding the researcher was to allow them to look at their data through the eyes of the third member for more rigorous data analysis. The added researcher wrote her responses to the autobiographical data of the original autoethnographers, who later reflected on the reactions for deeper analysis of their assumptions.

In all of these partially collaborative studies, "non-autoethnographer" researchers participated in the collaborative process although they did not have shared personal experiences with their research teammates as a White, a bulimic, or a Jew respectively. However, their contribution to the process was notable. We do not argue that all collaborative autoethnographies should utilize a sounding board-methodologist-writer, but some research teams may benefit from adding such a member. If your research team is made up of novice autoethnographers, a methodological expert can coach you through the autoethnographic research process—data collection, analysis, interpretation, and writing process. In addition, she or he can render an outsider perspective by asking, clarifying, and probing questions. The outsider voice may affirm your stories and challenge your assumptions for further examination.

The Size of an Ideal Research Team

What is an ideal size of a CAE team? There is no magic number for a perfect team. Published studies of AE based on group work have involved as few as two and as many as 11 researchers. In Chapter 2, we provided many examples of CAE by differently sized teams. We noted that more works by two-person teams are available in the literature, but there are many exemplary collaborative autoethnographies produced by mid-size (three to four persons) and large teams (five or more persons).

As you decide the size of your research team, you need to consider benefits and challenges of working in a large or a small team. Collaboration is tighter when a smaller number of researchers are involved. Sharing of intimate stories may be accomplished better in smaller group settings. Coordination of logistics may be simpler for smaller groups than larger groups during data collection, analysis, and writing. Blending voices of research participants may be simpler for smaller groups, and negotiation is more manageable in smaller groups than in larger groups. In comparison, collaboration among a larger group of researchers appears to be looser where individual stories are presented. In larger-group studies, collaborators appear to have begun sharing individual stories in differently intended meetings, which evolved into a collaborative writing project (Geist-Martin et al., 2010; Hernández et al., 2010; O'Shea et al., 2011). In large-group studies, researcher voices tend to be more juxtaposed in multivocal presentations than blended in one voice in final writings (Weems et al., 2009).

Communication among Team Members

Another important factor to consider in forming an effective research team is how well co-researchers can communicate with each other. It is possible for members to collect data together and then part ways to do their independent analysis, interpretation, and writing up with the collective data. Or members may stick together at all steps of research until an AE is coauthored. In any case, clear expectations need to be communicated from the beginning. The more people you have in your team and the more unfamiliar you are with each other, the greater the need to lay out your mutual expectations at the beginning of collaboration. Explore what everyone wants to accomplish by this collaborative project and how committed everyone is to sharing personal stories, constantly probing each other, and completing the project on time. Although initial agreement can be altered once collaboration begins, unless co-researchers have a shared understanding of fundamentals regarding collaboration, the autoethnographic process, and expected outcomes, it could be very challenging to carry on and complete the intensely personal and shared project.

You cannot anticipate all issues that you will need to discuss and resolve from the beginning. However, some issues would be better resolved at the start. For example, who will have access to the collective data? What will happen to the data already collected if one of you drops out of the research team? Who will author written products? Who will get credit as the first, second, and so on, author? Easterby-Smith and Malina's (1999) study, involving multiple management scholars from the United Kingdom and China, shed great insight about how they agreed to solve the data access and authorship issues:

> In order to facilitate individual contributions, the overall team affirmed that all data collected on the project should be considered equally the property of every member, that pairs and subgroups would be encouraged to write together wherever there were likely to be common interests, and that all members would inform the national coordinators of their writing plans so that an overall list of work in progress could be maintained. (p. 81)

In addition to communicating expectations at the onset of the research, we cannot overemphasize the importance of continuous communication and relationship building among team members. Since you will be sharing many personal and sensitive stories with each other, trust and open communication will be absolutely necessary. Thus, how co-researchers communicate with others will greatly contribute to the joy or the burden of the CAE process. At the stage of forming a research team, it may not be easy to discern everyone's personality and communication style. Add to your beginning communication an open discussion about how you like to communicate with each other to resolve conflicts if they arise later.

Although you may feel that you have communicated as much as you could at the planning stage, conflict and tension is inevitable in the collaboration process. Therefore, it would be wise for you to understand how your team members like to resolve conflict. Creamer (2004) argued that "long-term collaborators fell into one of three groups: like-minded, with a shared philosophy that rendered conflict unlikely; triangulators, who described their differences of little consequence; and multiplists, who found resolving differences a customary component of their work" (p. 859). These three groups of people would have different levels of comfort for consensus and differences, as Easterby-Smith and Malina's study (1999) illustrated. Communicating your differences and similarities early will provide structure for dealing with conflicts when they arise.

Keys to the Group Success

As we have discussed so far, multiple factors contribute to the success of collaborative autoethnographic teams. Critical to success are composing a manageable-sized research team with compatible members, taking time to discuss fundamentals about group dynamics, and keeping communication channels open based on mutual trust and respect. Paulus, Woodside, and Ziegler (2008) shared the wisdom from Barry et al. (1999), drawn on their collaborative research involving health professionals. In writing about the formation of this research team, they observed: (1) "We had sufficient common ground amongst us at the start"; (2) "None of us has a strong personal need or desire to work within a pyramidal hierarchy structure"; and (3) "We share a willingness to be open and a preparedness to learn from each other" (Paulus, Woodside, & Ziegler, 2008, p. 226). Wray (2002) also emphasizes the importance of collaboration among "those who were epistemic equals," namely equal positioning between collaborators (p. 859), concurring with the second point above. Although Barry et al.'s (1999) and Wray's (2002) conclusions grew out of their own disciplinary research, their insights are informative. If you are share common interests with your CAE team members, and you are willing to work together with collegial respect and open-mindedness, you are likely to overcome challenges associated with collaboration.

Deciding on a Research Focus

Forming a research team and finding a research focus can be a chicken-or-egg question. It is possible to form a research team first and then find a research focus based on group consensus or to decide on a research focus first and then form a research team. Whichever sequence of action you select, you need to understand that the first step will determine the next step to follow. If you form your research team first, your research topic should emerge from group consensus. On the other hand, if you have a pre-selected research topic, interested fellow travelers will join you because the topic resonates with their experiences and they are willing to collaborate in the endeavor. In this section, we provide guidance for finding and refining your research focus in either case. We also provide examples of research topics covered by other collaborative autoethnographies.

How to Find Your Topic

If your group is already formed before looking for a research topic to explore together, consider the following exercise to identify a research focus for your group. Create a list of topics about which your members are passionate and on which they can offer personal perspectives. Since you need to ensure full, willing, and enthusiastic cooperation from all members, aim for consensus rather than a majority voice.

Our experience illustrates the importance of careful deliberation at the initial step (Ngunjiri, Hernandez, & Chang, 2010). When we decided to do AE together and looked for a research focus in 2008, our common experiences as faculty of immigrant backgrounds in the U.S. academy surfaced quickly as a possible research topic. Knowing each other's background before we formed our research team certainly helped us choose the topic easily. We took time to discuss how we might explore our common interest from different angles after our seemingly easy decision on the topic, yet this general topic was good enough for us to get started.

If your group has not been formed and you want to initiate a collaborative autoethnographic project, you as an initiator have freedom to shape the focus of the research. You may find a topic with potential participants in mind. Chang's study with Bleil, Fornicola, and Dillman (2010) exemplifies the first approach. When Chang initiated a CAE project about the layoff experiences of women executives, she had knowledge of participants' recent layoff situations. So she selected the topic and invited the three women to the collaborative project. Chang did not share the same experience with them; however, her sympathetic alliance with them earned her a team member status, and all those who agreed to participate initially had full commitment to the chosen topic. Toyosaki et al.'s (2009) approach to their community AE resembles Chang's study with her students. After deciding on the research focus of investigating the "identity and materiality" of "whiteness in education," Toyosaki and colleagues described their process of forming the team as follows: "I (Satoshi) invited a student from my intercultural communication class (Nate), my colleague from my former doctoral program (Sandy), and her student (Kyle) to participate in this autoethnographic endeavor as 'coauthors' or 'community members'" (pp. 59–60).

In some cases, you may select your research topic and recruit interested strangers to your CAE team. Recruiting unknown members could pose the most challenges to the success of the collaboration project, resulting in mixed results. Here, I (Heewon) want to illustrate three cases that had differing results. In 2008, I formed an AE writing community with my work colleagues who wanted to explore their cultural identity. Recruits came from all ranks of the organization, some familiar and others unfamiliar to me. Loose connection among members, the broad research focus, and the lack of articulation for collaboration contributed to the fluctuation of membership over the academic year and ultimately to the disbandment of the group. Only a few surviving members from the group ended up producing individual autoethnographies for my coedited book (Chang & Boyd, 2011) and the initial effort birthed my long-term collaboration with Faith and Kathy-Ann (the co-authors of this book).

The second case involved my doctoral students. Due to my long-term interest in leadership mentoring, I recruited students who were interested in expanding their class projects on mentoring research and incorporating their mentoring experiences into their collaborative project. Although CAE was a component of this collaborative study of leadership mentors, maintaining their enthusiasm about the autoethnographic component was challenging to me partly because collaborative wrestling with the topic was not always comfortable and easy when collegiality among members was still forming. Although some students continued with their individual projects beyond the class, the research team as a whole did not survive.

The third case involved my Master's in Education students who were enrolled in an advanced seminar of multicultural education focusing on gender equity. Although I did not pick students for this course, a CAE project exploring the interplay between race, ethnicity, and gender identity resulted in an article for presentation (Chang et al., 2007). The success of this project, despite initial unfamiliarity among students and the pre-selected research focus, was due to the following factors: (1) the class had only three students, which made intimate collaboration possible; (2) the students and I came from multicultural backgrounds—Korean American female, African American female, Ethiopian male, and White American male—which made us eager to learn about/from each other; (3) we had to reach a consensus in order to commit to conducting and completing collaborative autoethnographic project as a class project; and (4) once the students decided unanimously to run the class as a research project, I participated in the research as their equal.

These cases of CAE projects shed light on how to plan for a project with your pre-selected topic and initially unfamiliar co-researchers. Since the research topic you will explore together is the only binding factor for your research team, we suggest that you articulate the research topic and expectations of team members as clearly as possible. In addition, you will need to participate in the collaborative process actively, leading every step of the process, sharing your personal stories, and sensitively nudging others to open up.

Sample Topics

Compared to single-authored autoethnographies, CAE has begun to appear in publication more noticeably within the last five years. Like solo autoethnographies, collaborative autoethnographies cover a wide range of topics, discussed in the many examples cited so far. By definition, all autoethnographies, individual or collective, touch on personal matters. However, some reveal more personal "confessions" than others. Although it is difficult to classify collaborative autoethnographies by clear-cut topical categories, we can identify them broadly by personal, societal, and professional topics.

Focusing on personal matters, some researchers invited readers into their intimate personal stories through "evocative" autoethnographies. Here we repeat some examples we offered in Chapter 1 and add new ones that are collaborative in nature: bulimia (Ellis, Kiesinger, & Tillmann-Healy, 1997) and teen pregnancy and mental illness (Muncey & Robinson, 2007). Other personal topics are not about personal confessions but are intimate nevertheless. Lietz, Langer, and Furman (2006) discussed their Jewish spirituality, whereas O'Shea et al. (2011) focused on infusing spirituality with their public professional work as professors. Some chose to discuss mothering (Geist-Martin et al., 2010) and others work-life balance (Cohen, Duberley, & Musson, 2009).

Some collaborative autoethnographers chose to explore women's or feminist topics as social issues. Defrancisco, Kuderer, and Chatham-Carpenter (2007) focused on the topic of women and self-esteem. Kalmbach Phillips et al. (2009) discussed their journey of "trying on, being in, and becoming feminist poststructural thinkers/inquirers/teacher educators" (p. 1455). Klinker and Todd (2007) added an age dimension to gender when examining their journeys of becoming professors as middle-aged women.

Racial, ethnic, and immigration issues have also been adopted by academics as a subject of collaborative exploration. Racially focused, Randolph and Weems (2010) shared their own experience of discrimination as African American faculty, while Toyosaki et al. (2009) explored the meaning of whiteness in education as Whites and non-Whites. Ngunjiri, Hernandez, and Chang's (2010) study investigated the intersection of ethnicity and gender as they navigated U.S. higher education as immigrants from Kenya, Trinidad, and Korea. Similarly, Nuñez, Murakami-Ramalho, and Cuero (2010) focused on teaching in a Hispanic-serving institution about how their backgrounds as Spanish-speakers informed their pedagogy. Reyes Cruz, Moreira, and Yomtoob's (2009) study adds immigration as a topic of boundary stretching to the literature of CAE.

Other academics chose to discuss issues pertaining to the world of academia. Boje and Tyler (2009) presented separate narratives but a collaborative analysis of workaholism prevalent in their academic life. Cann and DeMeulenaere (2010) implicitly critiqued the exclusivity of the academy by sharing how they extended a boundary of the academy by teaching in K–12 environments while pursuing a career as professors.

They intended to bring two different worlds together in pursuit of providing quality education. Doctoral mentoring has also been the focus of two studies coauthored by students and faculty (Chapman & Sork, 2001; Chawla & Rawlins, 2004); Gardner and Lane's (2010) study involved a tutor-student relationship in undergraduate nursing education. Other studies, conducted solely by students, focused on their academic journeys in their respective doctoral program (Espino, Muñoz, & Kiyama, 2010; Murakami-Ramalho, Piert, & Militello, 2008) and in different programs (Gurvitch, Carson, & Beale, 2008).

Academics not only explored their own experiences in the academy collectively but also reflected on their research activities. For example, Subedi and Rhee (2008) discussed their positionality as researchers in relation to the researched and challenges imposed by power differentials between researchers and the researched. Lashua and Fox (2006) shared autoethnographic stories of their involvement in "arts-based research through learning about and co-producing leisure with Aboriginal youth making rap music" (p. 268). Marshall, Rosen Eil, and Armstrong (2009) discussed how their archaeological project investigating a women's peace camp during a war affirmed and extended their feminist thinking.

As demonstrated here, the topics of CAE are varied. Yet, since academics are often initiators of these self-reflective and self-analytical endeavors, the topics of investigation appear to favor academically related topics. This natural tendency should not be misconstrued as the superiority of such topics. We suggest that autoethnographers think broadly as they choose topics so that collaborative works could contribute new knowledge beyond the topics relating to the academy.

Remaining Flexible

Whichever focus you initially select for your study, we advise you to remain open minded about the ultimate direction of your study. For a study to be truly collaborative, equal participation of each member should expected; thus, during the group process your initial topic could be altered and redirected. Watch and analyze how the direction of your study is unfolding. Keep your methodological journal so that your group can also discuss the process. Morphing of your initial topic could occur at different stages of your research process: during data collection, when you discover that richer data could be mined on a certain subtopic rather than your original topic; during data analysis, when your data point in a different direction than your original intent; and/or during data interpretation, when new insights illuminate certain aspects that your group had not thought about initially.

Cohen, Duberley, and Musson (2009) discovered, during their study of how relationships between work and home were conceptualized in women's lives, that the initial conceptual framework did not serve them well as they continued data analysis:

> As we attempted to analyze our data, it became clear that our initial discussions centered very much on discussing the ways in which we integrated and segmented various aspects of our home and work lives. Guided by Nippert-Eng's (1995) analysis, we talked at length about the ways in which we constructed home and work realms, the boundaries between them, and the symbols we used to show that we were crossing from one into the other. However, as the discussions continued it became apparent that there were limitations to this approach. (p. 233)

Ultimately, Cohen, Duberley, and Musson (2009) ended up considering "the permeability of home and work boundaries, the various ways in which one sphere of activity affected the other, and how that caused us to feel" (pp. 233–234). Their new insight about the relationship between home and work was gained during data analysis and interpretation because they did not insist on their initial conceptual framework of "segmentation" but allowed themselves to be open to a new framework of "permeability" that emerged from the data.

One of the characteristics of qualitative research is design flexibility (Creswell, 2006, 2012; Maxwell, 2004; Wolcott, 2010). Design flexibility refers to the possibility that the research focus could be adjusted from the original intent because researchers usually start with a broad topic and allow it to be narrowed and refined as they are informed by their research participants. The design flexibility is grounded on the epistemological orientation of qualitative inquiry in which researchers take the learner's positionality instead of imposing their pre-selected frameworks as an authority. By remaining flexible about the direction of your initial research topic, you will appreciate listening to each other's stories, probing each other with questions grounded on your collected data, and analyzing data from the bottom up, namely from the emic (insider) perspective, instead of imposing the predetermined frameworks of leading researchers. This flexibility will help you enjoy the process and reach deeper interpretation closer to the core of your collective data.

SELECTING A COLLABORATION MODEL

Now your research team is set and you have selected a research topic. You may feel like jumping right into data collection. Wait. Although it may mean a bit of delay in your process, your team will eventually be happy about the wait. We suggest that you first discuss how your team will proceed with data collection and how much you will collaborate with each other. Clear articulation of expectations for each other can save you agony in the future and help preserve your relationship.

Full or Partial Collaboration

Since we have provided detailed information about the extent of collaboration in Chapter 2, we address here only relevant information that can assist your team in determining how much collaboration is preferred. Your team can collaborate fully at all stages of research. This means that you will contribute your autobiographical data to the common pot of data, convene to ask probing questions of each other for clarification and expansion of data, and collaborate in data analysis, interpretation, and report writing. Your full collaboration may conclude with an article. Or your team's writing efforts may extend beyond writing one research report to multiple articles and books.

Your team can also collaborate partially at different stages of the research process. Different combinations of researchers can collaborate at different stages of research. For example, your team may collaborate only at the data collection stage. In this case, you will share and combine your stories to increase data points and the number of participants. With mutual agreement that all team members will have equal access to the combined data in the future, you may choose to depart from your team and individually complete your data analysis, interpretation, and write-up. Your team can also partially collaborate beyond data collection. Some of you may stay together to complete data analysis, interpretation, and writing, whereas others may depart from the project. Another possibility of partial collaboration is to include an additional member such as a "sounding board," described in Chapter 2, to enhance the productivity of your research team. Although you cannot anticipate changes in life that may precipitate departures of some members in the middle of your project, it is best to determine the extent of collaborative efforts prior to the start of the project.

Concurrent or Sequential Collaboration

In addition to the decision of full and partial collaboration, you will also want to decide on your procedural model—sequential versus concurrent. They are explained in detail in Chapter 2; we will again briefly review each model here.

The sequential model allows researchers to contribute to the pot of data one person at a time: When collecting autobiographical data, one researcher writes about his or her experience and passes his or her writing to the next researcher who then adds his or her account before passing it to the next person. This sequential model allows your stories to build on each other's and expand not only in quantity but also in depth.

In contrast, the concurrent model would allow researchers to write individually about a selected topic and then share their stories concurrently. The process of writing individually and sharing collectively is iterative. This model keeps your teammates from influencing each other's thought and allows each member to stand on equal footing when you share your individual stories. One member's failure to write and share will not immobilize the group process. As Klinker and Todd (2007) indicated, you will also gain deeper insights about your topic and research direction by asking probing questions and conversing with each other regularly after each writing episode.

With an understanding of the procedural distinctiveness and methodological benefits and challenges of these models, articulated in details in Chapter 2, you will need to decide on a model or models fitting your research timeline and collaboration situation. The good news is that you do not need to select one model over the other for an entire project. Unlike full or partial collaboration, the selection of the sequential and concurrent model is flexible in that it is possible to combine both models or stick to one kind.

Defining Roles and Setting Boundaries

Now that you have addressed some of the structural issues of CAE, it is time to deal with some relational concerns inherent in this kind of work. Now it is time for your team members to have a heart-to-heart talk about what you expect from each other, what you do or do not like to do, and what you should and should not do. Paulus, Woodside, and Ziegler (2010) argued that tension and conflict are part of group process, even when friends make up a team. Although you cannot anticipate all possible conflicts and problems, it is important to voice your concerns and make earnest efforts to address them before the study develops momentum.

Consider defining responsibilities and roles needed for the group. Meeting scheduler, discussion facilitator, communication coordinator, literature review coordinator, data keeper, and data analysis coordinator are some examples. In Chapter 6, we discuss some expanded roles and responsibilities of members particularly focusing on writing. Some responsibilities and roles remain constant and others may become obsolete as your study progresses. New responsibilities and roles may be added as your group advances in your research process. Although you may need to add flexibility to role assignment, dividing responsibilities will save you from much confusion and delay in the process. Keep the process democratic, collaborative, and flexible; however, you may need a "task-master" project manager for your team.

You may also want to set clear boundaries about what you as a group and as individuals should or should not do. Especially because your data contain intimate and personal stories, you should articulate how you want to keep confidentiality of personal information and how much each of you could utilize others' autobiographical data for your individual research or writing beyond the agreed CAE.

For academics, another important consideration is the authorship of your collaborative writing. It is a tricky business to determine the extent of contribution to writing, especially when the text blends voices of researchers. Paulus, Woodside, and Ziegler (2010) observed, "[W]e often could no longer tell who had written which portions of the manuscript . . . our individual voices diminished over time as our collective voice strengthened through our work together" (p. 858). So, then, what criteria will you use to determine the order of the authorship? How should credits be given to collaborators in their future writings when initiated by different individuals? It would be wise to set rules and boundaries about the authorship for your collaborative publication early in the process. Such decisions can help you delineate expectations for researchers in different placements of authorship.

It is also wise to have a shared understanding of the rights and obligations of each member. It is possible for a member to drop out of the research team in the middle of or after data collection. Ethical guidelines surrounding participants' rights in research studies indicate that participants can withdraw from a study anytime. Depending on when it happens, it can have different implications for the on-going project. For example, if a person drops out early during data collection, the impact of such a departure on the study may not be as great as if a person drops out later in the process. Whenever it happens, the question arises as to what to do with the autobiographical data of the departing member. It can sometimes be challenging to extract the data of the departing member immediately when data from the members are intertwined with others and removing some could destroy the continuity and cohesiveness of the data. We suggest that you think through options for your team to protect your group data and process as well as individual rights. Before you begin your research process, clarify and get consent from team members about what you would do with data in case some of them remove themselves or are removed from your group process.

CONCLUSION

So far we have suggested that the planning phase of a CAE project involves making informed decisions relevant to four tasks: (1) forming a research team; (2) deciding on a research focus; (3) selecting a collaboration model; and (4) defining roles and setting boundaries. Although you may have delineated a well-crafted research design for your CAE, if you have not considered ethical issues pertaining to your collaboration, the design is incomplete.

As highlighted in this chapter, teams must also ensure that their CAE projects are in keeping with ethical guidelines. Among ethical standards for research set forth by the American Educational Research Association (2011), several principles are particularly relevant to social science research involving human subjects: avoiding harm, "confidentiality," and "informed consent." They are articulated as follows:

- "Education researchers take reasonable steps to avoid harm to others in the conduct of their professional work" (p. 147).
- "Education researchers ensure that confidential information is protected" (p. 149).
- "Education researchers do not involve a human being as a participant in research without the informed consent of the participant or the participant's legally authorized representative" (p. 149).

These principles should be followed to protect your co-autoethnographers, those referenced in your stories (Morse, 2002), and yourself (Chatham-Carpenter, 2010).

An official step toward protecting research participants is to receive approval from the institutional review board (IRB) of your institution. IRBs review research proposals to ensure that researchers incorporate ethical standards in their design and that they follow their approved design. Yet questions have been raised about whether autoethnographic research requires IRB approval. One school of thought argues that it does not require an IRB approval because the study does not involve human subjects other than the researchers; therefore, potential harm to human subjects does not exist. Ellis (2004) noted that her IRB colleagues argued that AE did not require IRB approval because it was considered as fiction or dealt only with researchers and their interactions with family members. Another school of thought argues otherwise. Morse (2002) argues that AE researchers should be concerned about confidentiality of people who are included in the autoethnographic data of the researcher. Foster, McAllister, and O'Brien (2006) recommended pseudonyms be used for others included in one's AE and for the writer, if necessary, if their work is to be published. Each research team should determine the requirements for IRB approval dependent on the specifics of their institutions.

Even if AE proposals had received approval, the following IRB requirement would have met only one kind of ethics: "practical ethics" (Ellis, 2007). Ellis makes a case for meeting "relational ethics" by protecting privacy of people implicated in autoethnographies without informed consent. Especially when others referenced in such writings are portrayed negatively or in uncomplimentary terms, ethical issues surrounding the protection of confidentiality become tricky. It may not be possible or even necessary to acquire consent from those who did not participate in actual research activities as interviewees or subjects of direct observation for the purpose of research. They appear in autoethnographic narratives because they are part of researchers' autobiographic data/life stories. Nevertheless, even in such cases, autoethnographers are advised to apply ethical standards of doing no harm, protecting confidentiality, and balancing research with relational concerns (Ellis, 2007; Hernandez & Ngunjiri, 2013).

Whether you try to protect fellow autoethnographers, "involuntary participants" referenced in your stories, or yourself, we suggest that you understand the full implication of ethical principles of social science research and make your best efforts to protect privacy of each person. Ethical concerns should be discussed at the start of the study and throughout the study process because the team cannot always anticipate all the potential ethical quagmires that arise in due course. Thus, consider procedural as well as relational ethics as the study progresses (Ellis, 2007; Guillemin & Gillam, 2004). In the next chapter, we discuss various data collection strategies for CAE projects.

CHAPTER 4

Data Collection

By now, you should feel ready to begin the exciting phase of collecting autoethographic data.[1] If you have read general qualitative research books (Creswell, 2006; Maxwell, 2004; Patton, 2001; Wolcott, 2010) or AE methodology books (Chang, 2008; Ellis, 2007; Muncey, 2010), you should feel less intimidated about taking the first step of data collection. By taking one step at a time, you will reach a point where you feel you have sufficient data to begin analyzing and writing about about. However, data collection is not a mechanical and linear process. Rather data collection, especially in collaborative autoethnography (CAE), involves not only familiar techniques addressed in qualitative research methods books it also involves multiple negotiations with your research colleagues. It will take many rounds of conversations with them to reach creative compromises across your differences while gathering a variety of materials. In this chapter, we cover issues surrounding data collection and types of materials you may collect individually and collaboratively as well as your collaboration strategies.

COLLECTION OF DIVERSE DATA

You can collect a variety of data for your CAE. In addition to conversational and interactive data, there are other types of data that can be collected. It is typical that autoethnographers use self-generated personal memory data and other autobiographical material as the foundation of their studies. Chang (2008) adds that researchers can utilize data from external sources—family, friends, colleagues, and documents—to complement self-data. Your collaborative data will be enriched by your self-data, materials from your external sources, and a variety of data from your research teammates. You will also collect different types of data. In addition to personal memory data, you and your fellow autoethnographers can observe, reflect on, and analyze your self-identities; collect archival documents about yourselves and your sociocultural contexts; and interview others and each other. Table 4-1 summarizes various types of CAE data you can potentially collect. We identify different types of data, with the time focus and the source/authorship, and provide examples for each data type.

We elaborate on different types of data in the next few subsections. Although self-memory and recollection are likely to dominate your data, you can still determine what additional data you can add to enrich the study. We argue that rich data coming from multiple sources will contribute to the "thick description" of your life and sociocultural context and will enhance the credibility of your stories and interpretation through triangulation of data sources.

Table 4-1 Autoethnographic data types.

Data Type	Time Focus	Source/ Authorship	Examples
Personal memory/ recollection	past	self	snapshot writings created by researchers from memory on various topics: events, people, places, objects, researcher behaviors and thoughts, utterance, and senses
Archival materials	past	self or other	public and personal documents created by others about the researcher (e.g., certificates, acknowledgments, etc.); text, video, sound, or graphic materials about the researcher (e.g., recommendation letters, newspaper articles, multimedia material, photos, etc.); or self-focused materials created by the researcher (e.g., diary, publications, photos, media material, etc.)
Self- observation	present	self	observation notes created by the researcher to document his or her own activities and actions as they unfold at the present time of the study (e.g., self-observation log, memos capturing one's stream of consciousness, etc.)
Self- reflection	past & present	self	free-form (without any predetermined schema) journals or self-reflective writings, less factual and more interpretive, created by the researcher regarding his or her past and present experiences and sociocultural issues affecting them
Self-analysis	past & present	self	self-focused writings or charting created by the researcher with predetermined schema, framework, or forms
Interview	past & present	self-other or other	interview with research teammates; interview with other sources beyond the research team

PERSONAL MEMORY AND ARCHIVAL DATA

Both personal memory and archival materials bring the past into the present light for autoethnographic research. On the one hand, personal memory captures what you recall about your past and surroundings for the purpose of the study. It is about the past but captured at the present time of the study. On the other hand, archival materials refer to physical evidences of the past that you and others had created for other purposes. They are about the past and created in the past but are collected for the present use. Therefore, for your study you generate/create your memory data, whereas you collect preexisting archival materials.

Personal Memory Data

Personal memory data include writings that you will create as you jog your memory about past events, people, places, objects, behaviors, thinking, and utterances. By activating your memory of sight, hearing, taste, smell, and touch, you may be able to bring out many vivid details about your past when collecting these types of data. Although you may try to recall your past as accurately and completely as possible, your personal memory data are disappointingly "imperfect."

Lapadat (2009) argued that memory work is not a random recalling process. Rather, it is a "causal and interpretive" process because "the storyteller begins the analytical process in even the choice of story to tell, how to tell it, and the moments" (p. 43). Instead of being inhibited by the limitation, researchers embrace and take full advantage of the subjective nature of memory work in their study. Their acknowledgment of subjective memory resonates with Dillard's (1987) argument that memory of the past is illusive, selective, and distortive. Namely, we recall what we want to recall and how we want to remember the past. Therefore, the primary purpose of memory work is not about collecting perfectly accurate details about your past; rather, it allows you to recollect your past as you remember it.

With acknowledgment of its limitation, begin the collection of personal memory data. If you have a subject related to your research topic of which you have rich memory, this is a good place to begin. It is best to start writing your memories in free-flow; write down as many details as possible that you remember about the specific aspect of your past. You will have many opportunities to reflect on and interpret what you recall later. For now, focus on capturing what surfaces in your mind as you start pulling out what has been buried in the depths of your mind and soul. At this point, you need not worry about formatting and mechanics of style; just write.

While some of you may be successful in letting your memories gush out onto your paper (or computer screen), others may need external assistance in stirring their memory bank. For such people, we offer some "stir sticks," such as inventorying exercises that Chang (2008) suggests. Inventorying exercises refer to making lists of items pertaining to your research topics. For example, before you write about a specific topic, you may make a list of people, events, or places related to your topic. Recalling small bits of information, without the huge burden of writing about them all at once, may be a more manageable step. Out of the list, you may select a few items to describe more extensively. You may add both the list and the detailed writings to your "pool" of data for analysis and interpretation. The following is an example of Heewon's mentors-in-life list that she created for her CAE on mentoring and leadership with a dozen leaders of color in faith-based higher education:

My mentor list includes 13 people. I identify them here with different characteristics:

- Mother: female, Korean, past-present, senior, personal/spiritual/professional mentoring, family-origin, currently moderate relationship
- Father: male, Korean, past-present, senior, personal/spiritual/professional mentoring, family-origin, currently moderate relationship
- College group minister: male, Korean, past, senior, spiritual mentoring, church-origin, currently no relationship
- Dissertation advisor: male, U.S. White, past-present, senior, professional mentoring, work-origin, currently moderate relationship
- Department colleague: male, U.S. international White, present, senior, professional mentoring, work-origin, currently strong relationship
- Department colleague: female, U.S. international Black, present, peer, personal/professional mentoring, work-origin currently strong relationship
- Department colleague: female, U.S. international-Black/Hispanic, present, peer, personal/professional mentoring, work-origin, currently strong relationship
- Former neighbor: female, U.S. White, present, senior, personal/professional mentoring, community-origin, currently strong relationship

From the list, Heewon focused her description on mother and dissertation advisor later.

Although she initially developed the inventorying exercises as activities for individual autoethnographies, Heewon applied them to her own CAE. When the inventorying exercises are used in a group setting, we suggest that you still give yourself some alone time to create a list before sharing it in the group. During group sharing, your team may brainstorm together to expand your combined list. This hybrid model of solo and group activities is likely to allow your group to benefit from the unadulterated independent thinking of individuals and group synergy.

Archival Data

Archival data complement personal memory data. Archival materials include a variety of public and private documents that others or you have created for different purposes prior to your AE study. They include (1) official documents (e.g., birth certificates, diploma, official letters, etc.), publications (e.g., newspaper articles, biography, website information, etc.), video, sound, or graphic materials as well as physical artifacts that others have created; and (2) writings, journals, artifacts, and personal items that you have created. Some of them may focus on you, illuminating specifics of your past, and others on your immediate and broad sociocultural contexts. One source of valuable archival material is a personal journal you might have kept in the past. Gurvitch, Carson, and Beale (2008) demonstrate the value of their personal journals kept for two years during their studies, which were used for their CAE of doctoral experiences.

In addition to adding new details to your existing data and helping you jog your memory, archival materials can play an important role as the basis for the triangulation of your personal memory data. You can cross-check, verify, and correct your recollection against archival data collected from various sources. Archival data not only complement but also augment personal memory data. In a dialogic writing of mentoring relationship between a doctoral student and her dissertation advisor, Chawla and Rawlins (2004) utilized Chawla's writing assignments (archival material) submitted to Rawlins in the course of one semester as a basis for their CAE constructed later. The archival data from the time of Chawla's doctoral work laid the foundation and framework for the reflection and analysis at the time of their collaborative research. Since the authors were able to interlace their memory data with their archival data, their CAE gave readers confidence in the credibility of their analysis and interpretation.

SELF-OBSERVATIONAL DATA

Unlike past-oriented data such as personal memory and archival data, self-observational data capture your present actions and thoughts as they unfold before your eyes at the present time. In a technical sense, it is impossible to collect unadulterated data about your present moment because as soon as you attempt to record them, your thoughts and actions are disrupted and your present moments flee. Despite the challenge, there is value to jotting down your fleeting thoughts and actions in the present moment as swiftly as possible.

Rodriguez and Ryave (2002) developed systematic self-observational data collection techniques that utilize structured recording forms to assist self-observation. Chang (2008) applied this data collection technique to the autoethnographic research method. For example, she suggested that researchers record activities, time, and people involved in the activities as they are engaged in them for a set period of time (p. 92). Such records can help you gain self-knowledge about your preference of activities and people. During self-observation you can keep track of your feelings and emotions as well.

Your present thoughts and behaviors can also be captured during interactive interviews with your team members or interactions with others during your natural activities. Let your audio or video recorder run while you are conversing with others or are involved in your routine activities. Be mindful of ethical guidelines when recording your conversations. Obtain consent from others beforehand. When you are engaged in natural activities, you may not always censor your behaviors or speeches. By reviewing your recorded moments, you will have opportunities to observe yourself as if from "outside." This method of data collection is valuable in capturing your thoughts and behaviors at the least-rehearsed and self-regulated moments.

SELF-REFLECTIVE AND SELF-ANALYTICAL DATA

Self-reflective and self-analytical data capture your present thoughts and perspectives as well as your past. Although Cann and DeMeulenaere (2010) and Lapadat (2009) refuse to separate interpretation from recalling of the past, in this section we intentionally isolate self-reflection and self-analysis from personal memory work so that we can encourage you to become an astute observer of your own cognitive process. Unlike personal memory data or archival data that are raw (i.e., least-processed) data on the past, self-reflective and self-analytical data are processed data about meanings and impressions of recalled events, people, place, and/or objects. Furthermore, we discuss self-reflection separately from self-analysis. Although they may happen concurrently, they are conceptually two different activities in data collection.

Self-Reflective Data

When you reflect on your past or present, your past experience and perspectives vigorously enter your thinking process. You not only construct stories of what happened, who was involved, and where it took place, but also think about the meaning of the event, person, and location and assess their values to you. Since interpreted meanings are shaped by your present experiences, self-reflective data mix the present and past and can adapt to the present moment of data collection. For example, during Chang's collaborative study of female executives' layoff experiences with her doctoral students (the article is under review by a journal), her co-researchers recalled what happened on the day of layoff and subsequently. At the same time, they reflected on the impact of the event on their lives; their feelings toward their former bosses, coworkers, and subordinates; and their identity as the unemployed. Whereas their memory data focused on what happened factually, their self-reflective data captured their changed impression of the event over time and their emotional responses to the event over time. We also noticed that over the course of six months of data collection, their reflection of pain associated with layoff had changed its intensity and shade from "hot" to "cool" colors.

Self-reflective data do not have to be tied to single events, locations, persons, or objects. You can utilize self-reflexivity on broad or general topics related to your life or sociocultural issues. For example, in Chawla and Rawlins's (2004) CAE, their reflexivity guided their research as the first author reflected on different stages of their evolving student-mentor relationship and the second author responded to the first one. Hernandez's (2011) AE of teaching and assessment drew from her recollection of encounters with students as well as her self-reflection on her teaching and assessment practices; Galman's (2011) AE also utilized her perspectives on integrating Jewish faith with work and family. These writings illustrate that autoethnographers' self-reflexivity is integral to their research process and production.

Self-Analytical Data

In some occasions, you will collect more cognitively processed data. Cognitive processing involves higher-order thinking skills, according to Bloom's taxanomy, such as evaluation, application, and creation (Bloom et al., 1956; Krathwohl, 2002). Instead of simply recording what happened in the past, for example, you may assign meanings to and evaluate simple events as you recall them. Other times, you may compare your data with others, applying some comparative criteria; still other times, you may synthesize concrete details into simplified abstraction or create hypotheses in your mind. You may also form perspectives and opinions based on your past experiences. When your mind works on your past experiences, you end up recording the results of your cognitive processing rather than merely describing what you recall. Here we introduce three tools for self-analytical data collection: culturegram, relational diagram, and comparison diagrams.

Chang (2008) constructed the culturegram as a self-analytical tool to help autoethnographers visualize their multicultural identities with various cultural groups. Figure 4-1 shows a refinement from her previous work. This exercise would compel you to identify your cultural familiarity and competence in various cultural categories such as race, ethnicity, gender, religion, nationality, class, language, profession, and interest groups. You can add more cultural categories deemed relevant to your context. You are encouraged to identify your affinities in each category and to rank the affinities in order of their importance to you. The underlined ones indicate the most important identity in the category. Ultimately, you are asked to identify the three most important self-identities that you perceive at a given moment. To complete a culturegram, you will need to look at your life holistically, analyze your cultural membership, evaluate the importance of each membership to you, and synthesize the relation of different identities to the overall perception of yourself.

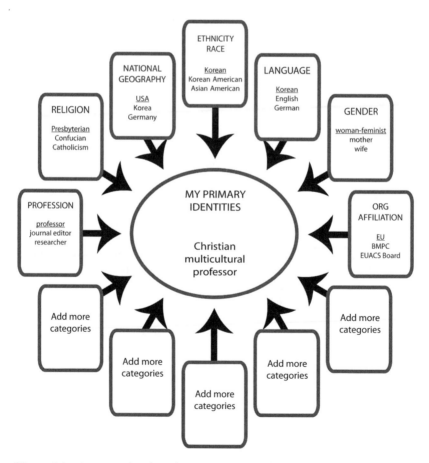

Figure 4-1 An example of a culturegram.

Relational diagrams include kinsgrams, sociograms, and professional network chart. The kinsgram is one of the tools that anthropologists commonly use to chart relationships among members of communities that they study during fieldwork. It visualizes relationships by birth, marriage, attachment, and association. Figure 4-2 shows symbols used for a kinsgram; Figure 4-3 includes an example of a kinsgram. You can chart your family and community relationships in your kinsgram. By comparing kinsgrams among your team members, you can discover how your kinship influences—differently or similarly—your social functioning.

Sociogram refers to a visual display of social network. Katz et al. (2004) define a social network as follows:

> A social network consists of a set of actors ("nodes") and the relations ("ties" or "edges") between these actors. . . . The nodes may be individuals, groups, organizations, or societies. The ties may fall within a level of analysis (e.g., individual-to-individual ties) or may cross levels of analysis (e.g., individual-to-group ties). (p. 308)

You may construct your sociogram with personal friends, associates, or professional colleagues. A typical sociogram would look more like

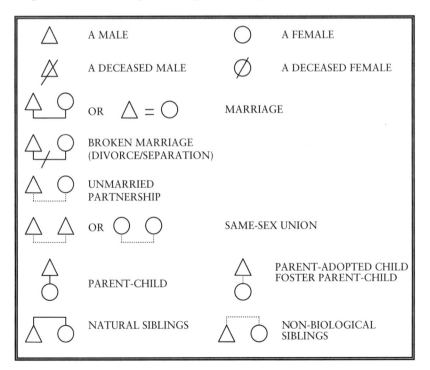

Figure 4-2 Symbols used for a kinsgram (Chang, 2008, p. 83).

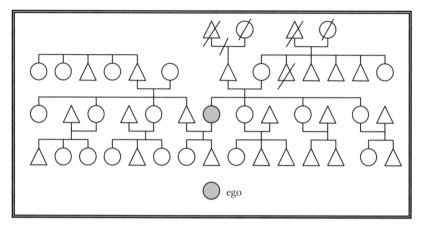

Figure 4-3   An example of a kinsgram (Chang, 2008, p. 84).

Figure 4-4. In this chart, you indicate emotional and social closeness by the length of the connecting line.

Heewon used similar principles in her exercise of charting constellation of relationships to guide her CAE team (see Figure 4-5), with the following instruction of how to use it:

> This chart will allow you to plot people in your constellation of relationships. Add to your inner circle (the second closest circle to self) those who inspire you, nourish you, mentor you, care about your growth, like to be with you, and/or provide you with developmental opportunities; add to your middle circle (the mid-sized circle) those who work with you well but are not emotionally close to you; add to your distant circle (the largest circle) those who have working relationships with you but with whom you have difficulty. Think about the following questions:
> - How are those in your inner circle qualitatively different from those in the middle or distant circles?
> - What have you learned from those in the inner circle, in the middle circle, and in the distant circle respectively?
> - What have you learned about self from this exercise?

This diagram can easily be adapted for charting your social and professional network. For each person to whom you are connected, you can analyze the connection of that relationship to other individuals or organizations and social circles to which you belong. You can also analyze the demographic characteristics of your social circles and the intensity of the relationship. By analyzing your sociogram, you will be able to draw conclusions about your relation to "others of similarity" (those who share similar cultural values with you and with whom you

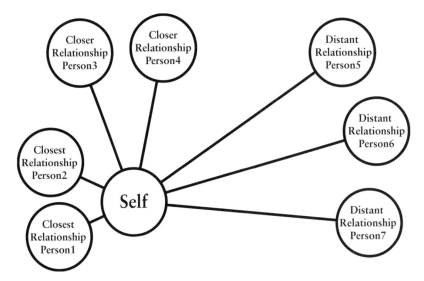

Figure 4-4 An example of a sociogram.

feel comfortable), "others of difference" (those from cultural groups that do not share similar values and that you are not familiar with), and "others of opposition" (those who come from groups that have opposing values and whom you consider "enemies") (Chang, 2008, pp. 26–29). Others of similarity are likely to show up on your sociogram more frequently. Therefore, the analysis of your sociogram will help you discover your relational propensity. Identifying relationships per se may not always be the goal of your AE. However, the analytical data of relationships provide you with rich contextual data about yourself.

The comparison chart is another data collection tool to collect self-analytical data. For example, a Venn diagram works well when you draw comparisons within the group. The method of comparison also helps you display both similarities (commonalities) and differences between you and others. Many collaborative autoethnographies focus on commonalities that emerge among participants despite their seemingly distinctive backgrounds.

Three CAE studies illustrate such convergence based on shared commonalities. Muncey and Robinson (2007) focused on the commonality of marginalization in society that resulted from having been a teen mother and a mental hospital patient respectively. Nuñez, Murakami-Ramalho, and Cuero (2010) explore "how their cultural backgrounds inform their pedagogical approaches toward equity" in their Hispanic

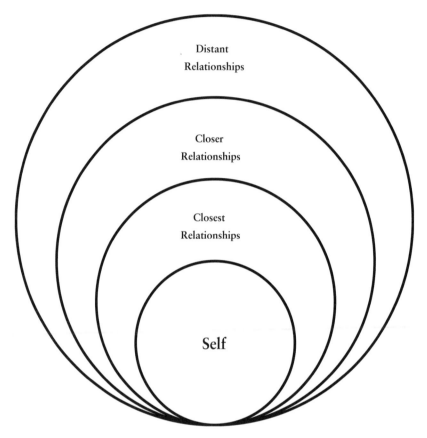

Figure 4-5 A constellation of social relationships.

serving institution despite their different ethnic and racial backgrounds. Cann and DeMeulenaere (2010) found the commonality of justice-orientation across their gender (female vs. male) and racial (Black vs. White) differences and present their co-narratives of dual responsibilities as a K–12 teacher and college professor.

Not all collaborative autoethnographies focus on commonalities. Chapman and Sork (2001) highlight and problematize differences between a female feminist graduate student and male non-feminist doctoral supervisor. Our own CAE of immigrant faculty of color in the U.S. academy explores the interplay between different ethnic backgrounds and similar professional experiences. Figure 4-6 illustrates how our similarities and differences might be expressed in a Venn diagram.

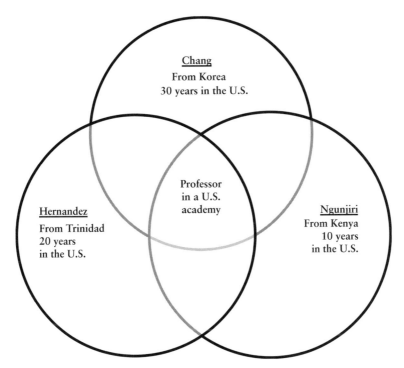

Figure 4-6 A Venn diagram of our similarities and differences.

Along with self-reflective data, self-analytical data help you examine yourself and your teammates in a different light from self-memory, archival, and self-observational data because these cognitively more processed data push you further in the direction of data analysis. So far, we have examined types of data you can use in either solo or collaborative autoethnographies. Now let us turn our attention to data unique to CAE.

CONVERSATIONAL AND INTERACTIVE DATA

Unlike individually collectible data, dialogic data cannot be collected by solo efforts of individual researchers. Collection of conversational and interview data must engage one or more partners in conversations; therefore, interaction among research teammates becomes a unique source of data for CAE. Whether formal or informal, systematic or casual, face-to-face or virtual, conversations have been incorporated in all CAE processes at some points. Ellis, Kiesinger, and Tillmann-Healy (1997) called them "interactive interviews" and argued that they facilitate an "in-depth and intimate understanding of people's experiences with emotionally charged and sensitive topics" (p. 121). Three sets of collaborative autoethnographers also articulated the values of interactive interviews in their study (Cann & DeMeulenaere, 2010; Cohen, Duberley, & Musson, 2009; Toyosaki et al., 2009). Cann and DeMeulenaere noted that their living room conversations such as the following gave birth to their CAE, saying: "Many actual conversations that have occurred between the authors over the past two years, often times in one of our homes, in the car as we shuttle our kids to a snowy day activity or via cell phone while juggling other tasks" (p. 41).

Similarly, Cohen, Duberley, and Musson (2009) utilized their conversations, termed "autoethnographic conversations," as their primary data source (p. 230). Unlike Cann and DeMeulenaere, who relied on face-to-face conversations, Cohen and colleagues conversations took place in person as well as via e-mail over four months. Toyosaki et al. (2009) took their conversations to the virtual world. Instead of face-to-face conversations, they carried out conversations in systematic and sequential manners, with one researcher writing and passing the "writing stick" to the next person who did the same, in round-robin fashion.

Others also utilize conversations as important supplemental sources of data and intersperse them with other data collection strategies. In our study (Ngunjiri, Hernandez, & Chang, 2010), we collected a variety of data individually and came together to discuss what we gathered and to ask probing questions.[2] By alternating between solo data collection and interactive interviews among ourselves, we were able to take advantage of the probing sessions to clarify meanings of our data and to determine subsequent steps in our research process based on our collaborative wisdom. We recorded our probing sessions and added our conversations to our collective data pool.

Data Collection Strategies

It may be clear by now that you can collect a variety of data from different sources. In our discussion of data types, we have offered information, even if not explicitly, about how you may collect them. In this section, we discuss some specific data strategies. How much do you want to work separately to collect your autobiographical data? How and when do you want to engage your teammates in collaborative data collection? What kind of data should you collect individually or collectively? If you have not already thought about these questions, this is the time to do it.

Individual Data Collection

Let us imagine that your group has decided on your research topic. Now you will need to determine which information is necessary to collect and where you can locate it. It may be accessible from your memory bank, personal journals, file cabinets, parents' attic, or other places. The next question is how you will retrieve necessary and relevant information. As a primary agent of control, you sometimes need to act alone, recalling, self-observing, self-reflecting, or self-analyzing your personal data. Even in CAE research where others become catalysts in your data collection process, your individual work is necessary. Ellis and Bochner's (1992) study of abortion and Lietz, Langer, and Furman's (2006) study of Jewish spirituality started with the solo work of data collection—writing down their experiences—before sharing their experiences with their teammates. Other research teams started with interactive interviews with each other about their topic of interest before setting out to do individual writings and data collection (Ellis, Kiesinger, & Tillmann-Healy, 1997). Whichever direction your team takes, individual data collection is vital to CAE.

Solo data collection opportunities will give you serious self-reflective time without being influenced by your teammates or succumbing to your own desire to conform to your group's unintended peer pressure. When researchers are permitted to take a "free walk" for a while for their solo data collection, this unadulterated time may yield unexpectedly rich data unique to individual researchers. Therefore, researchers should not be too anxious to coordinate individual data collection activities too quickly and too completely. However, prolonged individual data collection without converging as a group can result in wide digression among individual data sets. We suggest that you be mindful of topical boundaries that you have agreed to explore as a group. The boundaries could be as broad as "your leadership experience while growing up," as in the case of our faculty of color study (Ngunjiri, Hernandez, & Chang, 2010) or as specific as "my layoff moment," as in the case of Heewon's study with her doctoral students.

During your individual collection process, you may collect various types of data that have been discussed so far. You do not need to collect all types and all data at a single session. Especially at the beginning of your data collection process, it is beneficial for you and your teammates to intersperse individual data collection sessions with collaborative discussion sessions regularly, which we discuss in more detail a bit later in this chapter. Although you should allow some flexibility in planning your individual data collection sessions, we suggest that you also think ahead about types of data you want to collect during these sessions.

We used three different levels of planning in our three collaborative autoethnographies.[2] In our study of immigrant faculty of color, our planning for individual data collection sessions was most relaxed, which allowed us to control individual directions of data collection. We agreed on certain data collection activities, such as each one constructing a culturegram; we also wrote on different topics pertaining to our leadership expereinces. For example, Faith wrote about her personal mission statement and critical incidents on discovering gender and age discrimination; Kathy-Ann wrote about constructions of blackness; and Heewon wrote about the chronology of leadership experiences and her gendered perspective on professorship among other topics. Due to our already established collegiality, minimal power differentials as faculty colleagues, and knowledge and experience with qualitative research methods, we allowed ourselves to determine our writing topics within given boundaries. We then used our diverse individual writings as stimuli for our group sessions in which we discussed our different and similar experiences, probed unexplored issues, and generated new topics to write about in subsequent individual sessions.

Heewon approached her layoff study with a medium level of structure and advanced planning. In the study of women executives' layoffs with her doctoral students, she gave more structure to data collection because her fellow researchers were learners of the AE method and needed more guidance.

At the beginning, Heewon posed a writing prompt: "Describe the moment when you heard you lost a job." Three participants wrote their responses to the prompt in a sequential mode. Eventually, multiple rounds of responses to this prompt and each other's writings became the focal point of discussion when the research team met. At group sessions, topics for the next rounds of individual writings emerged: "being cut off," ". . . the first few days after," "the beginnings of healing," "lessons about leadership," "your old job," "reasons for being let go," and "resiliency."

The data collection process of this study is characterized by two features: (1) the data collection framework (the sequential model in this case) and the first writing prompt were pre-planned before the data collection began; and (2) flexibility was built into the data collection plan to allow researchers to decide subsequent data collection topics based on previous data and the group process. The combination of these two features helped balance structural predictability with flexibility in data collection. We attribute the fitness of this data collection approach to the unique makeup of the research team consisting of a research expert and emerging autoethnographers who had already established relationships among themselves. The emerging researchers' familiarity with qualitative research was helpful when extracting possible topics from already collected data for further exploration.

Heewon's third CAE study, focusing on mentoring experiences of leaders of color in faith-based higher education, took yet another approach to data collection. The research design of this study imposed the most structure to data collection when compared to the other two studies. At the beginning, two leading researchers out of a team of 12 members planned the study in advance because the recruits for the study came after the plan. In this research design, participants were expected to contribute two writings responding to two online discussion prompts set up in Blackboard®[3] each month and participate in one of two monthly virtual conferences (see Appendix A for the writing prompts).

For six months of data collection, participants interspersed monthly group sessions with individual data collection activities. Although researchers allowed deviation from pre-planned writing and discussion topics, participants followed the most prescribed data collection plan. In this study, the structure in data collection was necessary because leading researchers entered into this project with a large group of strangers who were not familiar with the AE or qualitative research methods. So the research process was designed to teach participants about the research method by doing it.

As you can tell, all our studies have not only combined individual and group data collection activities but also interspersed individual sessions with group sessions. Solo data collection was important to our study; group data collection was necessary.

Group Data Collection

When autoethnographic data are collected individually, you may ask where and when group work should enter in this supposedly collaborative process. CAE involves balancing between individual and collective data collection, although the combination of "collaboration" and "autoethnography" appears to be inherently oxymoronic. If you think of solo work and group work as overlapping activities, it will help reconcile the inherently dichotomous terms. For example, even when you do individual data collection, you operate within the parameters and framework that your group has set for individual researchers.

When individual and group data collection activities are alternated systematically, you will see how individual work becomes the inspiration for group discussion and how decisions emerging from group sessions spill over into the next stages of individual data collection. Occasionally punctuating solitary data collection periods with group conversations maximizes the capacity of collaborative autoethnographic efforts. Unlike AE, collaborative autoethnographers combine their energy and data to create a richer pool of data from multiple sources. In this section, we build on our previous discussion of sequential and concurrent model of collaboration to describe how your group can utilize either model for group data collection.

Sequential Model. If your group has decided to try a sequential model, select a topic you want to explore together. The initial topic should be broad. One of you starts writing about or writes a response to the selected topic and passes the writing to your group. Anyone who wants to respond to the previous writing can take the next turn. Each of you should think about adding something new to the string of conversations, instead of merely affirming other writings. When you respond to your teammate's contribution, you can select one strand of thought and expand on it with your new information or you can affirm or contradict your teammate's thought and offer your differing perspectives. You can also end your writing with a question to facilitate the conversation. There is no set rule about how to respond to each other. In all of the CAE studies we have designed and participated in, we agreed in advance that we would not only affirm others' thoughts and experiences but also honestly contribute our unique and sometimes contradictory perspectives to the conversation. Our mutual respect even in case of disagreements helped us preserve our collegiality. When your team feels that data collection has reached saturation on one prompt, move on to another topic for a new prompt and a new sequence of discussions. The sequential model is illustrated in Figure 4-7. (R1, 2, and 3 indicate different researchers.)

When you implement the sequential data collection model, you do not need to be rigid about the sequence of contributors. In our own research about the layoff, we did not prescribe the order of participants. Three participants took turns without pre-scheduling the turn; instead, one began and upon completing, she invited others to contribute. As a result, and depending on each researcher's schedule, everyone freely participated in responding to online forums set up for their data collection whenever they wanted to. It turned out that some contributed more to certain forums and less to others. Ultimately, the two remaining researchers ended up contributing to the collective pot of data equally.

This data collection model has at least two benefits. First, the sequential data collection model is useful when your research team wants to stay focused on your data collection on one subtopic at a time. Since your data on a certain subtopic are strung together, that can help you focus when analyzing data. Streamlining data collection and data analysis can be useful for novice collaborative autoethnographers, although this convenience can backfire during data analysis and interpretation (potential concerns are explained in the next chapter). Second, this sequential data collection model is also beneficial in stimulating each

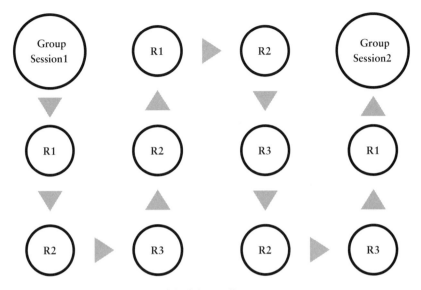

Figure 4-7 The sequential model of data collection.

other in data collection. By reading contributions made previously, the next researcher can affirm, question, and expand on what has already been written about. The focused expansion can help data collection reach a level of depth and breadth with which each member can be satisfied before moving on to another topic.

Concurrent Model. The concurrent model assumes that every member of your research team participates in a same schedule of data collection. All members collect their individual data alone but during the same time period with the same expectations. With their individually collected data they converge for group sessions. Our study of immigrant women took this model as illustrated in Figure 1-3 (Chapter 1). DeFrancisco, Kuderer, and Chatham-Carpenter (2007) illustrate their process in a concurrent model. With 10 participants, they found a simple way of sharing data with each other: "Each woman wrote her life-journey with self-esteem and a month later we shared them via email" (p. 238). When they met for group conference, their writings became the central material for discussion.

When your research team meets in person or virtually for group discussion, you will invariably end up gathering new information, analyzing and interpreting to make sense of your collective data, and discussing next steps. It is worthwhile to record the group sessions for future analysis. This type of data is what we referred to as conversational and interview data in earlier sections in this chapter.

The concurrent model also has benefits. As discussed in Chapter 2, researchers in the concurrent model can think and collect data independently from their teammates during their solo activities. This independent thinking of the researchers could enrich types, sources, and content of data when your research team is not too prescriptive. Diverse thinking of individual researchers broadens possibilities for your data sources. Another benefit of the model is the delineated phase of collaboration following individual data collection. During the collaboration phase, researchers can touch base with each other, bring diverse data to collective interrogation, and negotiate differences among themselves. Since multiple group sessions are likely to be built into the CAE process, you will feel the forward movement through data analysis and the interpretation through the group sessions.

Iterative Process. The combination of individual and collective data collection often takes place in an iterative process. Cohen, Duberley, and Musson (2009) described the iterative process clearly. They initially collected data by brainstorming ideas via e-mail, met in person to discuss their collective ideas and to probe each other in "interactive introspection" sessions, and followed their discussions with e-mail exchanges:

> We began the process with a flurry of e-mail exchanges during which we brainstormed ideas about incidents that had been critical to us in terms of the dynamics or our work and nonwork lives. We then held three meetings where we had in-depth discussions about various aspects of our lives and the ways in which we had experienced tensions in trying to manage the interplay of home and work life. These meetings were at times emotionally charged as one or the other of us talked about highly personal issues we were facing. Conversations typically lasted around four hours and followed a similar format. One person started off discussing issues particularly pertinent to her at that time and then the other two chipped in, asking questions, making comments, and then talking about their own situations. This enabled a process of "interactive introspection" (Smith, 1999) to take place in the conversations as we told our own stories and responded to each other's interpretations of events.
>
> The meetings were followed up by e-mail exchanges among the three of us. These included notes of what had been said and attempts to conceptualize our experiences. Thus, our discussions and e-mails contained both our memories of our experiences and our developing attempts to theorize them. (p. 233)

As you undergo the iterative process during data collection, alternating individual and group sessions, you will be able to narrow or redirect your focus. Also, it is not uncommon that researchers redirect their research focus, especially when they start with certain theoretical frameworks.

Cohen, Duberley, and Musson (2009) experienced such a shift when they discovered that their experience of work-home dynamics did not fit the conventional discourse of compartmentalization and fragmentation between work and home boundaries. Rather, as they noticed their experiences with one sphere of life affecting the other, they changed their discussion of how they balance their lives to how they maintain order as well as experience disorder. We encourage you to return to Figure 1-3 to see the visual presentation of the iterative process in our research (Ngunjiri, Hernandez, & Chang, 2010).

CONCLUSION

In this chapter, we explained a variety of data you can collect for your CAE—self-memory, archival, self-observational, self-reflective, self-analytical, and conversational and interactive. We also expounded on individual and group data collection strategies. As you can imagine, you cannot collect all types of data all at once. Find your own mix; experiment with different strategies for your study.

When you collect data, remember three interdependent principles: (1) rich data are a prerequisite of a good product; (2) data collection is not an end in itself; and (3) data are like scraps with little value until something beautiful is made out of them.

First, without rich raw materials you cannot produce an excellent research report. Whether you dig deeper into a few sources or collect widely from a wide variety of sources, strive to collect rich data. Rich data—diverse and substantive—add details, vivacity, and excitement to the "thick description" of the phenomena you investigate (Geertz, 1973). Also, data from various sources help you triangulate your data as we discussed earlier.

Second, we introduced various data collection strategies—individual, collective, sequential, and concurrent. It may appear that data collection is a major business in itself. Although we expect you to do a great job collecting data, we want to remind you that data collection is not an end in itself. We have seen too many researchers who were so invested in the process of data collection that they were left with little energy to continue the study once data collection was "completed." They forgot that there is a finish line to cross and a long way to get to the finish. Think beyond data collection. We will discuss what lies beyond data collection in the next two chapters.

Last, it is important to remember that data have little value until they are analyzed and interpreted. Data need to be analyzed and synthesized. They need to be pulled apart and dissected. Data fragments need to be moved around and grouped with other relevant ones. In the process, the data may be ripped apart; seams of reattached pieces may look insecure, requiring repairs; and newly assembled data fragments may need to be sewn together with new thread. This metaphor illustrates that data are there to serve a higher purpose—to support the ultimate interpretation of the sociocultural phenomena your group is investigating. Do not love your data too much. Do not feel too attached to your data. If you do, you will have a problem disturbing or discarding your data when it is necessary to do so. If you let your beloved data stay, your final product will end up looking like a patchwork with too loose threads. In the next chapter, we present guidelines for how to work with data and make something beautiful out of it.

CHAPTER 5

Data Analysis and Interpretation

By now, you may have gathered various materials relevant to your research topic for a while. As you watch collection of text, graphics, audio, and other data grow, you may be anxious to make meaning of them as soon as possible. You may wonder about when the right time is to begin data analysis. Do not be surprised to hear that you have already begun your data analysis as you collected, organized, and managed your ever-growing data. Autoethnographers (Lapadat, 2009; Muncey, 2010) would argue that data analysis begins with memory work; when you select memories, you examine, evaluate, and analyze them as you decide which ones fit with your autoethnographic exploration. For qualitative research, the phase of data collection is usually seamlessly connected to data organization, analysis, and interpretation. Furthermore, many qualitative researchers do not differentiate data analysis from data interpretation because they are often intertwined in the activities of "working with data" (Creswell, 2006; Glesne, 2011; Maxwell, 2004; Shank, 2002). Despite interconnectivity among data organization, data analysis, and data interpretation, qualitative methodologists acknowledge the importance of explaining data interpretation separately from data analysis (Denzin, 2004; Geertz, 1973; Patton, 2001; Thorne, 2008; Wolcott, 1994). We agree that it is useful to discuss them separately in order to highlight the distinctive goals of each activity. Therefore, in this chapter we discuss the three processes—data organization, data analysis, and data interpretation—in separate sections. We also discuss benefits and cautions about using computer-assisted qualitative data analysis software (CAQDAS) for data analysis. We highlight the purpose of data analysis and interpretation in supporting your writing goals to produce a polyphonic or multivocal text, one that adequately captures the areas of commonality and divergence in your experiences.

Data Organization and Management

As your data collection progresses, you will notice that the volume of data grows quickly. If steps are not taken to store these data in an organized manner, you can lose track of them. In this section, we make suggestions about how you might organize and manage your data in preparation for data analysis and interpretation. Data organization and management precedes analysis and interpretation. Although we discuss these activities in that sequence, steps to complete the collaborative autoethnography (CAE) process, like other qualitative research, are not linear and inflexibly sequential. In reality, organizing data and the initial steps in analysis often happen as you are collecting your data. Saldaña (2009) discusses organization as a prerequisite step in data analysis: "First, you need to be organized. This is not a gift that some people have and others don't. Organization is a set of disciplined skills that can be learned and cultivated as habits" (p. 28).

Data organization begins simply by filing away what you collect for your study, whether it is material from your personal memory or a physical object. You store them in logical places where they can easily be retrieved for your use later. As you continue to collect data, your current organization of data will be disturbed to make room for new data or to accommodate reorganization of data. Constant rethinking of the relationship between old and new data is part of good data analysis. Therefore, you should remain flexible about your organization of data.

The process of data organization and management not only gives order to piecemeal and messy data but also provides opportunities to engage in preliminary analysis indicating how the pieces fit together. When you gain a global perspective of where a variety of data fit and where deficiency lies in your data set, you are already underway with data analysis. To assist you with initial data organization and management, we suggest labeling, sorting, and storing strategies.

Labeling and Storing Data

The first and simple step of organizing your data begins with labeling each item with the date of collection, the identity of the collector, the source, and the type of data. The contextual information is critical when analyzing data. When multiple researchers are collecting data, it is easy for each researcher to develop his or her own system, which can be confusing. By agreeing on a system for labeling data from the beginning of your research process, you can avoid confusing and mixing up data and save many headaches later, as well as prevent the possible loss of valuable materials. Much of your textual, visual, and audio data may be captured in electronic files. Electronic files need to be labeled and filed away in appropriate folders and project names. If your team desires, you may want to group same types of data together in one place (for computer files, in one folder). In Heewon's study about the mentoring of leaders of color in higher education, her research team ended up producing six different types of data: (1) text data collected via online discussion; (2) audio recordings of virtual conferences; (3) transcriptions of the audio recordings; (4) participant surveys; (5) participant pre-participation essays; and (6) other application materials for the leadership institute from which we recruited the researchers. The leading researchers initially organized these data by types in separate folders.

Your research team should discuss the organizational structure of your data files and folders early in the research process. The collective decision making will help your team keep alive the spirit of distributed leadership in this research process. Based on your agreement, you will also need to determine who will organize and manage data. Although such responsibility may fall on one person, your team needs to be reminded that autobiographical data contributed by all researchers need to be handled as a co-owned property with a clear stipulation of who can and cannot use them and for what purposes the data may be exposed through public presentations and publications. When all members of your collaborative research team have equal access to data as well as knowledge of how to access data, you will practice the democratic principle of CAE.

It is also helpful that all data are stored in one place, rather than scattered in different places. When you come to analysis and interpretation, you will appreciate that you can get to data easily and quickly. When it is impossible to put personal artifacts or other physical materials together in one place, you may want to create a location chart to help find such physical data quickly when needed. It may also be helpful to take photos of such materials and scan documents so you can keep them as electronic files.

We have utilized a variety of computer-assisted tools to label and store our text, visual, and audio data, which are then made accessible to all members of our research teams. For example, in our study of immigrant women faculty of color (Ngunjiri, Hernandez, & Chang, 2010), we utilized an online discussion forum in Blackboard® to collect our personal memory, self-reflective, and self-observational data. We have continued to keep the online discussion boards, where we had shared our autobiographic material, open so that each of us can access our collective data anytime. We also utilized qualitative data analysis software, called NVivo®, to organize and analyze data. Again we shared NVivo files containing raw and analyzed data with each other. In another CAE involving a dozen higher education leaders of color, Heewon used Google Docs® to store and share data and other research-related material. As an online space, Google Docs has allowed all members, residing in different parts of the United States, to access all materials equally and concurrently.

Transcribing Audio Data

Transcribing audio data is a mainstay of qualitative interviewing. In most of our collaborative autoethnographies, we found recording our interactive interview/discussion sessions useful. At these sessions we probed each other to clarify what we had previously collected for our individual data and to draw out what we had not captured in our data set. Since such sessions not only validated but also augmented other types of data, the transcription of such audio data enriched our data set. Since some qualitative data analysis software such as NVivo have features to code audio data without transcription, it is also possible to utilize audio recordings directly for analysis. However, if you plan to use text data as the basis of your data analysis, it is advisable to transcribe your audio data in preparation for analysis.

LOGISTICAL CONSIDERATIONS FOR DATA ANALYSIS AND INTERPRETATION

Data organization and management systems are means to an end. Ultimately, you will need to analyze and interpret your data. Some qualitative methodologists treat data analysis and data interpretation synonymously because both activities work on fragmented data to discover cohesive "stories," "themes," and "patterns" (Creswell, 2012; Glesne, 2011; Maxwell, 2004; Saldaña, 2009; Shank, 2002). For example, Glesne moved from a discussion of data analysis to "writing up qualitative data" in her textbook on qualitative research. The assumption is that researchers will be able to unpack meanings from themes and cohesive stories that they have discovered during data analysis. Acknowledging the reality that many qualitative reports lack in-depth interpretation, other scholars deliberately differentiate data analysis from interpretation. For this school of thought, data analysis involves segmenting, coding, classifying, and regrouping data to find essential elements and to describe them, whereas data interpretation involves the holistic examination of meanings of analyzed data within the sociocultural context of the data and through the theoretical and conceptual lens drawn from the literature (Denzin, 2004; Patton, 2002; Wolcott, 1994).

Within autoethnography (AE), there is no consensus as to whether a stage of data analysis and interpretation even exists. Some autoethnographers argue that the process of writing personal stories involves analysis and interpretation because researchers make choices about which stories to tell. Ellis's (2004) methodological novel on AE includes a section on "analysis in storytelling" (pp. 194–201). She argues that "there is nothing more theoretical or analytic than a good story," because, "when people tell their stories, they employ analytic techniques to interpret their world. Stories are themselves analytic . . . their goal is to evoke a situation the author has been in or studied" (pp. 194, 195–196). Similarly, Richardson (2000) argues that writing is inquiry. We offer this chapter on analysis and interpretation in the spirit of making explicit what is normally hidden in the narratives, poems, short stories, and other autoethnographic and qualitative publications—how to make meaning of your data in order to construct the written product of your CAE. We acknowledge the overlap between analysis and interpretation but prefer to separate them here for the purpose of illuminating each process.

When to Start

When should you begin data analysis? You should not wait until data collection is completed to begin data analysis because analysis helps you narrow your research focus and steer the direction of collection toward richer and more relevant data. As we explained in the previous chapter, qualitative research generally begins with a broad focus because the research topic is either not well researched or because researchers delay narrowing of the focus to allow a wide range of potentially relevant information to emerge during the early stage of data collection. In the process of narrowing the focus, data would direct researchers to where to focus more, where to steer away, and where to delve deeper. As Maxwell (2004) argues, the qualitative researcher "begins data analysis immediately after finishing the first interview or observation, and continues to analyze the data as long as he or she is working on the research, stopping briefly to write reports and papers" (p. 95). To illustrate how data analysis works during data collection, let us go back to the example of our immigrant faculty study in which we adopted a concurrent data collection model. After we completed our individual culturegrams and shared our writings, we gathered to discuss what stood out from each other's writing (the culturegram was our first iteration of individual autoethnographic data collection). For instance, we asked questions such as:

- What does it mean for you to be Korean American? At what point did you determine that as your identity?
- What changes have you noticed in how you define your identity?

This process of probing deeper enabled us to clarify our individual identities, even as new information emerged that we recorded and used as a guide/prompt for the next round of individual autoethnographic writing. In this case, data analysis began when we read each other's writing and probed each other about the autobiographic stories. The point here is to think of data collection-analysis-interpretation as iterative rather than linear processes.

In the study focusing on the layoff of women executives that was referenced in the previous chapter, data analysis also began during data collection. After several iterations of writing about layoff moments, the team felt they had reached saturation. They then moved into sequential writing on the next topic that emerged from those discussions. The intermittent meetings throughout the data collection process provided opportunities to discuss and assess data, which is again part of data analysis.

When we explain to our students the dynamic relationship between data collection and data analysis, one informing the other, they often ask, "Won't early data analysis bias the direction of data collection?" The question indicates their concerns about researcher subjectivity affecting data analysis and further data collection. They want to know if researchers would somehow arbitrarily change the direction of data collection midway to satisfy their preexisting assumptions. Their concerns reflect the deeply ingrained epistemology of objective scientism—that researchers are able to curb their subjectivity by following a preset research protocol. We explain that qualitative researchers do not begin with presumptions about their research outcomes; thus, there are no predetermined assumptions to satisfy along the research process. In addition, we also assure them that further data collection is based on what researchers find from their previously collected data, not on their predetermined assumptions.

We would argue that there is another reason to start data analysis earlier rather than later. The reason is not concerned with the research process; nevertheless, it is worth mentioning, especially for the sake of novice CAE researchers. CAE data collection is an arduous process that takes time and emotional energy. Therefore, researchers often think that when data collection is completed their research process is almost over. If researchers have been juggling the balls of data collection, analysis, and interpretation concurrently, this perception is correct. However, those who still front-load their research process with data collection need to know that data analysis and interpretation are just as arduous and time consuming as data collection. We advise novice CAE researchers to balance their time between data collection, analysis, and interpretation so that they can avoid rushing through data analysis and interpretation. Overlapping data collection and data analysis interpretation will give researchers methodological advantages as well as enhancing the logistics (such as which questions to ask next or what topic to cover in the next iteration of individual writing).

Who Should Be Involved

Who should be involved in data analysis in CAE? Ideally, all researchers should get involved in preliminary data analysis leading to further data collection. Since the early stage of data analysis interacts with data collection, input from all researchers should be incorporated, which will contribute to power sharing among researchers and enrichment of data with multiple perspectives.

It is even better if all researchers can participate in the full course of research until the data of all participants are analyzed, interpreted, and written up. This requires a long-term relationship that can last from several months to multiple years. When collaborating in a study, it should be commonly understood that all researchers have equal rights to analyze collected data collaboratively and produce a coauthored writing. In our study of immigrant women faculty, for instance, we were able to reach the ideal situation where we used the shared data to co-produce a CAE (Ngunjiri, Hernandez, & Chang, 2010).

However, situations may not always be ideal with co-researchers participating in every step of the process. Some researchers might need to drop out in the middle or at the end of a data-collection stage. If that happens, the research team needs to resolve who has the right to the shared data and who should carry on to complete the remaining phases of research to reach publication. We do not have a formulaic answer to offer. However, we suggest that each research team have a conversation to gain common understanding and avoid hard feelings among colleagues while assuring completion.

DATA ANALYSIS

The purpose of data analysis is to discover what is going on in the data, which is a prerequisite for interpretation. Differentiating analysis from interpretation, Wolcott (1994) argued that data analysis is directed at "the identification of essential features and the systematic description of interrelationships among them—in short, how things work" (p. 12). He also speaks about the possibility of explaining "why a system is not working" in data analysis. Similarly, Glesne (2011) observed that the goal of data analysis is to "describe, compare, and create explanation" (p. 184).

The process and procedures of qualitative data analysis are articulated in general qualitative research textbooks such as Creswell (2006), Glesne (2011), Maxwell (2004), Patton (2001), Saldaña (2009), and Wolcott (1994). Useful information about qualitative data analysis can also be gleaned from many method books specific to different traditions of qualitative research, including AE (Chang, 2008; Ellis, 2004;

Muncey, 2010), action research (Mills, 2010), case study (Moustakas, 1994; Yin, 2009), ethnography (Fetterman, 2010; Wolcott, 2010), grounded theory (Birks & Mills, 2011; Charmaz, 2006; Strauss & Corbin, 2008; Strauss & Glaser, 1967), and phenomenology (Smith, Flowers, & Larkin, 2009). You may utilize strategies, techniques, and ideas about how to do qualitative data analysis from such method books as you analyze your collective data. Keeping with the spirit of liberating you as a creative qualitative researcher, we present our ideas as suggestions that you may add to your repertoire of data analysis tools. In this chapter, we focus on three clusters of activities regarding data analysis: (1) reviewing data; (2) segmenting, categorizing, and regrouping data; and (3) finding themes and reconnecting with data. The approach to data analysis and interpretation presented here is most appropriate for analytical-interpretive AE utilizing a systematic approach to qualitative research methods. Those writing CAE from more imaginative-creative or confessional-evocative approaches may also find this chapter useful, even though data collection, analysis, and interpretation are often blended in those approaches because here we make explicit the process of analyzing and interpreting data that is often implicit in most published autoethnographies. As Ellis (2004) indicates, "The author might or might not decide to add another layer of analysis by stepping back from the text and theorizing about the story from a sociological, communicational, or other disciplinary perspective" (p. 196). Below, we show you how to add that layer of analysis beyond the selection of stories and how to do this collectively.

Reviewing Data

Reviewing collected data is a simple but necessary step toward data analysis. Reviewing involves reading text data; examining archival materials, graphic data, and physical artifacts; listening to audio recordings; and watching video recordings. You will benefit from two different kinds of reviewing: macro and micro. A macro-review is usually done when you feel ready to undertake serious and concentrated data analysis. At this level, you do an uninterrupted and undisturbed review of your entire data set to gain a holistic sense of what your data are about. Although you may not be able to complete a macro-review of all data at one sitting, we suggest that you consider taking large blocks of time to review the data so that you gain a global perspective of them. Such a global reading provides a bird's-eye view of data, allowing you to see the basic contour of your data, the density of materials for certain areas, deficiency in other areas, and distinctiveness of certain features. There is a temptation to shortchange this process because you may be anxious to get down to coding as soon as possible. Succumbing to such a temptation affects the quality of your data analysis. Allow yourself to soar around over your data a bit longer! By allowing yourself to be completely open to all possibilities that your data can offer, you will find many surprising and unexpected nuggets in them.

During the macro-review of your data, we suggest that you take notes of what you see and what you do not see in your data. Jot down your thoughts regarding recurring topics, unique details, emerging patterns, relationships among data, methodological insights, critiques, and ideas for further work. Such note taking is commonly practiced in other qualitative research traditions: for example, action research (Mills, 2010) and ethnography (Chang, 1992). This activity of note taking is also called "memoing" by grounded theory researchers (Strauss & Corbin, 2008). Strauss and Corbin defined memos as "a specialized type of written records—those that contain the products of our analyses" (p. 117). Hunter et al. (2011) expanded the meaning of memos:

> Memos are liberating component of classic GT [grounded theory] as they allow researchers to write down any and all ideas they have concerning their data. This creates a fund of memos that when properly stored—in this instance, in a database—allows the memos to be re-worked and sorted in preparation for theory development. (p. 7)

Through writing memos, you capture your initial understanding and "mini-analysis" of the data as a whole. Saldaña's (2009) label, "analytic memo," highlights the analytic nature of this activity (refer to pp. 32–44).

Reading and rereading data and writing memos are not only for the initial step of data analysis; you will engage in this activity throughout your data analysis. Strauss and Corbin (2007) affirm the continuous engagement of memoing: "Writing memos should begin with the first analytic session and continue throughout the analytic process" (p. 119). As you continue with your data analysis, you will move beyond the macro-review to the micro-review of data. At the micro-level, you review data within segments divided by data types, collection periods, data sources, and researcher cases. In other words, you may read different researchers' autobiographical materials separately to gain a deeper understanding of each case. You may also review the data of the past separated from the data of the present. By reviewing, for example, interactive interview data separately from personal memory data, you can gain differentiated perspectives between these two data types. As you segment and code your data and group data segments by topical categories, a need may also arise to review data within different categories. Reviewing data within different topical categories is a critical activity in the data analysis. We will expound on it later in this chapter.

These activities of macro- and micro-review will help in three ways: (1) acquaint you with unfamiliar data collected by your research colleagues; (2) reacquaint you with your own data in relation to others; and (3) help you gain relational perspectives among a variety of data. The more you are familiar with the intricacy of your collective data, the more thoroughly you will be able to analyze your data and offer meaningful interpretations within the larger context.

Segmenting, Categorizing, and Regrouping Data

The results of your macro-review can facilitate the next step of data analysis: segmenting/fragmenting or coding data. In one way, you can construct a preliminary list of topics emerging from the data during your macro-review and use the topics as your initial codes. In another way, the results from your macro-review can act as a separate analytical lens at the later stage of data analysis.

The macro-review may provide the initial codes for analysis. A code refers most often "to a word or short phrase that symbolically assigns a summative, salient, essence capturing, and/or evocative attribute for a portion of language-based or visual data" (Saldaña, 2009, p. 2). Coding is an activity of fragmenting data by topical distinctiveness and assigning each fragment to a code. Recurring topics can easily become codes. For some segments of data, the codes you have already constructed from your macro-review may be sufficient. For other segments, the preconstructed codes may be insufficient. In such cases, you will make up new codes as you go along. Even if you need to add new codes, the initial codes that emerged from your macro-review will become a solid foundation for your data analysis.

Some qualitative researchers start coding from scratch without any preconstructed list of codes. They tend to utilize micro-coding (sentence by sentence or a small sentence unit by unit) to identify codes specific to the fragmented data. Such micro-coding would look like what is displayed in Figure 5-1. This micro-coding ensures that every sentence of data is examined carefully and included in initial coding.

Coded data become "mobile" decontextualized fragments that can be easily taken out of their contexts and grouped with other data fragments. These fragments are not useful by themselves. For the data fragments to contribute to your ultimate interpretation of data, you will need to put them back together to create a meaningful picture. The mobility of coded data allows you to move them around to group them with others with a similar topical focus and label the bigger categories of fragmented data. Such topical grouping is called "categorizing." The results of macro-review can also be useful at this stage. You may use your analytic

Data (modified from one of our studies)	Code
1. [The first critical moment that comes to my mind is when I was asked to serve my college as the interim dean for multicultural affairs.]	1. Becoming interim dean as the critical moment for leadership
2. [As I believe I have stated elsewhere, I had not had any desire nor plans to become a full-time administrator.]	2. No intention to become an administrator
3. [After a failed national search for a new dean, I met with my provost at his invitation. . . . As I met with the provost, he stated his concern for letting the position go unfilled. He also listed a number of reasons why I would be a good interim dean . . . tenure at the college, previous department chair, demonstrated commitment to campus diversity goals, knowledge of policies and areas do tension, and I was an alum.]	3. External encouragement to accept the leadership position
4. [I, in turn, listed all the reasons that I would not be good for the position.] . . .	4. Resistance to becoming an administrator
5. [The most meaningful moments . . . the provost asking me, my department chair enthusiastically supporting me, and my husband's support.]	5. External encouragement to accept the leadership position
6. Though I had been a department chair, as chair I felt more like "It's your turn" to be chair rather than "You are suited to be chair." I also think that I am a better dean than I was chair.]	6. Self-affirmation of leadership

Figure 5-1   Micro-coding example.

memos as a mirror against which to hold up your categories. Although your bird's-eye view of data would not have captured details that your coding and categorizing activities might have, these different ways of processing the same set of data converge to enhance consistency among your own interpretations.

As you continue to code data and categorize coded data, you may also feel the need to merge multiple categories into one, divide a category into multiple categories, or regroup divided categories. These activities of segmenting, categorizing, and regrouping iterate in a dynamic process. Ultimately, you want to reach a manageable number of categories that can show topical distinctiveness from each other. If you start with a preconstructed set of codes that have a certain level of conceptual generality (e.g., administrator), it may not take too many rounds of categorizing and regrouping to arrive at a manageable number of conceptual categories. If you begin with micro-coding that focuses on specifics in your data, it may take multiple rounds of categorizing and regrouping to arrive at the same level of abstract categories. The first approach is more efficient. If you have done a thorough job with the macro-review, your preconstructed codes and categories will represent your data fairly.

Despite the prolonged data analysis process of the second approach, we want to point out the unique benefit of this approach: Since you will pay close attention to details of your data, you will be able to appreciate the nuances embedded there and your categories will reflect the complexity and intricacies of your data.

Finding Themes and Reconnecting with Data

The purpose of reducing topical categories to the essential minimum is to serve the ultimate goal of data analysis—identifying themes. A theme refers to "a phrase or sentence that identifies what a unit of data is about and/or it means . . . a theme 'at a maximum describes and organizes possible observations or at the maximum interprets aspects of the phenomenon'" (Saldaña, 2009, p. 138). Figure 5-2[1] expresses the relationship among codes, categories, and themes. Grouping codes helps identify categories, and themes emerge out of the process of reviewing content within each category, combining categories, and reflecting on relationships among categories.

Themes may be identified in different, albeit not mechanical, ways. Figure 5-2 illustrates three different ways that you may discover relevant themes for your study. We will explain constructing themes/theming (discovering a theme) from simpler (Theme 1) to more complex (Theme 3). Theme 1 in Figure 5-2 makes a summary observation of what coded data within a category represent. For example, in Heewon's on-going

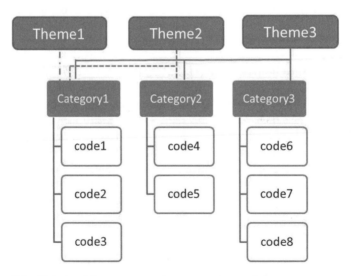

Figure 5-2 Relationships among codes, categories, and themes.

mentoring study, her research team gathered in the category of "mentoring experiences" all kinds of fragmented data relating to a variety of mentoring experiences that higher education leaders of color had with different types of mentors. Out of this category, a tentative theme emerged: the prominence of personal and spiritual mentoring but the dearth of professional mentoring that the majority of female leaders of color had experienced in faith-based higher education.

Theme 2 in Figure 5.2 illustrates a theme captured by combining or intersecting data from two or more categories. Again, let us use Heewon's mentoring study to explain how this second type of theming worked for her research team. The team had two categories: gender mentoring and mentors. The first category contained data relating to gender issues and cross-gender mentoring; the second related to different types of mentors and their gender and the types of relationships they had experienced. Looking at how data from both categories intersected, the research team made a tentative observation that, although both male and female participants had experienced cross-gender mentoring in their professional lives, more female participants experienced cross-gender mentoring than did men, such experiences were more concentrated in hierarchical relationships necessitated by their academic or work situations.

Theme 3 in Figure 5.2 represents a theme that articulates relationship(s) among multiple categories. To make a relational observation, you need to rise above detailed data and individual categories to see how topical categories relate to another one. Making such a thematic observation requires a comprehensive understanding of your data. Let us return to the example of Heewon's mentoring study. Out of multiple categories—gender and mentoring, age and mentoring, race/ethnicity and mentoring, mentoring experiences, and organizational culture of higher education—the research team tentatively identified a comprehensive theme articulating that personal factors relating to the race, ethnicity, gender, and age of mentors and participants affected the participants' mentoring experiences but, above all, the institutional factors unique to higher education more significantly affected their mentoring relationships or lack thereof.

After you identify your themes, you need to explain what themes mean, how categories add details to the themes, and how your data support and illustrate them. When the time comes to write your narrative, which we will discuss in the next chapter, your explanation of each theme should be so substantive and sufficient that it can stand alone without your data excerpts. When data excerpts are displayed along with your explanation, they provide evidence to support and illustrate each theme. When displaying data, we suggest that you use only a few selected ones instead of cramming your report with too many data quotes for each theme. While data excerpts are integral to qualitative research report, they cannot replace your explanation or discussion of themes. Selecting only a few excerpts out of mountains of data is a painful step. It may sometimes feel like cutting of your limbs or discarding your beloved treasures. However, we want to remind you that you should not love your data too much to leave some behind. Data are there to serve your explanation—the results of data analysis.

You may wonder whether you would have the same problem if you take a more narrative approach to your CAE. We argue that the problem persists across different approaches to CAE. You will always collect more data than you can actually include in your final writing. It does not mean that what is left behind was useless to collect. Such data help you arrive at your findings. Regardless of methodological approaches and writing styles, you will face the same challenges of selecting a few segments from abundant materials from your life and of packaging your selection in order to support and illustrate your explanations of social phenomena. After all, if you are writing a journal article or conference presentation, there are page limits whether you are writing as two people or 10; such limits then force you to select from the data those quotes, anecdotes, poems, songs, and stories that best illustrate the themes on which your paper is focusing.

Theme searching activities of segmenting and regrouping data disturbs the data as they were collected. Some autoethnographers consider data analysis an invasive treatment of data. For example, Defrancisco, Kuderer, and Chatham-Carpenter (2007) chose not to do an analysis of themes after their research team of 10 women shared their self-esteem stories out of respect to their individual stories. The last author wrote,

> We could not simply do an analysis of themes as we had done in our earlier published research. To do so seemed inconsistent with what had been a very holistic learning experience and would feel disrespectful to the women who had opened their lives and vulnerabilities to us. How could we reduce their painful and rich sharing to isolated, reductionistic data methods that might devalue the very real and vibrant differences among the women? Such an approach now seemed void of the very thing we were attempting to study—the self—the emotional, anxious, intuitive, informative self. (p. 239)

Therefore, they decided to focus on their "own reactions to the research process using the transcripts from the audio-taped group discussion" (p. 239). Many evocative autoethnographers are likely to take a similar path of infusing analysis and interpretation into their narratives instead of the "invasive" process of data analysis. Whichever direction you take, you need to remember that CAE is more than a patchwork of multiple stories.

TO USE CAQDAS OR NOT, THAT IS THE QUESTION

Before computer-assisted qualitative data analysis software (CAQDAS) began to appear in 1980s, qualitative researchers had completed many high-quality studies without the assistance of computer software. They typed or sometimes word processed their data. They read and reread their data printed in hard copy and manually coded data on the margins of their hard-copy data. Most qualitative researchers, including collaborative autoethnographers, are likely to continue their data analysis without CAQDAS. We do not doubt that qualitative studies will continue to be successfully completed without such assistance. We have completed multiple studies without computer software; we also have used two different CAQDAS in our research studies. Instead of sharing our experiences with specific products, we will keep our discussion at the conceptual level.

CAQDAS has become more accessible to qualitative researchers within the last 15 years, and its capacity and user-friendliness have expanded to facilitate the qualitative research process effectively and efficiently. Here, we will discuss what CAQDAS is and how useful it can be.

CAQDAS is available as both proprietary and open-source products (Lewins & Silver, 2007, 2009; Wikipedia, n.d.). Proprietary products require the purchase of a user license. We are currently aware of 10 such products: A.nnotate (a.nnotate.com), ATLAS.ti (atlasti.com), Aquad (aquad.de/en), Ethnograph (qualisresearch.com), HyperRESEARCH (researchware.com/products/hyperresearch.html), MAXQDA (maxqda.com), NVivo and XSight (qsrinternational.com), Transana (open source but purchase required: transana.org), and QDA Miner (provalisresearch.com/QDAMiner/QDAMinerDesc.html). Open-access products are also available freely via the Internet and include CAT (cat.ucsur.pitt.edu), Qiqqa (www.qiqqa.com), and Weft QDA (www.pressure.to/qda).

Depending on capabilities and features of the software, you can use it to perform a variety of tasks efficiently: organizing raw data, coding text data (sometimes video, sound, or graphic data), grouping coded/fractured data into topical categories, retrieving coded data, and comparing coded data based on set criteria. Some of the products have sophisticated search functions that allow you to look for selected words and phrases in your data and to create matrices based on selected variables. Some have drawing functions to assist you with creating charts and tables from your data. Some products, such as Nvivo, facilitate multi-user collaborative data analysis more efficiently than others. Lewins and Silver (2007,

2009) have provided a useful comparison among selective proprietary products, such as ATLAS.ti, MAXQDA, NVivo, HyperRESEARCH, QDA Miner, QUALRUS, and Transana. However, since the products continue to evolve, information on individual CAQDAS becomes quickly outdated. It is best to visit the homepages of respective products to learn about their distinguishing features.

No computer software by itself can enhance the effectiveness of qualitative data analysis. Researcher competence and skills of induction, deduction, abduction, synthesis, evaluation, logical, and critical thinking as well as comfort with ambiguity, flexibility, and creativity (Saldaña, 2009) will ultimately influence the quality of data analysis and, in turn, the quality of the research. Lewins and Silver (2009) articulate the importance of the researcher even when CAQDAS is used: "[CAQDAS is] not to provide you with a methodological or analytical framework . . . as the researcher you should remain in control of the interpretive process" (online). You, as a researcher, are still responsible for fragmenting data, assigning codes, categorizing codes, and regrouping coded data. With this premise understood, we are convinced that CAQDAS, when used effectively, can facilitate the data analysis process, especially with massive data.

DATA INTERPRETATION

Finding themes is an important task in data analysis, enabling you to explain to the community of scholars what you have discovered from your data and how your data support your claims. Unfortunately, many qualitative researchers stop at finding themes and leave unanswered the ultimate question: "So what does all this mean?" Data interpretation helps you answer this so-what question, focusing on what your overall discovery from the data means; how your discovery advances the understanding of the phenomenon/topic you have explored; and how your discovery is connected to the existing literature (Creswell, 2006; Maxwell, 2004; Wolcott, 1994). In self-focused research such as AE and CAE, the task of data interpretation is critical because it allows you to discuss matters beyond yourself and to connect yourself with others and the sociocultural context. In other words, data analysis is a pathway to interpretation that "begins with elucidating meanings" (Patton, 2001, p. 477). Without making meaning of your analyzed data, your discovery will be limping on one foot.

Meaning-making in CAE is, of course, not limited to the data interpretation stage of research. During iterative dialogic interactions when collecting and analyzing data, co-researchers are already engaged in collective meaning-making. Paulus, Woodside, and Ziegler (2010) articulated such a dynamic process: "In collaborative research, meaning-making is the dynamic and iterative process of connecting researchers, empirical materials, interpretations, and theory to better understand the phenomenon under study, all within one or more institutions and the wider research community" (p. 860). This process of meaning-making continues into the more intense data interpretation stage.

Data interpretation is also closely tied to writing—the productive process. It connects data analysis with the writing of the findings but does not dwell on data bits. Denzin (2004) articulates such relationship as follows:

> Interpretation is a productive process that sets forth the multiple meanings of an event, object, experiences, or text. Interpretation is transformative. It illuminates, throws light on experience. It brings out, and refines, as when butter is clarified, the meanings that can be sifted from a text, an object, or a slice of experience. So conceived, meaning is not in a text, nor does interpretation precede experiences, or its representation. Meaning, interpretation and representation are deeply intertwined in one another. (p. 453)

Chang (2008) also argues, "Meanings are not available from the data as ready-made answers; rather they are formulated in a researcher's mind" (p. 127). This means that you will need to construct meanings based on what you know from the literature, what you see in the relationship between your data and outside world, and what is implicit or buried deep down in the data.

The first strategy in searching for meaning is looking for conceptual and theoretical tools from the literature to explain your findings. Thorne (2008) suggested that researchers return to their "original literature," which she dubbed as "the 'old friends'—those key pieces of empirical knowledge that you will have critiqued and challenged in justifying your study in the first place" (p. 196). You may or may not have started this CAE journey with a serious literature review. Yet, we imagine that as scholars you have lived with many old friends from your disciplinary literature who have shaped your interpretive lenses in scholarship. Look into what you already know to see if any original literature could lend a satisfactory explanatory framework for your findings. Have literature conversations among your research teammates to bring to light concepts and theories with which you are collectively familiar. Such conversations will help your research team identify the focus of your literature search.

Thorne (2008) also advised us to turn to "new literature" on "insights, observations and ideas" that emerged from the data that your original literature review has not covered. The new literature search can be quite challenging because this may mean that you need to go beyond your familiar territory of interpretive paradigms and perspectives and familiar topical areas. Our experiences attest that we have greatly benefited from working collaboratively with scholars from diverse disciplines and backgrounds because we were able to pull from a variety of literature, paradigms, and perspectives to explain our findings. By utilizing what is available in the literature, you are ultimately able to connect your research findings with works of others.

The second strategy of searching for meaning encourages you to explain your findings within the sociocultural context. Thorne (2008) explains this strategy as "extending interpretation" (pp. 200–202). This approach encourages you to take on a standpoint or an interpretive paradigm or perspective such as feminism, critical race theory, Marxism, postpositivism, and so on (Denzin, 2004). The standpoint or paradigm you are adopting may help explain your data. Examine how contextual factors—cultural, social, economic, political, organizational, and interpersonal—might have affected your findings, and speculate about how the findings might have turned out differently in different contexts.

In addition, explore how demographic identifiers of self—gender, ethnicity, race, religion, education, class, language, locality, and nationality—might have affected your research team members' experiences with the social phenomenon you have investigated. Again, the literature review might give you a foundational understanding of the societal contexts. As you try to interpret the interplay between your experiences and contextual and demographic factors through a particular interpretive paradigm relevant to your findings, compare your findings with what is available from the literature. Are your findings consistent with what has been reported in the literature? Look for new insights as your findings may critique and/or extend the existing literature. This is where your unique experiences as individuals and co-researchers inform, challenge, and/or expand current literature.

The third strategy of searching for meaning is looking for what is obviously missing in your data. During data analysis, you work with what is present in data. Therefore, you tend to neglect what is absent from them. Data interpretation gives you an opportunity to pay attention to cues that may be potentially critical in gaining a fuller understanding of the phenomena. There are many reasons why certain data are missing from your collection. Researcher-participants might have intentionally held back information (e.g., to protect themselves from harm, ridicule, or over-exposure, or to protect intimate others); they might have been neglectful of such data because they were deemed insignificant; or social or personal limitations could have contributed to the absence of data. The reasons may go on and on. By examining reasons for absent data, you will be able to indirectly decipher the sociocultural meanings of present and absent data.

Data interpretation is not a formulaic activity. No one correct interpretation exists. Even within your research team, you may not always come to consensus. So how will you reconcile multiple perspectives and interpretations? It will be too unwieldy to present all of the individual interpretations in your write-up of CAE. Therefore, your team needs to dialogue to reach a reasonable agreement about your interpretations. When you are divided between two different interpretations, consider juxtaposing such differences to display the multiple voices in your research team. Different voices juxtaposed in one text can make significant contributions to the literature and is one of the primary contributions of CAE research (Chapman & Sork, 2001; Chawla & Rawlins, 2004). Contrasting interpretations may illuminate irreconcilable perspectives, which are valuable as they demonstrate the diversity and complexity of human experience.

Conclusion

This chapter began with a discussion of how to organize and manage a variety of data in preparation for data analysis and interpretation. Data analysis serves a different purpose from data interpretation. Data analysis identifies essential features from the data and describes how they are interrelated, whereas interpretation explains what the findings mean in relation to the sociocultural context. Although they are functionally and conceptually different from each other, data analysis and interpretation are often done concurrently, even during data collection. As Paulus, Woodside, and Ziegler (2010) argued, interpretive meaning-making takes place when researchers dialogue during data collection and interact with data during data analysis. It also happens when writing up a research report. So, delve into the borderless process of data collection, analysis, interpretation, and writing. Allow yourself to zoom in and out of the data to gain both a bird's-eye view and a microscopic look at the data. Undertaking a search of the literature during your interpretation phase enables you to find explanatory frameworks and to engage the marketplace of published ideas by extending, critiquing, illustrating, and challenging existing explanations.

CHAPTER 6

Collaborative Autoethnographic Writing

Writing up the results of your collaborative autoethnography (CAE) research project for presentation or publication is the final step in the research process. Whether writing for publication is done as a solitary exercise or in a CAE community, it is perhaps one of the most challenging parts of research. In the process of writing this book, we read several articles employing autoethnographic and collaborative autoethnographic methods to examine how writers worked together to turn their research studies in publishable works. We found only a few articles (see, e.g., Espino, Muñoz, & Kiyama, 2010; Lapadat, Mothus, & Fisher, 2005; Nuñez, Murakami-Ramalho, & Cuero, 2010; Paulus, Woodside, & Ziegler, 2010) in which researchers discussed openly the writing process and some of the unique challenges that occur in turning a work involving many writers, stories, and voices into a cohesive piece.

In this chapter, we try to make the process of collaborative writing more transparent. First, we discuss some of the persistent challenges in turning research into publishable pieces, challenges from which we ourselves are not immune, as well as the opportunities and challenges that occur when this is done as part of a CAE team. We then break down the writing process into three phases: (1) pre-CAE writing; (2) CAE writing; and (3) post-CAE writing.

THE WRITING CHALLENGE

Though scholars are well aware of the need for publication to secure advancement in the academy, the central challenge remains how to turn that knowledge into focused action. Each of us is at a different stage in our own publication journey, and our stories and struggles with the publish or perish paradigm reflect different pathways to the end goal; yet, there are striking similarities about what has worked for us in our attempts to advance in that direction. Among the three of us, there have been four book publications to date and several book chapters, book reviews, and journal articles. Heewon is the editor of an open-access journal, and all three have served in various capacities as guest editors/

reviewers for peer-reviewed journals, including the *International Journal of Multicultural Education* and the *Journal of Research Practice*. Yet each of us also has an extensive list of research projects (solo and collaborative) that have remained in the pipeline between presentation and publication for much longer than we think is effective.

We each lament our lack of time, given the professional and personal demands we face as women in the academy, juggling family life and professional responsibilities. We recognize the lack of time as a somewhat constant challenge within the academy (Page-Adams et al., 1995). But some still become prolific writers in spite of this limitation. What, then, are some persistent challenges to writing? And what are some ways that CAE group work can help mitigate these challenges? How can CAE writing help develop a habit of writing (Toor, 2010)?

Some of the factors that create a sense of writing inertia are perhaps inherent in the traditional paradigm of the writing act. Writing has been viewed as a solitary task—a moment in time when the writer, once armed with pen and paper, now computer, grappled with these tools to give voice to words and ideas that rebelliously refused to become part of the printed page without some inward struggle. The iconic image of a writer stuck behind a typewriter, with one sentence on the page and crumpled pieces of paper tossed carelessly on the floor, has been played out over and over in many a movie script. Images like these have perpetuated the idea that writing is a chore, a challenge, and a solitary exercise. Moreover, if one is not able to master this writing as a solo/solitary act paradigm, then writing becomes a giant colossus that is difficult to conquer. The approach of collaborative research and writing proposed in this book and this chapter is a direct affront to this traditional view of writing for publication and, if used well, can propel you to become a more productive writer nested in a more supportive writing context.

Research suggests several factors can create inertia when it comes to writing. These include fear and uncertainty about the writing and publication process (Lee & Boud, 2003) and lack of momentum (Boice & Jones, 1984). One persistent reason given by faculty and students alike is not being part of a supportive group (Hale & Pruitt, 1989). Additionally, as scholars have noted, graduate work does not prepare us adequately for the work of writing for publication. Most doctoral programs devote much time to content knowledge specific to each discipline and ample instruction in research methodologies; there is little or no direct instruction relevant to writing in general and how to write for publication specifically (Cuthbert & Spark, 2008; DeLyser, 2003; Mullen, 2001). A year or more of solitary and painstaking dissertation writing follows two or three years of coursework. This is the last concrete impression of the writing process that remains with newly minted doctorates. It is perhaps not surprising, therefore, that writing is not a task that they are anxious to do.

THE COLLABORATIVE WRITING PARADIGM

Recently, more and more doctoral programs are stressing the importance of collaborative writing for developing the skills of their graduates and boosting confidence in writing (Ferguson, 2009; Maher et al., 2008). Some programs have students participate in doctoral/thesis writing groups once they have completed their coursework. The format these groups can take may differ across disciplines and universities. Some groups assume the role of a peer-reviewing circle as members complete various chapters or milestone toward the final dissertation. Some groups may meet for set hours to support each other through the discipline of writing. Other groups, whether or not they include various other types of support, also set aside time for participants to discuss and become educated on the process of writing, its challenges, and the strategies for persevering to the end. In each case, the idea of support as a critical element in navigating the writing process dispels the notion of the solitary writer and her or his instrument as the principal template; this type of supportive group process is well documented as being beneficial to participants (DeLyser, 2003; Ferguson, 2009; Galligan et al., 2003; Kinnucan-Welsch et al., 2000; Larcombe, McCosker, & O'Loughlin, 2007; Lee & Boud, 2003; Morss & Murray, 2001; Rose & McClafferty, 2001).

Participation in writing groups has both practical and psychological benefits (Ferguson, 2009). It helps "demystify" writing into a clearly defined process (Ferguson, 2009; Lee & Boud, 2003; Rose & McClafferty, 2001); participants can learn more about the craft of writing and writing conventions; gain a structure that offers accountability and schedule for writing (Morss & Murray, 2001); benefit from feedback presented by peers even as they hone their own reviewing skills; and benefit from the diverse mix of disciplines in multidisciplinary teams (Galligan et al., 2003). Psychologically, working in a supportive environment can lead to increased motivation to write (Morss & Murray, 2001; Murray & Newton, 2008; Pololi, Knight, & Dunn, 2004) and provide needed emotional support through the ups and downs of writing (Boud & Lee, 2005; Larcombe et al., 2007).

All of these benefits can be attained through collaborative autoethnographic writing. Although collaborative writing is common practice in academic and professional circles, the term itself often escapes definition. Collaborative writing has been classified under several labels, including collaborative authoring (DuFrene & Nelson, 1990), group authorship (Ede & Lunsford, 1990), and team writing (Bovee & Thill, 1989). Lowry, Curtis, and Lowry (2004) define collaborative writing as "an iterative and social process that involves a team focused on a common objective that negotiates, coordinates, and communicates during the creation of a common document" (p. 72). They add that the task of collaborative writing can involve pre- and post-writing activities and "the possibility of many different writing strategies, activities, document control approaches, team roles, and work modes" (p. 74).

This definition is consistent with how we would characterize writing in CAE. However, we see some important distinctions between a generic view of collaborative writing and CAE. First, unlike collaborative writing efforts in which teams may be formed for the specific task of completing a writing project, in a CAE study the writing is an integral part of the research process and a critical component for group meaning-making and analysis. As such, the CAE team comes into existence long before the collaborative writing aspect of the work begins, and without writing the research process would not be complete. Second, CAE writers have a greater investment in the final collaborative writing product because it not only has the potential to reflect their writing styles, it also includes content about their personal experiences that may be written in their own voices. For these reasons, CAE writing involves a complex and unique mix of relational and practical concerns.

As with most collaborative work, there are attendant challenges and opportunities in CAE writing. In the following sections, we adapt the framework provided by Lowry, Curtis, and Lowry (2004) for tasks and activities of collaborative writing and discuss some challenges and opportunities in CAE writing during pre-CAE writing, CAE writing, and post-CAE writing.

PRE-COLLABORATIVE AUTOETHNOGRAPHY WRITING

In the preceding chapters, we dealt with team formation, data collection, and data analysis. In working through these steps on a CAE project, team members would have already bonded and perhaps created informal, if not formal, operating guidelines. However, as teams get close to writing the final report, it is important to clarify the task, create a writing plan, and set guidelines and expectations for working toward the written final product. Alternatively, teams may have addressed writing concerns at the onset of their work and can use the juncture of commencing report writing to reiterate and reevaluate these operating principles. Pre-CAE writing tasks will vary based on the project and demands of CAE teams; however, we offer the following guidelines for creating a CAE writing plan and defining members' roles and responsibilities.

Creating a Collaborative Autoethnography Writing Plan

A practical aspect of writing is creating a plan to get it done. One of the first steps in this process is defining what kind of writing product the team is hoping to craft. Is it a paper for presentation, a grant application, a journal article, or a book proposal? Once this decision has been made, the accompanying tasks can further be delineated. These include deciding on the focus of the writing project (a journal article, for example, can focus on the methods or on the results), finding a suitable venue, creating a timeline for completion, and developing a system to facilitate collaborative writing.

Once your team has completed step one, the next step is to create a system of regular contact and communication to coordinate the writing activities. The question to be answered is: What processes and tools are we going to use to enable us to write collaboratively? We have a working model for each collaborative project we do. In writing this book, we agreed to meet bi-weekly for one to two hours to ensure that we were consistently working toward the project deadline. We assigned each other specific tasks and met to discuss progress, review, and plan the next steps in the process.

Shared context is accommodating to systems of frequent contact and communication. We have been fortunate to work at the same institution. We use regular face-to-face meetings, web-conferencing, and e-mail to stay in contact. Given the vagaries of our personal and professional commitments, at times we lapse in attending these meetings, but being in the same institution and department provides informal opportunities to briefly discuss where we are with the project between department meetings and tea breaks. Our proximity lends itself to enriching the writing experience and ultimately the final product. Discussions about the progress of the work can intrude into everyday communication and become rich data for further analysis and writing. Many CAE efforts have come from researchers who share some type of social context and benefit from this kind of closeness. Some collaborations have been conducted between spouses (Ellis & Bochner, 1992), among professors and students (Chapman & Sork, 2001; Ellis, Kiesinger, & Tillmann-Healy, 1997), and among colleagues on a topic of mutual interest (Defrancisco, Kuderer, & Chatham-Carpenter, 2007). Such collaborations provide built-in opportunities for frequent communication and contact.

However, shared context is not a prerequisite for CAE. Geist-Martin did not allow distance from collaborators to deter her

(Geist-Martin et al., 2010). She sent an e-mail invitation for individuals interested in participating in a panel discussion on mothering experiences at an upcoming conference. What ensued was a CAE project that involved writing and sharing individual stories, presenting them at a conference, and collaborating to turn this research into a journal article. CAE teams with members in different locations can use technology to support writing and communication efforts. During the summer months, although each of us might be at different parts of the globe, perhaps in our respective countries of birth of Korea, Kenya, Trinidad, and Tobago, we use technology (e-mail, Skype, Blackboard) to keep working on our CAE projects.

In selecting tools and technologies, you should consider how they can be used to facilitate and enrich the writing experiences. A number of questions need to be answered:

1. How much solitary versus collaborative writing will your team do? If so, how will documents be shared/analyzed reviewed?
2. Does your team favor a socially constructed approach to writing?
3. Is real-time sharing (synchronous) needed, or is posting of documents and follow-up responses (asynchronous) required? For real-time sharing, we have used Google Docs® so we can each be in different locations but look at the document and edit it simultaneously; other technologies that can be used include Blackboard, Wikis, and e-mail.
4. Will computer-assisted qualitative data analysis software like NVivo be used to analyze the data?
5. How will your team control the document throughout the collaborative writing exercise?

Answering these questions will help you determine which technologies can best meet the needs of the collaborative autoethnographic writing project.

Defining Member Roles and Responsibilities

CAE writing for publication involves several tasks beyond producing a written document. There are the practical considerations of actually writing the piece—reading, outlining, drafting, reviewing/editing, and revising. However, there are other aspects of working on group projects that Lowry, Curtis, and Lowry (2004) have identified as important supporting activities that also apply to CAE work: researching, socializing among members, communicating, negotiating, coordinating, and monitoring the progress of the group. If you have followed the suggestions in Chapter 3 for team formation, you will have given consideration to some of the prerequisites to forming a team that can work well together. We have all been a part of unproductive collaborative efforts. The goal here is team longevity and productivity.

In our case, we have been candid about our membership in this CAE circle and our desire to work together. Heewon approached Faith and Kathy-Ann to be a part of this collaborative research circle, initially with a focus on writing about our experiences as women of color in higher education. However, we have discussed openly why she chose to approach us and not other colleagues at our institutions. We had not worked collaboratively on other projects before, but we had observed each other's work ethic and passion for research. Hence, an important consideration for us, and one that your team should consider as you approach the writing phase, if not sooner, is how each participant can best contribute to the writing process. Given these varied tasks, it is useful for your team to tap into the synergy and skill sets that members bring to the team effort. Table 6-1 shows a breakdown of some supporting collaborative writing activities in which we often engage as we work on a CAE project.

These roles are not mutually exclusive. In many cases, team members will fulfill these tasks organically as they work together. Alternately, if these tasks are not done, a team may lack the kind of supportive glue needed to keep it healthy through the process of collaborative work. In our collaboration, we have learned the different skill sets that each member brings to the team, and this has been the basis for defining team members' roles and responsibilities. Although we often move in and out of roles, we lean on each other's skill sets in different areas to sustain our group efforts. As your team focuses on tasks that are directly linked to the written product, it is important to ensure that members are also fulfilling these roles and responsibilities.

A critical decision in assigning member roles and responsibilities is to determine who the project team leader will be. Such decisions are commonly based on who initiated or made the biggest investment in the collaborative project or may follow from a decision about who will be the lead author. Be aware! Decisions about who will be the first, second, or third author of a given piece can be a breeding ground for group discontent. Because all our work builds off our collaborative efforts and we strive to fully represent each other's voices in the final product, we claim each piece as being equally constructed by all members. However, the reality is that one person's name must appear before another. We have struggled with the present paradigm of different weights for first, second, and third authorship; it is not well suited to CAE in which, from our perspective, each of us is an equal contributor to the research process. Paulus, Woodside, and Ziegler (2010) have shared the challenges they have faced with this in their work. Barring an imminent change in the way authorship is viewed and rewarded in the academy, we choose to set expectations about authorship at the onset of each project and are

Table 6-1   CAE supporting member tasks and responsibilities.

Researcher	• Finding a suitable venue for the written product
	• Compiling a library of full-text articles/reference list with team members
	• Finding and forwarding information about new opportunities for scholarship
	• Finding editors/proofreaders to assist in proofing final drafts
Socializer	• Organizing events for team support and celebrations
	• Organizing member efforts to support members through personal crises
Communicator	• Sending e-mails and follow-up communications to facilitate the writing process
	• Responding to requests and/or communicating with graduate students and other scholars regarding our work
	• Communicating with journal editors, publishers, and granting agencies relative to project demands
Negotiator	• Intervening to settle conflicts among team members
	• Bargaining with publishers/editors in the interest of the team
Coordinator	• Coordinating members' schedules to create mutually acceptable timelines
	• Managing/circulating/sharing documents in various stages of the writing process
	• Scheduling team meetings and making logistical arrangements for room set up and technologies, lodging, and travel arrangements
Monitor	• Monitoring team progress in line with benchmarks for project deadline
	• Keeping a checklist of collaborative autoethnography projects and timelines for various activities in which the team may be engaged
	• Monitoring/keeping teams abreast of approaching deadlines and commitments

guided by a group understanding of how we will rotate ownership and authorship of our work in keeping with the ethics of our fields and our own sense of justice.

As a personal stance, we continue to advocate for equal merit, irrespective of the order of authors' names in a given manuscript by including a note to that effect in our publications.[1] We determine leadership in projects based on several factors: the number of competing projects on which each of us is working; who is next in line for rotation of first authorship, who has the best skills to advance the particular project; and who is willing to make the biggest contribution to the actual writing of the piece. We are not advocating our model as a better approach; it works for us, and that is why we use it. The important point here is for your team to be clear at the onset about members' roles and responsibilities and to create a system that is fair and transparent when it comes to team leadership and authorship.

COLLABORATIVE AUTOETHNOGRAPHY WRITING

Once the pre-writing phase is completed, teams are ready to begin writing. In this section, we discuss a choice of strategies for writing collaboratively, prominent typologies of CAE writing, strategies for how authors can deal with multiple voices in one piece of writing, and ethical concerns.

Writing Collaboratively

As we discussed in Chapter 3, your group may decide the level of collaboration that will take place at each phase of the researching and writing process and solidify these in the pre-writing phase. Now is the time to work your plan. We favor a full-collaboration approach: Each of us is fully invested and participates at each stage of the process (we discuss this in more detail later in this chapter). However, there are different ways in which members may agree to work together. Lowry, Curtis, and Lowry (2004) have identified the following as prevalent collaborative writing strategies: group single-author writing, sequential writing, parallel writing, reactive writing, and mixed-mode writing.

In group single-author writing, one person writes on behalf of the team. Sequential writing is a variation of this approach, in which one team member writes her or his part and then passes the document along to another to write her or his part. Parallel writing or partitioned writing (Ellis, Gibbs, & Rein, 1991) is the "divide and conquer" approach, in which the writing task is broken down into sections and team members are assigned different sections of the report, which are then compiled, reviewed, and edited at a later date. Stratton (1989) suggested a subdivision of this approach into two types: horizontal-division writing and stratified-division writing. Horizontal-division writing occurs when members are assigned writing segments without taking into account members' competencies. Alternatively, in stratified-division writing, assignments are given based on members' core competencies such as skills in researching, editing/reviewing, or role as lead author. Reactive writing (coined by Lowry, Curtis, & Lowry, 2004) is employed when writers are able to write a document synchronously; thus, they are able to react to and with the document in real time. Teams can use Google Docs®, for example, to have members interact and write the piece together synchronously. Finally, mixed-mode writing can include a combination of any of these collaborative writing strategies.

Each of these approaches has advantages and disadvantages. Single author and sequential writing lend themselves well to CAE models of partial collaboration and may be useful for teams that have some familiarity with each other's writing styles. Parallel writing lends itself to a more efficient use of the team's time since everyone is writing simultaneously and the task of compiling and putting the final document can become the task of the team leader. For teams that favor a full-collaboration approach, parallel and reactive writing may be the most useful strategies in line with this CAE approach. (For a more thorough discussion of collaborative writing strategies, see Lowry, Curtis, & Lowry, 2004.)

Collaborative Autoethnography Writing Styles

Your CAE project can be presented in a choice of style formats. Your team may choose to align itself with a more analytical approach or with the creative/evocative approach based on particular philosophical or disciplinary orientation, suitability of the approach to the topic being studied, intent to protect members' identities, familiarity with the style of writing, or a variety of other reasons. Four prominent writing styles for presenting CAE are identified in Table 6-2: imaginative-creative, confessional-emotive writing, descriptive-realistic writing, and analytical-interpretive writing.

Although each of these types of CAE writing styles has distinctive characteristics, writers often begin a CAE with a discussion of the purpose of the study, design, and methods and then use the rest of the article to present the work that best fits these typologies. With more creative/evocative approaches, this "front" matter is often shortened to give prominence to the rest of the writing. While we have attempted to discuss four distinctive types of CAE writing, we have done so merely for ease of exposition. Authors may use various approaches in a given piece. However, we have used the existence of a predominant writing style in what is normally considered the method section of a report to identify congruence with a particular approach.

These four typologies are organized in a continuum from top to bottom from a style of presentation that allows authors to remain closely aligned to the written piece to writing that provides a more detached perspective.

In imaginative-creative (IC) writing, authors make use of various literary forms to present their work. Unlike confessional-emotive (CE) writing, these forms are not characterized by an "outing" of personal experiences but instead deal with more general topics. Like CE writing, though, IC

Table 6-2 Prominent typologies of collaborative autoethnography writing.

Imaginative-creative writing (IC)	Authors use various creative literary genres, including drama, fiction, and poetry, to express autobiographical experiences.
	Example: McMillan, S., & Price, M. A. (2010). Through the looking glass: Our autoethnographic journey through research mind-fields.
Confessional-emotive writing (CE)	Authors freely interject their feelings, emotions, and opinions into the report, often in the process of "outing" themselves in their research.
	Example: Muncey, T., & Robinson, R. (2007). Extinguishing the voices: Living with the ghost of the disenfranchised.
Descriptive-realistic writing (DR)	Authors attempt an objective, detailed, and controlled description of experiences documented through autoethnographic research.
	Example: Murakami-Ramalho, E., Piert, J., & Militello, M. (2008). The wanderer, the chameleon, and the warrior.
Analytical-interpretive writing (AI)	Authors present work in the traditional research report format, often with stated research purpose, research question/s, methods, and findings. The findings are more explicitly analyzed and interpreted against a conceptual framework presented from the literature.
	Example: Geist-Martin, P., Gates, L., Wiering, L., Kirby, E., Houston, R., Lilly, A., & Moreno, J. (2010). Exemplifying collaborative autoethnographic practice via shared stories of mothering.

writing can be very personal and emotive and it can be presented in the form of poetry, play scripts, dialogues, and fiction. Some of these pieces are meant to be performed rather than read (e.g., Ellis & Bochner, 1992).

A good example of IC writing is entitled "Through the Looking Glass: Our Autoethnographic Journey Through Research Mind-Fields." In this piece, McMillan and Price (2010) use a call and response allegory format, based loosely on Lewis Carroll's *Alice in Wonderland*, to share their experiences of teaching naturalistic inquiry methods at an institution and the opposition they encountered. The article begins with a departure from form by offering the script first and then discussing the relevant literature and research design methods employed in the study at the end. The script is meant to be performed for full effect. The authors use the following argument for utilizing this medium to present their study as a means of protecting themselves within their institutions:

> Having long recognized the unfortunate similarities between our own academic careers and Alice's illogical romp through "Wonderland," we opted to interweave Lewis Carroll's *Through the Looking Glass* and *Alice's Adventures in Wonderland* throughout the scripted portions of our autoethnography. Alice had made it safely through her Wonderland, had she not . . . ? Perhaps Alice's negotiations of externally imposed limitations could shed new light on some of the ways in which we and others like us could circumvent our own. Incorporating a fictional format into our storytelling provided a safe place for us to do so. (p. 145)

Use of fictionalized retelling of the collaborative autoethnographic experiences is a good strategy for protecting not only authors but also others implicated in such accounts. However, writers can draw on several literary formats for other purposes in presenting these accounts. Another example is an ethnodrama that two African American academics Randolph and Weems (2010) constructed based on their experiences with racism in the academe. They examined "the social/political context of racism in higher education and its manifestation in institutional practices" through their drama script with nine characters (p. 311).

In confessional-emotive writing, the form owes as much to the topic under study as it does to the actual writing style. While there are several examples of this kind of writing in autoethnographic research (see, e.g., Chatham-Carpenter, 2010; Jago, 2002; Tillmann, 2009), a few are emerging as collaborative pieces. In CE writing, authors are at center stage in the narrative. The form of inquiry and reporting provides the scholarly space to finally "out" themselves in their research. This is the case in the article by Muncey and Robinson (2007). These authors find commonalties around the irony of one being a user (Robinson) and the other almost a user of nursing care facilities where they now work. Muncey writes about her experience as a teenage mother in the United Kingdom, where a few years earlier, she could have been labeled a nymphomanic and placed in a mental institution. Robinson, on the other hand, writes about his experiences being in a mental care institution. Both recount earlier attempts to write about their experiences, but they often felt restricted to do so in disguised accounts or with the use of pseudonyms. Through this account, they "serve as a conduit and support to the wider audience of publication denied to the majority of healthcare" (Muncey & Robinson, 2007, p. 79). Another example is Gallardo, Furman, and (2009) work focusing on personal and familial experience with depression. They utilized poetry in their CE writing.

Descriptive-realistic (DR) writing is a stark departure from CE and IC accounts. However, DR still employ an engaging writing style. The purpose of the writing is to represent researchers' stories as realistically as possible, and researchers often use a narrative style of writing. After presenting a standard literature review, Murakami-Ramalho, Piert, and Militello (2008) described their experiences of developing researcher identities as doctoral students of color. Combining the portraiture method, developed by Lawrence-Lightfoot (Lawrence-Lightfoot & Davis, 2002), with CAE method, these researchers framed their self-narratives with the metaphoric images of "wanderer," "chameleon," and "warrior." To describe their evolving identities within the doctoral program, the wanderer wrote, "My graduate school experience has been like so many of my life experiences: constantly setting a course on a new adventure, and constantly becoming introspective about questioning my own esteem and abilities" (p. 821). The chameleon recounted her adapting history:

> In my search for an identity in the doctoral program, I continued to reconnect to life experiences, as well as new experiences, which entailed adapting to new countries and moving from an administrative position and respected professional status to that of a full-time student. I left a full-time job in a K–12 American international school and moved to the university with my two sons. Adapting to a new social context as a family was not easy. (p. 823)

Finally, after describing an "incident," the warrior described his doctoral journey as the negotiation between war and peace:

> Reflecting on this doctoral journey, I conclude that encountering the paradox of war and peace has been a necessary component of shaping my identity as an educational researcher. The presence of war or struggle has generated the agitation that I needed to resist being molded into a predetermined paradigm of an educational researcher. (p. 826)

As illustrated here with excerpts from their writing, this collaborative work describes their doctoral experience in a creative but realistic discourse.

Analytical-interpretive (AI) writing most closely resembles the traditional format of presenting social science research, beginning with an introduction to the research topic/problem, reviewing the literature, presenting guiding questions and methods employed in the study, results and conclusions. Although they may utilize IC, CE, or DR devices in the work, what distinguishes this most from the other forms is its congruence to the prescribed approach to presenting research and a further distancing of self from the narrative than is apparent in the other typologies. The article by Geist-Martin et al. (2010) in Appendix B provides a good example of this approach. Although the focus of this article is on the collaborative method employed in this study, the authors maintain a third-person point of view throughout the article, provide guiding research questions, discuss the methods employed in the study, and select excerpts from transcripts to illustrate prominent themes that emerged from their collaborative work. This is the general format that we have come to expect from other kinds of social science research projects.

Strategies for Dealing with Multiple Voices

CAE writing allows for the merging of multiple voices to tell one cohesive story. This is a salient strength of this kind of inquiry. Multiple perspectives, voices, theoretical lenses, and experiences of participants can enrich the final product across varied contexts. The potential for rich inquiry is mind boggling. The challenge is how to present it as one written piece. What is kept in the final piece? What is omitted? Should the article be written in one voice or many voices?

Teams must negotiate and answer these important questions. Ultimately, in the interest of the final product, tough decisions will have to be made about what to omit and what to keep. Failing to do this can lead to a disjointed piece that never makes it past the peer review stage of publication. While serving as reviewers for a special issue of the *Journal of Research Practice*, we read the submission from a group of researchers, in which "excerpts" from the data collection went on for over seven pages. The piece itself was a good fit for the special issue and the methodology was sound. However, in attempting to represent each participant equally, the article had degenerated into several competing stories. After seven pages of individual researcher reflections, the reader lost sight of the initial purpose of the article. Moreover, though there was some attempt to categorize the stories into distinct themes, the sheer volume of prose wearied the reader and demanded that she shift from one storyteller to the other. With a little coaching, they were able to revise and submit a more cohesive story. However, as they later confessed in the published piece, revising the piece in line with our suggestions was not easy:

> We felt the "cut" of shortening these stories quite deeply; every time we shortened the narratives, our (once rich and descriptive) autoethnographic narratives felt more shallow . . . and of course the question also emerged on a seven-person author team of "who decides what to cut?" We see this as a compromise between highlighting theory/context and method;

we contemplated removing some stories and highlighting others, but this led to the question of "whose autoethnographies are most valuable?" (Geist-Martin et al., 2010, p. 4)

In choosing how to represent multiple voices in CAE, tough decisions must be made. In this case, the authors chose to give mini-excerpts from all seven narratives to offer readers a glimpse into the data of what was an article focused on their method of doing CAE.

In several CE collaborative autoethnographies, authors have chosen to share their stories using multiple voices. Writing from different institutions, Brown and William-White (2010) recount their experiences of being African American women at majority White institutions by telling their stories side by side. A similar approach was used by Espino, Muñoz, and Kiyama (2010) when they recounted their personal experiences of successfully navigating doctoral work as a supportive group of Latina women with multiple identities. After participating in writing individual stories and several telephone conversations, they chose to use "*Pláticas*" to weave together a collective story that, although not an exact transcript of their accounts, illustrates the commonalities of their shared experiences. Guajardo and Guajardo (as cited in Espino, Muñoz, & Kiyama, 2010) define a *plática* as "a collaborative process comprised of sharing stories, building community, and acknowledging multiple realities and vulnerabilities in an effort to enforce strong bonds among the members of that social network" (p. 805).

Multiple voices can also be presented by using more creative genres. Gallardo, Furman, and Kulkami (2009) utilized their autoethnographic poems as primary data for the investigation of depression. The article begins with an introduction to the topic and background information on autoethnography and expressive arts research. What follows is a juxtaposing of a poem on experience depression or living with a spouse who has depression against the author's narrative reflection on the piece. Following is an example from the first author's narrative reflection, followed by a poem about her experience with a spouse who was experiencing clinical depression:

My husband, rather than seeking traditional treatment, spent most of our marriage, using alcohol, drugs, and infidelity to attempt to "feel" better and break the cycle of depression. Not surprisingly, to many of us, this escalated his experience with depression and sped up the cycle, leading to larger valleys throughout our married life.

Emotion

Sadness seeps into my soul,
Anguish, real and hot heats my heart,
Molten anger filled with dreadful despair. (p. 297)

The use of poetry and personal reflection is effective in capturing the strong emotions around the topic of depression and the use of different voices allows each author to tell his or her story within a unified piece of writing. Other creative approaches include writing play scripts with a cast of characters with the intent that such pieces be performed rather than read (Ellis & Bochner, 1992) and using fictional devices to present characters (McMillan & Price, 2010).

In more analytical approaches to CAE, teams may write with one voice but still acknowledge diverse perspectives. In fact, for teams that choose such an approach, the act of working toward negotiated meaning can add another layer of transparency to the work and give readers a backstage view of the collaborative writing process. Although we favor this approach of presenting our writing with one voice, we are careful to indicate instances when our views and experiences were not identical. Here is an example of how we were able to do that in one of our ongoing projects on the experiences of how, as foreign-born women of color in U.S. higher education, we have been confronted with the dilemma of integrating our spiritual selves with our academic selves:

> Balancing our spiritual identity in the context of US secular higher education is a persistent challenge. In this milieu, we were encouraged to compartmentalize our private and public life, to push our religious identity under the table. For Kathy-Ann and Faith these attempts at being socialized to compartmentalize have not taken root. We are cognizant of who we were as spiritual beings and are intent on judiciously letting our faith continue to be a part of our professional lives. For Heewon, having been socialized in this academic context during graduate studies, she has found it "foreign" to discuss the integration of faith into scholarship and incorporate spirituality discussion in the public domain of academic life until working in a faith-based university. Whereas our interpretations of integrating faith into academic life differ, all three of us are committed to being women of faith in the academy. (Hernandez, Ngunjiri, & Chang, 2011)

Whichever approach your team uses in dealing with multivocality in collaborative writing, it is useful to provide readers with a rationale for your choice as well as a transparent view of the process of weaving these voices into one story. As we have highlighted here, dealing with multiple voices in collaborative writing is a persistent challenge. At the same time, multivocality is a unique aspect of this kind of work that can enrich the final product.

Ethical Concerns

We have discussed ethical considerations in previous chapters. However, this issue becomes more pronounced during the writing phase. Autoethnographic work inevitably implicates others. Personal experiences involving significant others during the data collection and analysis phase of research must be rethought as your team considers the possibilities of presenting these stories in the public sphere. Tolich (2010) has argued that waiting until one is ready to publish an AE study is too late to consider ethical issues; autoethnographers need to obtain informed consent from individuals implicated in their stories early in the research process. However, in many academic institutions, autoethnographic work, which, by definition is a study of "self," does not require institutional review board (IRB) approval. Nonetheless, teams should have ethical concerns regarding how they choose to represent others and themselves in CAE writing.

There are two types of ethics in qualitative inquiry: procedural ethics and ethics in practice. Guillemin and Gillam (2004) observe that procedural ethics, for example, involve IRB approval, whereas, ethics in practice are "situations that are unexpected when doing research that can potentially have adverse consequences" (p. 264). Ellis (2007) discusses some of these types of situations under the term "relational ethics" and advises that researchers balance research concerns with ethical concerns. She also offers sound advice for addressing relational ethics in writing (Ellis, 2007). Some strategies to employ involve being selective about what to include and exclude in the writing, writing with pen names, fictionalizing pieces, creating composite characters, and, where feasible and possible, obtaining informed consent early in the research process (Hernandez & Ngunjiri, 2013).

POST-COLLABORATIVE AUTOETHNOGRAPHY WRITING

After the project is completed, what comes next? Teams can use this time to celebrate, conduct a post-mortem of the group process and lessons learned, and make plans for the future. Alternately, teams may choose to disband. However, since one of the best strategies for advancing scholarship is to team up with other scholars in your area of interest as coauthors, why not take advantage of a ready-made research team to pursue ongoing scholarly work and to provide a supportive network?

Celebrate, Review, Reflect, and Plan Next Steps

Working together collaboratively is hard work. Even though we knew this when we began this book project, there was much that we still had to learn from the experience itself about how to best control the document, manage the process of writing and rewriting, and clearly define role and responsibilities. There are also important lesson to be learned about idiosyncrasies of teammates that may emerge under stressful conditions of trying to meet deadlines. This will probably be the case for most groups given the varied tasks (practical and social) and multiple personalities involved in collaborative efforts. Ultimately, working together on a collaborative project creates challenges that impact member relationships. Lapadat, Mothus, and Fisher (2005) discovered these dynamics when they worked together on a classroom study. They write:

> What we discovered, as three researchers engaged collaboratively in a classroom observation and intervention study was that our perceptions of our own researcher roles and of our role relationships with each other as co-researchers, which had at first seemed invisible and unproblematic, transformed into an elephant. (p. 2)

Similarly, Cann and DeMeulenaere (2010) describe this aspect of writing collaboratively as follows:

> And even the process of writing collaboratively is an on-going act of forging such discordant communities. It is an act of friendship that confronts each other on both our ideas and our practice even when (especially when) the two seem in contradiction. It requires open and honest communication and sometimes quite lengthy conversations when we realize we have been talking past each other. (p. 51)

Although this is not what most collaborative autoethnography teams think about when they embark on collaborative work, it is an inextricable part of working together. Collaborative autoethnographic work can forge community or push people apart.

As a result, after each writing project, teams should set aside time to celebrate, review, and reflect on both the practical aspects of the team work and the interpersonal aspects. Celebration is important to recognize the accomplishment of the team effort and as a supportive element in fostering team cohesion. Equally important is the need to review and reflect on what worked and what did not work, what lessons were learned, and what best practices emerged from the group process for use in future projects. Socially, teams should address how members feel about the process, strategies that can be implemented to improve communication and support among teams member, manage stress levels, and create a mutually enjoyable working relationship. Addressing these concerns is particularly important if the team plans to continue working together.

Ongoing Collaborative Scholarly Efforts

Teams can choose to engage in ongoing collaborative scholarship beyond the CAE project. This is the route we have taken. After our initial team formation as part of an AE workshop, we bonded together over our mutual desire to write for publication and our common research agendas. Through the collaborative process, we have been able to use the strengths of our team to work on multiple projects simultaneously. While one team member is spearheading a book project, another works on an article, and the third works on an upcoming workshop. Apart from our collaborative work, we each have our own circles of collaborators for our individual research agendas and may or may not have solo projects on which we are working. This practice just makes good sense in the academy.

Since we began working together on CAE projects in 2008, our research efforts have become so entwined that we are usually working on several projects: collaborative projects as well as individual research projects. Through the collaborative process, we have created a library of references, draft presentation, papers, workshops, and ongoing projects on which we can build to advance our scholarly work. For example, at the time of writing this book, over the course of a month we were able to accomplish the following as direct outgrowths of our collaborative efforts: Heewon wrote a book chapter (Chang, 2013); Kathy-Ann and Faith also wrote a book chapter that came as an invitation based on the work we had done on CAE (Hernandez & Ngunjiri, 2013); Heewon and Kathy-Ann presented papers at the Tobias Leadership Conference in 2012; Kathy-Ann took the lead on submitting a grant application to American Educational Research Association for a proposed CAE workshop to be conducted by us; and Faith crafted the joint proposal to the International Leadership Association for a paper presentation at the annual conference in 2012 (all done while we were also working on this book). Alone, we would not have been able to accomplish this, but together it was possible.

Evidence of this kind of scholarly collaboration is ubiquitous in academic circles and in CAE efforts. For example, Paulus, Woodside, and Ziegler are all employed as associate professors in the Department of Educational Psychology and Counseling at the University of Tennessee and have authored several CAE pieces together (Paulus, Woodside, & Ziegler, 2008, 2010; Woodside, Ziegler, & Paulus, 2009). Similarly, Ellis and Bochner (Bochner & Ellis, 2002; Ellis & Bochner, 1992, 2000), the famous couple most responsible for expanding and popularizing the method of AE, have collaborated on several projects. Norris and Sawyer (Norris, Sawyer, & Lund, 2011; Sawyer & Norris, 2004, 2009) have produced multiple collaborative writings focusing on duoethnography; Nabavi and Lund (Lund & Nabavi, 2008a, 2008b; Nabavi & Lund, 2010) have collaborated on justice and activism work using duoethnography. Each collaborative team effort brings with it the potential for ongoing collaboration to facilitate advancement in the academy.

Supportive Networks

CAE efforts can create a support network that provides emotional support and encourages presentation and publications long after projects are completed. Our collaborative work has engendered a "sisterhood" among us that provides not only emotional support but also a supportive structure that has enabled us to significantly improve our scholarship efforts. Through CAE, participants are presented with opportunities to "become confidants to each other's secrets and voyeurs into each other's self-described life experiences" (Hernandez & Ngunjiri, 2013). Our relationships inevitably become strengthened though this kind of sharing, and the intimacy is further solidified through the collaborative writing process.

In addition to any prior preexisting relationship that coauthors can bring to CAE, working through the writing process collaboratively can create a supportive relationship. Brown and William-White's (2010) account of their experiences as African American women in predominantly White institutions provides gripping tales of similar experiences in different academic institutions. As sisters, it is probable that they talked through these experiences in casual conversations, but the process of putting those experiences into a joint writing effort inevitably connected them though these shared experiences and simultaneously served as a source of support for their respective journeys in the academy.

These types of connections can continue beyond the CAE project. Consistent with qualitative methodologies, CAE research can generate copious data—more than is needed for one project. One publication from a CAE project may leave other parts of the research topic unexplored. These data can become the focus of another project and lead to more data collection and analysis. Teams can decide that this kind of ongoing collaboration is of mutual interest and agree to work together. Even if this is not the case, there is the possibility of forming a supportive writing circle. In the following chapter, we share the story of our collaborative journey.

CONCLUSION

The ultimate goal of research is dissemination of findings. We conduct research to draw attention to important issues that are often not well represented in academic and public circles. As such, it is important that our research becomes a part of the corporate knowledge base. This means that the results of CAE project need to be written up for public presentation and/or publication. CAE projects provide a built-in circle of support that mitigates some of the persistent challenges that often stymie writing efforts. Writing in community is a preferred strategy for demystifying the writing process and for providing practical and psychological support as the team works together to create a written product.

Teams can advance successfully toward the goal of sharing their findings by being attentive to the task and activities in CAE pre-writing, writing, and post-writing. Moreover, CAE projects can spiral into ongoing scholarly collaborations and relational networks long after a project is completed, providing scaffolds for team members to advance scholarship efforts individually and collectively.

CHAPTER 7

Applications of Collaborative Autoethnography

The emergence of collaborative autoethnography (CAE) as a dynamic research approach that involves collaborative voice in the research process adds an important element to the academic landscape. As we have detailed in the previous chapters, CAE offers opportunities for researchers to interrogate salient issues relevant to their own research agenda in supportive environments. However, its utility is not confined to the academy or to a specific discipline. The power of CAE as a research approach lies in its ability to enable collaboration among a team of researchers and to create a community of practice through collaboration in contexts where that might not have existed before.

Numerous collaborative autoethnographies have resulted from collaboration across disciplines (O'Shea et al., 2011) and across institutions (Geist-Martin et al., 2010; Toyosaki et al., 2009). Whether the collaborators start off as colleagues/friends or as strangers, their joint efforts at engaging in autoethnographic research engenders community among them, which then often extends their relationship to include more research, ongoing collegiality, and friendship. Perhaps it is as Parker Palmer has argued. "No matter how you slice it, the basic mission of the academy—knowing, teaching, and learning—is, at bottom, communal. That mission cannot be pursued successfully in the absence of cultural support for community" (Palmer & Zajonc, 2010, p. 43). We argue here that research is indeed communal—CAE engenders the practice of community and collaborative learning. In this chapter, we summarize the uses and benefits of CAE as research methodology. We begin with CAE as it is used in the classroom and then demonstrate its use as activism research, in empowering co-researchers, and for professional development.

PRACTICE IN THE CLASSROOM

Collaborative autoethnographic methods can be employed in the classroom for teaching qualitative research and design, where students are involved in collecting, analyzing, and interpreting autobiographical data collectively and writing individual final assignments (reflection papers) and/or collaborative manuscripts. CAE is also used to help graduate students think about their future research goals through pilot studies. We discuss both approaches below, supported by our own praxis and published literature.

Teaching the Qualitative Research Process

Within the academy, CAE has been used as a tool to teach qualitative research. For example, Heewon has used it to teach qualitative research to doctoral students at Eastern University. The qualitative research course is taught in a cohort-based doctoral program in organizational leadership that follows the hybrid model of instruction. Each semester of the program consists of three components: (1) one-week online pre-residency; (2) one-and-a-half-day residency (six one-and-a-half-hour face-to-face sessions); and (3) 10 off-campus online weeks.

During the pre-residency week,[1] Heewon requires students to submit a personal memory writing of two to three pages about a mentor who has significantly influenced their leadership development. Students write about their family member, work supervisor, work colleague, spiritual elder, or personal friend as their leadership mentor. A cohort of 20 students end up collecting 20 pieces of personal memory writings by the beginning of their first face-to-face class.

During the residency, Heewon requires students to interview each other in pairs or in a small group to probe further on their writing. Students take notes and record their interviews. Heewon then uses collective autobiographical writings and interview data to teach students how to do qualitative data analysis and interpretation. By the end of the residency, students form a research team of three to four members with similar backgrounds (e.g., education leader, business leader, nonprofit leader, and women leader).

Each research team expands their research project by interviewing other leaders with similar backgrounds as themselves about their leadership mentoring experiences. Each team could exercise their freedom to decide whether to add their autoethnographic data (initial writings and interview) in the interview data from new participants to complete their data analysis and interpretation for their final project. This collaboration model enables students to collect a sufficient amount of data within a short time period to experience meaningful qualitative data analysis and interpretation.

The pedagogical model of CAE, combined with the interview method, not only gives students hands-on experiences with the qualitative research process but also valuable lessons on ethical considerations regarding both participants and researchers. Their empathic understanding comes because they experience the vulnerable position of participants as well as the powerful position of researchers. Previous coursework has resulted in several conference presentations of students at the International Congress of Qualitative Inquiry (Bleil, 2010a), International Leadership Association (Bleil, 2010b; Wolf & Ober, 2010), and Mid-Atlantic Leadership Conference (Asenavage-Loptes, 2012; Meader, 2012; Nussbaum, 2012). After the course was completed in 2009, Bleil, Fornicola, and Dillman (2010) applied CAE to their independent project with Chang, focusing on executive women leaders' layoff experiences, which resulted in a journal article currently under review.

Coia and Taylor (2009) have also used the collaborative autoethnographic approach in the classroom with pre-service teachers; their published article is a reflection on their experience in helping the student-teachers become more reflective practitioners. In their conference presentation, Coia and Taylor (2006) discussed how they used CAE to teach educational research, for "reflective teaching" in a teacher education program:

> Combining the defining features of autobiography with the methods of ethnography while foregrounding collaboration, co/autoethnography is a method whereby we share our stories and the stories of our pre-service teachers as a way to understand our practice and discover ways to navigate the crises that we face . . . co/autoethnography insists that the meaning of our teaching practice can only be fully understood if it is constructed in collaboration. (p. 60)

In this case, CAE helped Coia and Taylor and their pre-service teachers in heightening their self-awareness, "becoming more knowledgeable about our identity development as teachers/agents of change/teacher educators" (p. 60). They indicated that they used it to strengthen pre-service teachers' identity formation as teachers and to "practice a pedagogy of mutuality." Further, they note:

> Co/autoethnography looks slightly different when we invite our students to use it. We invite students to begin to think about their past experiences as learners and as teachers, both inside and outside schools, as a lens for the ways in which they think about who they are becoming as teachers. We attempt to replicate the co/autoethnography process we use ourselves. We encourage our students to form small groups in which they work for the entire semester. We format the process in a deliberately open-ended way, inviting students to write, share, ask questions about, reflect on, and re-write their narratives. We ask that at the end of the semester, they put together a co/autoethnographic reflection that includes what they have learned about their beliefs about teaching and learning through the co/autoethnographic process. (p. 61)

It is clear from this description of Coia and Taylor's use of CAE in pedagogy that it is useful for students to learn how to be reflective as they prepare for their teaching roles and for professors to be able to further their reflexivity in relation to their identity as teacher educators. As Coia and Taylor indicate, they hope that as the student-teachers co-construct autoethnographies, "their construction of relationships and community among themselves as teachers ideally resembles those created with students" (p. 59).

Lapadat has also used CAE in a qualitative methods class; she and her (now former) students published a CAE article in which they explored identity development (Lapadat et al., 2009) and another article with another group of (now former) students focusing on a life challenge (critical incident) that each had experienced and its influence on their lives (Lapadat et al., 2010). Lapadat (2009) reflected on the two different qualitative methods classes and the lessons she learned about CAE: "Learning by doing is an immediate, powerful way to learn and it demystifies processes of qualitative research" (p. 957); and "[t]he what and how of research become meaningful and personal through doing it" (p. 956). Further, Lapadat (2009) indicated that using CAE in teaching qualitative research enabled her to learn about power, voice, co-researcher relationships, and reflexivity. As her students learned how to engage in qualitative research including designing the study, collecting (autobiographic) data, analyzing data, and writing the final product, she was learning and reflecting on her role as a professor and co-researcher who was attempting to reduce the power differential in the co-researcher relationships. Issues of anonymity, ethics, institutional review boards, and mentoring graduate students were also part of her lessons learned.

A number of common principles emerge from all the descriptions of using CAE in the qualitative/educational research courses:

1. The professor(s) provide the class with a topic to cover throughout the course. The topic may also be co-constructed through discussions with the class. Having the professor choose a topic is probably more time efficient so that from the very first day of class, she or he can come prepared with relevant course readings on both the topic of choice and the methods to be employed. The dialogic route has the advantage of having more student buy-in; however, in most classes that may still mean that the majority wins over the minority voices.
2. The course is designed around the broad topics of data collection, data analysis, interpretation, and writing.
3. Data collection involves individual writing as well as collaborative/collective writing assignments.
4. There is also evidence of individual of collective meaning-making.

5. The final written assignment may either be collaboratively written or involve individual writing. In either case, there are instances of both individual and collaborative writing assignments throughout the course.

In some cases, the professor co-creates knowledge with the students in the form of a published manuscript after the fact. It is also possible that there are many instances of using CAE in the classroom that do not result in a published outcome. However, when the CAE project is intended for presentation or publication outside the classroom context, professors and students should check with IRB guidelines at their institution. This will ensure that they are adhering to ethical guidelines early in the research process.

We hope this outline provides faculty with information that they can use in crafting their own CAE-infused qualitative research courses. As Lapadat (2009) reflected, using CAE is a powerful teaching approach because it makes qualitative research come alive for the students, making it more personally meaningful as they use their own data in the process of collection, analysis, interpretation, and writing.

Conducting Collaborative Autoethnography as a Pilot Study

CAE can be employed as a pilot study prior to conducting a larger study, perhaps to test the themes that may be explored later on with a more comprehensive sample. In our initial conceptualization of our study, our intention was to begin with our own stories, as we prepared to engage in a much larger, mixed-methods study about women of color in the academy. That larger study has not yet commenced, as we failed to secure funding and also as we needed to go back to the drawing board and conceptualize it to better fit with our individual and collective research goals. In the interim, as mentioned previously, our collaborative project has resulted in several CAE workshops at conferences including the American Anthropological Association (Philadelphia, 2009), International Leadership Association (Prague, 2009; Boston, 2010), and International Congress of Qualitative Inquiry (Urbana-Champaign, 2009). Further, we have published one article after coediting the special issue of *Journal of Research Practices* focusing on autoethnography (AE) (Ngunjiri, Hernandez, & Chang, 2010) and we have two other papers in progress. This book grew out of our realization of the need for a text that would help people learn a step-by-step process of engaging in CAE, particularly after the first couple of workshops that we presented. In that sense, the pilot study has become a full research agenda that has kept us busy and productive over the past three years.

Another avenue for utilizing CAE as a pilot study is to incorporate students' dissertation topics in qualitative research courses such that instead of the professor providing the topic of research (as Lapadat did in the studies mentioned previously), students would use their own topics. In that scenario, students can be grouped into teams depending on the topic's closeness to their own dissertation area.

Faith and her colleague, Sharon Gramby-Sobukwe, are using that approach; they have conceptualized a study of Black women clergy and invited four doctoral students who are interested in the topic to join their research team. In a partial collaborative process, they invited the students to join them in conceptualizing one phase of the study, during which they agreed to have focused group discussions with Black women pastors, ministers, and those in training. They also collected autobiographic data utilizing critical incident approach. The two data streams were to be analyzed collectively and dialogically in e-mails, Skype®, and face-to-face meetings, with the purpose of producing manuscripts to submit for a special issue of the *Journal of Pan African Studies* on the stained-glass ceiling.

Two projects came out of that work, both of which were published in a special issue of the *Journal of Pan-African Studies* on the stained-glass ceiling (Vol 5, Issue 2, 2012). Two of the other students in the research team were not able to use the forum/CAE project further, due to the demands of their work. However, one student from the team is using it as a pilot study; her dissertation will be exploring the life stories of Black women clergy in the Philadelphia area.

In another example, the CAE study of Bleil (2010a, 2010b), focusing on mentoring of women executives, has developed into her dissertation; Bleil, Fornicola, and Dillman's study (2010), focusing on layoffs of women executives, has evolved into Fornicola's dissertation about women executives managing the aftermath of layoffs.

Although we have not found other examples of CAE being used as pilot studies for graduate student research, we surmise that it is a rich resource for that kind of work because, as Lapadat (2009) observed, learning by doing is a powerful, personal, and meaningful way for graduate students to learn how to do qualitative research.

BUILDING COMMUNITY

The CAE process can be used to build communities with familiar colleagues or strangers. It helps the communities develop solidarity through discovery of self and others.

Solidarity

The three articles by Lapadat and her co-researchers (Lapadat, 2009; Lapadat et al., 2009; Lapadat et al., 2010) together illustrate the utility of CAE in building community among co-researchers, such as between faculty and their graduate students. In their CAE project on "life challenges" (Lapadat et al., 2010), the class was made up of students from different graduate programs. Their journey together enabled them to develop a community of practice: Even five years after the class they were able to work together getting their article published. The other CAE project (Lapadat et al., 2009) involved students from a graduate counseling program who already knew each other well, yet even there, it furthered their development of community and enabled the professor to be somewhat integrated into their experience. For the students involved in the two class projects, the CAE project helped them recognize their solidarity; namely, they were all in it together.

Although the concurrent CAE that we undertook (Hernandez, Ngunjiri, & Chang, 2011; Ngunjiri, Hernandez, & Chang, 2010) and the sequential CAE that our doctoral students conducted (Bleil, Fornicola, & Dillman, 2010) did not start out with community building as a goal, it was one of the outcomes of the collaborative research journeys. For example, as we practiced concurrent CAE, we learned a lot about each other's backgrounds that we would not have talked about except in that environment. This learning contributed to feelings of comfort with vulnerability, and we found ourselves willing to dig deeper into earlier experiences of home, school, immigration, and education. We could not have grown deeper in our collegiality and friendship without that willingness to be vulnerable, as vulnerability is the other side of intimacy. Furthermore, in the process, we find that we are able to support each other in our teaching roles because we have that deepened relationship, going above and beyond the calls of duty.

We also support each other outside of the university setting as friends, visiting Kathy-Ann in the hospital after the birth of her daughter and attending and participating at Faith's Quaker wedding ceremony. We support each other and recognize our friendship as a deeper layer of our collegial relationship. It is unlikely we would have grown in our relationship without our collaborative project, which brought us together as often as every fortnight during the active period of data collection and analysis. Moreover, that project became the genesis for further engagement in collaborative work, including the book project, journal editing, and several CAE workshops, and conference presentations. Our chapters of autoethnographies on spirituality in higher education (Hernandez, 2011; Ngunjiri, 2011) in a book coedited by Chang and Boyd (2011) were further continuation of our collaborative activities. We have definitely benefited from interacting and co-researching with each other; our solidarity as immigrant minority faculty in a Christian institution has helped spawn all those projects mentioned above.

Discovery

CAE can be used as a tool for developing community by eliciting discovery, when researchers with different perspectives interrogate their diverse subject positions and experiences. For example, Toyosaki et al.'s (2009) community autoethnography is aptly named, as one of its primary purposes is to develop community among the co-researchers. As discussed in Chapter 2, community autoethnography borrows a participatory approach from community ethnography and a way to learn about and build relationships from Ellis and Bochner (Bochner & Ellis, 1995). In community AE, building community among the participants is part of the goal. In the example, the four researchers interrogated their experiences of whiteness from different perspectives and subject positionalities—as a middle-class White, an Asian immigrant, a poor White, and a female White—that together aided in a deeper understanding of whiteness while also contributing to growing their relationship as co-researchers. Their collaboration helped to develop community in the midst of their diversity.

Further, Lund and Nabavi (2008a), a White male and a female of color examine issues of race, identity, and activism among young people. When they first met, Lund was the researcher/activist while Nabavi was a youth leader in a youth activism environment. Later on while Nabavi was a graduate student, they started duo-ethnographic research reflecting on their experiences. Their ensuing studies and publications demonstrate how two researchers who have a power differential make the transition from a hierarchical relationship of difference, to a co-researcher relationship interrogating those differences (Lund & Nabavi, 2008a; Nabavi & Lund, 2010). As they indicate, "We accept the complexity of gendered and racialized relations and have conducted this research from differing subject positions" (Lund & Nabavi, 2008a, p. 2).

As a tool of discovery in a community of difference, CAE serves the purpose of demonstrating multivocality (Lapadat, Mothus, & Fisher, 2005; Lapadat et al., 2009) whereby the different voices of the co-researchers are "heard" through the text. CAE enables researchers to bring their different voices together, sometimes creating a coherent whole (McMillan

& Price, 2010) and other times ensuring that individual voices are not lost in the name of consensus (Geist-Martin et al., 2010; Lapadat et al., 2009; Murakami-Ramalho, Piert, & Militello, 2008).

RESEARCH AS ACTIVISM

CAE can be utilized in building community for the purpose of collective action and agency, particularly in the context of the search for more equitable social and institutional arrangements. Here, we are thinking that when two or more people get together in the spirit of sharing, co-learning, and collaboration, it becomes that much easier to solicit for action on behalf of themselves as representatives of a wider group or on behalf of others. The sharing and vulnerability involved can be a stepping-stone toward collective action, and the empowerment that co-researchers experience can be used toward collective agency. For example, the edited book that is a collection of autoethnographies/collaborative autoethnographies by women of color in academe (Robinson & Clardy, 2010). We envision that kind of project as useful in raising awareness about the working conditions that minority women experience in higher education, a book that other women of color could use to make their case without necessarily using their own stories. That is, since we (talking about minority women in academe) we can identify with the autoethnographies in that book, we could reference this book in advocating for change while in the process protecting ourselves from further harassment.

So, rather than our administrators and university officials reading our stories about how we experience their leadership and structural injustices, they could read about the other women whose stories are indicative of our experience. This is possible because as we learn from the experience of one of the authors in that book, who wrote a CAE piece about experiences as a Black woman in academe including her current institution (Brown & William-White, 2010), it is not always safe to publish our own stories without facing repercussions in our social context (William-White, 2011). Using published CAE works instead would offer a level of protection to minority faculty who need an avenue toward advocating for themselves.

Where colleagues feel brave enough to use their own stories, co-constructing CAE work can be used toward aiding collective action. Let us imagine that using the same topic—minority women in higher education—a group of women in a particular institution come together, create a CAE project, write it up, and use that to advocate for change. Again, we have not found examples of such published works; however, we did find articles such as McMillan and Price (2010) in which they explicate their experiences within their university using a performative autoethnographic approach, offering promise for activism research. There is potential for the use of collaborative approach to engage several co-researchers whose experiences bear similarity, then utilizing that material for the purpose of advocating for change. This is perhaps one place where utilizing the more evocative and performative writing styles of AE would be quite effective, as the writing has potential to not only inform the readers on the experiences/plight of the researchers, but also evoke the necessary emotion to prod the reader toward action. CAE research for purposes of activism is currently unutilized but has tremendous potential.

TOOL FOR CRITICAL WORK

CAE has tremendous potential for transformative intellectuals who intend to use their work to disrupt "the inequitable distribution of power and resources in society" (Cann & DeMeulenaere, 2012, p. 2). Here, we are thinking in terms of using CAE not so much for disrupting power relations in our own institutions as suggested in the previous section, but more so for disrupting inequity in society. Autoethnographers could engage community members as co-creators of knowledge and employ AE in a process of action research.

Empowerment and Collective Voice

One of the areas in which collaborative autoethnographic practice can be of particular use is in empowering researcher-participants (Lapadat, 2009), helping them find their individual and collective voice. Let us begin by narrating our own experiences to illustrate this point, then cite other published CAE articles. In our study focusing on our identities as women immigrants "of color" within the academy, we discovered a lot about our common experiences even though we come from three countries in different continents and have been in the United States for differing number of years (Hernandez, Ngunjiri, & Chang, 2011).

For example, in our struggle to articulate how we felt as outsiders-within, we discovered a common bond carried forth from our native cultures, whereby excellence is expected and rewarded. As such, we encouraged each other to continue to pursue excellence, particularly in our teaching, but also in our research, in spite of prevailing institutional culture. Hernandez (2011) captures some of that struggle well in her AE on teaching and assessment at our institution; collectively, we were able to come up with three strategies that we employ in navigating the culture of academic as well as of our particular institution: exploiting multifocal lenses, reconfiguring identities, and exercising tempered radicalism (Hernandez, Ngunjiri, & Chang, 2011).

Whereas this was an academic exercise whose outcome was a conference paper and a manuscript for publication, what we found was that it also became a journey in personal empowerment. The three strategies that we uncovered from our lived experiences might have remained hidden in our memory banks; instead, the dialogic process enabled us to own them actively and even see places in our work and family lives where we could utilize them explicitly or covertly.

Similarly, we have found that McMillan and Price's (2010) performative autoethnographic piece detailing their experiences in their institution has overtones of personal empowerment. By engaging in the collaborative reflexivity necessary to write their piece, they appear to have been able to "power through" the struggles they were facing with inter-departmental politics. They made it through the "rabbit hole" by writing through it.

We also see elements of personal empowerment in the article by Lund and Nabavi (2008a), too, mainly through the idea that a youth activist (Nabavi) is engaged in collaborative reflection and writing with a professor (Lund). During the process, they are able to co-construct knowledge in spite of the power differential that might exist in such a relationship. Their continued collaborative autoethnographic work (Lund & Nabavi, 2008b; Nabavi & Lund, 2010) suggests that the youth activist/graduate student was empowered to continue in the work of academic scholarship supported by the professor. This kind of empowerment of graduate students through collaborative research and writing with their professors is also evident in the work of Lapadat who has published two CAE articles with two different sets of students (Lapadat et al., 2009; Lapadat et al., 2010).

PROFESSIONAL DEVELOPMENT

Collaborative autoethnographic practice can be utilized as part of a professional development program within higher education and beyond. In higher education, we envision using CAE by bringing together a group of faculty and/or administrators who need to develop certain skill sets. For example, a faculty learning community can be instituted with the purpose of training faculty in research design and publication. Within such a group, the facilitator can use CAE with faculty collecting individual autoethnographic data on topics such as mentoring, teaching, student advising, or another element of the work within universities. The faculty would bring their individual data into the group for collective meaning-making, then later engage in further iterations of individual data collection, individual meaning-making, and collective analysis. The writing up could be either collaborative, or each faculty member could do his or her own writing and publishing. Thus, it can either be a full collaborative process or a partial one. O'Shea et al. (2011), for instance, focused on spirituality as a central topic for their faculty learning community, which resulted in a CAE.

With administrators and organizational leaders, a similar process can be employed. For example, Heewon engaged a dozen leaders of color from various colleges and universities in a CAE quest. The participants were recruited from a leadership institute designed to assist them in advancing as academic leaders. The collaborative research team participated in an online discussion on two leadership-related topics monthly for six months and met once a month virtually for focus group discussion (see Appendix A for writing prompts for the online discussion). Since the AE research method was new to the participants, they were learning about self-reflective and self-analytical strategies along the way. Through conversations with each other, participants learned leadership lessons from leaders who held certain posts that others desired. Not all participants decided to write up their individual autoethnographies at the end. However, all acknowledged that they had gained tremendous professional development experience through regular conversations over six months.

Published collaborative autoethnographies and our own works indicate that CAE can be applied to different situations and in numerous ways. We hope that you experiment with different approaches to find the best fit for your research team.

CONCLUSION

CAE is an innovative approach to research that provides researchers the space to work in community as they investigate topics of mutual interest. This approach to qualitative inquiry benefits the researchers and the research community.

In this chapter, we have discussed the various ways that CAE can be utilized, focusing mostly on its use in the academy. However, the scope for CAE extends beyond the university. CAE can be used in university-community partnerships or even be utilized in organizations outside of the university setting. For example, the use of CAE in activism fits well with university-community activism for issues such as equal housing, the fight against urban poverty, and partnerships with K–12 institutions. Similarly, CAE as a tool for empowerment can be used in the form of university-community partnerships. The professional component of CAE has potential for use in any kind of organization, where the university faculty or a trained consultant could facilitate the formation of learning communities for the purpose of training in specific skill areas.

Overall, CAE has the potential to be used in diverse ways, with many different audiences, and can therefore generate co-created knowledge that is actionable, personally meaningful, and empowering for all involved. Whether used in the classroom, with faculty and/or administrators, within organizations, or as partnerships between university and community groups, CAE offers potential that is yet to be fully utilized. We invite you to take advantage of the method in your own sphere of influence. Our experience as collaborative autoethnographers has solidified our view that CAE is much more than another approach to qualitative inquiry. It is a transforming process that allows scholars to build community, advance scholarship, engage in social activism, and become empowered in their social context.

Epilogue: Our Approach

When we first began our collaborative work, we had very little idea about what lay before us. Yet we forged ahead. Without the benefit of a book such as this, we stumbled on an approach to collaborative autoethnography (CAE) through a process of trial and error. Over the course of working on several projects, we have modified and adapted a model that works for us. In these parting words, we give you a behind-the-scenes look at our processes that, we must admit, are works in process. We begin with a brief recap of how our team got started and our initial project and discuss in-depth our collaborative writing efforts, which is often the most demanding aspect of this kind of work.

THE BEGINNINGS

We share a common passion for pursuing an active research agenda. However, at our current university, we face the challenge of heavy teaching loads, which leaves little time for research. After several informal conversations about this, we bonded over our desire to actively pursue a research agenda even at a "teaching university." Heewon approached Faith and Kathy-Ann to begin a project relative to our experiences of being foreign-born women of color in the academy. This collaborative autoethnography (CAE) circle was a natural outgrowth of a larger autoethnographic writing group of which we were a part. Using some of the data we had collected in the autoethnography (AE) workshop spearheaded by Heewon, we agreed to meet outside the group to make plans for how we would embark on the project.

Honestly, we had not given much thought to the strengths and skill sets among the three of us. The unifying elements were that we had all migrated to the United States to do graduate work and were each committed to advancing an active research agenda. However, as we began to work together, we saw how providential our meeting was. Each of us was at a different stage in our professional and personal development. Heewon, a naturalized citizen of the United States, was a full professor who had written two books and founded two online journals. She was also an empty nester and the oldest member of the team. Faith, was an assistant professor and the youngest member of the group. She had completed her graduate work in 2006 and was working toward permanent status as a U.S. resident. At the time, she was single and working on her first book along with a string of publications. Kathy-Ann, a recent permanent resident, was an associate professor and newlywed, having married in 2006. She had taken some time off from the academy to have her first child and was adjusting to motherhood while trying to play "catch up" with her publication efforts. Among the three of us, our status relative to our individual ambitions created rich fodder for much of the work that ensued from our collaborative efforts. In addition, because we were each at different junctures in our personal and academic journeys, we fell naturally into the roles of mentors and guides to each other for the challenges and possibilities that lay ahead in the areas of marriage, parenthood, promotion and tenure, and the advancement of an active research agenda.

PLANNING OUR DATA COLLECTION

At the end of the academic semester, when we finally had a chance to breathe, we had lunch at Panera Bread to talk about our proposed project. Once the chit-chat and eating were over, we just looked at each other and wondered: "So what do we do now?" With their expertise in qualitative methods, Heewon and Faith provided some directives for the way forward. We agreed on our research questions and our methods of data collection, which included completing culturegrams (see Figure 4-1 in Chapter 4; Chang, 2008) as graphic representation of our primary socio-identities, writing independent critical incidents, and conducting focus group interviews. In the first phase, we completed our culturegrams and wrote critical incidents independently, which we then circulated among the group. We reviewed each other's scripts and then met in a round of two-hour focus group interviews (they usually lasted about three hours as we love to talk). These interviews were recorded, transcribed, and independently coded, then we met to discuss codes and negotiate themes. This was an iterative process that led to more research questions, more independent writing sessions, and focus group meetings. We used Blackboard ®to share and store our files and eventually moved to Google Docs®.

These initial collections led to several projects and products, including submitting an NSF grant proposal, several presentations at the American Educational Research Association, the International Leadership Association, the American Anthropological Association, the Tobias Leadership Conference, the International Congress of Qualitative Inquiry, as well as book chapters, a coedited issue of the *Journal of Research Practice*, and journal articles at various stages in the publication pipeline.

COLLABORATIVE AUTOETHNOGRAPHY WRITING

In the course of our work together, we determined that each of us would be fully involved at each stage of the process; thus, we utilized a full collaboration model. Whereas each project has a unique approach, there is a pattern to how we approach collaborative writing after we have reached a relative stability in our data analysis and interpretation. The steps we take can be outlined as follows:

Step 1-Setting Up the Framework: Set the framework and timeline, select a journal, and discuss roles and responsibilities.

Step 2-Writing, Rewriting, and Meaning-Making: Embark on writing, ongoing revision of drafts, and group meetings to facilitate ongoing meaning-making until the final draft is submitted.

Step 3-Celebration and Reflection: Celebrate, regroup, revisit, reflect, and plan the way forward.

Although we categorize our approach to CAE as more on the analytical-interpretive end of the continuum and often choose to write with one voice, we think of these as generic steps that can be applied by CAE groups irrespective of their position on the creative-evocative versus analytic-interpretive continuum. Here is a glimpse of our process.

Step 1: Setting Up the Framework

In conceptualizing a research study, we begin with the end in mind. We teach research methods courses at our university, so we are well aware that the end result of research is dissemination of research findings. However, earlier in our career, we did not fully comprehend the importance of clearly defining our research agendas and developing a plan that moved our projects along the publication pipeline. As a result, we were often expending energies in many different directions and not effectively focusing our research agenda and efforts to diligently turn our presentations into publications. Now, in approaching a CAE project, we choose a topic that has some connection to each of our individual research agendas. This is an important consideration, since it ensures individual "buy in" to the project and allows each of us to continue advancing our own research agenda even as we are doing collaborative work. Once we have begun data collection and commenced data analysis, we begin thinking about the best venue for sharing our findings and a feasible timeframe for getting it done. At this time, we usually make decisions about who will lead this project and how we will coordinate the writing. We like to meet often and have fallen into a pattern of meeting almost every two weeks during the regular school year when we are working on a written piece.

Selecting a journal is an important consideration with respect to our work. While there are several peer-reviewed journals that focus on qualitative methods, several important considerations guide us in our selection process. We are concerned at this stage with several criteria in making our selection: reputation of the journal, aim and scope, types of articles considered, turn-around review time, number of issues per year, and composition of the editorial team. Apart from selecting peer-reviewed journal that has a good reputation is the issue of fit. How closely does the research project align with the aim and scope of a particular journal?

First, we consider if the journal focuses on the kind of topic that is the focus of our research article. We review the journal website as well as the table of contents and selected articles to see if our topic fits well with the journal. Next, we examine the kinds of articles that the journal publishes. Social science journals tend to specialize in one or a combination of four types of papers: theoretical and/or conceptual discussions, extensive literature reviews, empirical research, and methodological papers. We match our writing project to the appropriate journal after we have agreed that it is indeed a good fit for the article. Once we have completed these steps in the prewriting phase, we are ready to begin creating systems to support our writing of the project by establishing a division of the work based on members' core strengths.

Step 2: Writing, Rewriting, and Meaning-Making

We use a parallel writing structure that is consistent with Stratton's (1989) stratified-division writing in which we assign tasks based on our core strengths. Once tasks are assigned, we follow up with assignments in our bi-weekly meetings, to seek clarification on the writing, but mostly to provide a regular system of accountability and support for each other.

In our CAE team, Heewon has several core strengths. Since she teaches qualitative methods, she is often responsible for working on the methods section in an article. She is also the visionary, project instigator, and team socializer. It was her vision that first got us involved in autoethnography as a practical outgrowth of her book *Autoethnography as Method* (Chang, 2008). She called the group together and facilitated our introduction to AE. It was at this point that she selected and set up the technological tools (we chose to use Blackboard®, Skype®, face-to-face, and Google Docs®) and created systems of contact and communication as well as took the lead in engaging in supporting writing activities, coordinating our efforts, and monitoring our progress (Lowry, Curtis, & Lowry, 2004). As editor of a journal, she also has a good vantage point to see the steps that need to be done ahead to get the manuscript out on time. And she is generally the one to suggest lunch at a favorite restaurant or a get-together at her house.

Both Faith and Kathy-Ann have first degrees in English literature and are good writers. Faith is strong as a reader and reviewer of research articles. She reads prolifically and is often the one who begins crafting the literature review and theoretical frameworks and sharing insights into what and who we should be reading as we work on our various projects. She also has experience serving as the lead editor for a special issue of the *Journal of Research Practice*. Kathy-Ann is the writer and reviewer. She has experience as a copyeditor for *Mission Herald*, a publication of the Foreign Missions Board of Philadelphia, serves as a reviewer for several peer-review journals, and is a research consultant. With her background in quantitative research methods she brings a good balance and critical perspective to our choice of methods. She is great at conceptualizing a study and synthesizing research. She focuses on writing, editing/proofreading our drafts, and critiquing the unity and flow of the final written product. Even though each of us is strong in our individual roles, because we use a full collaboration model, we also move in and out of these roles and change roles based on particular projects.

Since we also want the work to be reflective of all of us, we go through several rounds of revisions by each team member until we all feel reasonably comfortable that the work represents the collective team. We each write our own sections; then the team leader merges the document and revises and edits it. This version is then re-circulated for one or two rounds of reviews, each of which is usually followed by team meetings. The final document is then edited and submitted to the targeted journal. It is through the process of reviewing and meeting to negotiate the final writing that we engage in another level of analysis that makes the final product represent our team effort. We would describe this part of writing as an iterative part of the analysis and interpretation of the data in response to our research question/s. Moreover, through the collaborative process, we recognize, as Paulus, Woodside, and Ziegler (2008, 2010) have articulated, that once the piece is finished it is impossible to distinguish what section belongs to which one of us. The work is simultaneously our reporting of our findings in response to the research questions, and a product of the group process.

In our collaborative work, therefore, we recognize these two layers of our research writing: (1) themes that emerge from the data as filtered through our process of negotiated group meaning; and (2) the *new* voice that emerges from our collaborative writing process. At the same time, we make room in the writing to emphasize different views and perspectives among us as we have shared in Chapter 6. These are critical elements that set our CAE efforts apart from our individual work. The final product does not represent any of us individually and could not be recreated singularly; it is socially constructed as part of the dynamic process that is inherent in how we choose to work together.

Step 3: Celebration and Reflection

Each CAE project is different and provides opportunities for us to grow individually and also as a team. Because we have been working together for several years now and are often working on several projects simultaneously, we tend to wait until the end of an academic year to celebrate our various CAE projects that have been completed. Our celebrations almost always involve food and tea (we are all tea drinkers). This is also the time to regroup and discuss projects that are still in the pipeline and make plans for how to move them along as well as what projects we want to tackle next. In response to a rejected article or one that might have been returned with a "revise and submit" recommendation, we discuss our options and how to proceed.

An informal setting also creates the right atmosphere to discuss what worked well on our last projects and what did not. Several ideas have come out of these sessions about how we can work better together. One source of continued challenge for us is how best to plan a timetable around projects that works for all of us, given our different commitments and personal levels of comfort working under tight deadlines. We have learned that writing always takes longer than we anticipate, so it is important to create a long project timeline and add an extra month beyond the time we think a project should be completed. Because our individual writing styles are so different, we have learned to negotiate meaning with respect to the content of the final product, but to allow the lead author's writing style to carry the piece. We have learned to be open to new ideas even as the field of AE and CAE continues to develop. Hence, even though we aligned ourselves with more analytic CAE paradigms, we are open to the idea of exploring imaginative-creative pieces and using multiple voices to represent our individual selves in future work.

After working together for the past couple of years, perhaps, the biggest lesson we have learned is consistent with the African proverb that reads: "If you want to walk fast walk alone, if you want to walk far walk together." In spite of the challenges in researching and writing together, we realize that we are more productive as a team than we could be individually and that we value the supportive "sisterhood" that has evolved out of our joint work. Therefore, we are forgiving of slights, miscommunications, and disagreements, accepting them as necessary growing pains in collaborative work.

In Retrospect

It is gratifying to write this epilogue as a book end (pun intended) to one of the biggest collaborative efforts that emerged from our beginnings in 2008. So much has happened since that fortuitous meeting. Our personal statuses have been updated. Faith became a permanent U.S. resident, got married, and is now associate professor. Kathy-Ann is now the mother of two little girls, and Heewon is enjoying life in a new house since the kids went off to college. We have celebrated life events and comforted each other through personal crises; we have traveled to Prague and London and various destinations in the United States, sharing our scholarship efforts on CAE in various forums.

Through this collaboration, we have become more prolific writers individually and collectively and have benefited from the nurturing and support of our collaborative circle. It has been an amazing experience! We wish you an equally rewarding collaborative experience.

Notes

CHAPTER 1

1. The full text of Geist-Martin et al. (2010) is provided in Appendix B.

CHAPTER 3

1. The study was initially presented as part of the Collaborative Autoethnography Workshop given by Chang, Ngunjiri, and Hernandez at the International Leadership Association Conference in 2010. The study has been written up as a journal article and is under revision.

CHAPTER 4

1. As a side note, we want our readers to be informed that, although not all autoethnographers use the term "data" comfortably, due to its association with quantitative approaches to research, we use this term because in this book we advocate a systematic approach to the research grounded on ethnography.
2. Ngunjiri, Hernandez, and Chang (2010) conducted a collaborative autoethnography focusing on their experiences as immigrant women faculty of color in a faith-based university; Chang conducted a collaborative autoethnography with Bleil, Fornicola, and Dillman (2010), focusing on the layoff experiences of two women executives (presented at a conference and submitted as a journal article); Chang is conducting a collaborative autoethnography with a dozen leaders of color in faith-based higher education. Our works are described in more detail in other chapters.
3. Blackboard is a proprietary learning platform in which participants contributed their writings to online discussion forums and engaged in online dialogue in writing.

CHAPTER 5

1. A similar chart appeared in Saldaña's book, *The Coding Manual for Qualitative Researchers* (2009, p. 12).

CHAPTER 7

1. Before the semester begins, Heewon acquires an IRB approval for the class project.

References

Abigail, R. A. (2011). By a crooked star: Developing spirituality within the context of a faith-based institution. In H. Chang & D. Boyd (Eds.), *Spirituality in higher education: Autoethnographies* (pp. 69–85). Walnut Creek, CA: Left Coast Press, Inc.

American Educational Research Association. (2011). Research ethics. http://www.aera.net/EthicsCode.htm (accessed on January 5, 2012).

Anderson, L. (2006). Analytical autoethnography. *Journal of Contemporary Ethnography*, 35(4), 373–395.

Anfara, Jr., V. A., Brown, K. M., & Mangione, T. (2002). Qualitative analysis on stage: Making the research process more public. *Educational Researcher*, 31(7), 28–38.

Asenavage-Loptes, K. (2012, March 24). Developing cross-cultural higher education leaders through mentoring. Paper presented at the Mid-Atlantic Leadership Conference, Newport News, Virginia.

Atkins, C. G. K. (2008). The choice of two mothers: Disability, gender, sexuality, and prenatal testing. *Cultural Studies↔Critical Methodologies*, 8(1), 106–129.

Atkinson, P. A., Coffey, A., & Delamont, S. (1999). Ethnography: Post, past and present. *Journal of Contemporary Ethnography*, 28(5), 460–471.

Barry, C. A., Britten, N., Barber, N., Bradley, C., & Stevenson, F. (1999). Using reflexivity to optimize teamwork in qualitative research. *Qualitative Health Research*, 9(1), 26–44.

Birks, M., & Mills, J. (2011). *Grounded theory: A practical guide*. Thousand Oaks, CA: Sage.

Bleil, P. (2010a, May 28–29). Mentoring experiences of women business leaders. Paper presented at the International Congress of Qualitative Inquiry. Urbana, Illinois.

Bleil, P. (2010b, October 27–30). Mentoring 2.0: Learning from the mentoring experiences of women business leaders. Poster presented at the International Leadership Association, Boston, Massachusetts.

Bleil, P., Fornicola, G., & Dillman, D. (2010, October 27–30). Collaboration autoethnography: Our collective stories of layoffs. Paper presented at the International Leadership Association, Boston, Massachusetts.

Bloom, B. S., Engelhart, M. D., Furst, E. J., Hill, W. H., & Krathwohl, D. R. (1956). *Taxonomy of educational objectives: The classification of educational goals; Handbook I: Cognitive Domain*. New York: Longmans.

Bochner, A. P., & Ellis, C. (1995). Telling and living: Narrative co-construction and the practices of interpersonal relationships. In W. Leeds-Hurwitz (Ed.), *Social approaches to communication* (pp. 201–213). New York: Guildford.

Bochner, A. P., & Ellis, C. (Eds.). (2002). *Ethnographically speaking: Autoethnography, literature and aesthetics*. Walnut Creek, CA: AltaMira.

Boice, R., & Jones, F. (1984). Why academicians don't write. *Journal of Higher Education*, 55(5), 567–582.

Boje, D., & Tyler, J. A. (2009). Story and narrative noticing: Workaholism autoethnographies. *Journal of Business Ethics*, 84(2), 173–194.

Boud, D., & Lee, A. (2005). "Peer learning" as pedagogic discourse for research education. *Studies in Higher Education*, 30(5), 501–516.

Bovee, C. L., & Thill, J. V. (1989). *Business communication today* (2nd ed.). New York: Random House.

Brown, A. F., & William-White, L. (2010). "We are not the same minority": The narratives of two sisters navigating identity and discourse at public and private White institutions.

In C. C. Robinson & P. Clardy (Eds.), *Tedious journeys: Autoethnography by women of color in academe* (pp. 149–176). New York: Peter Lang.

Cann, C., & DeMeulenaere, E. (2010). Forged in the crucibles of difference: Building discordant communities. *Penn GSE Perspectives on Urban Education*, 7(1), 41–53.

Cann, C. N., & DeMeulenaere, E. J. (2012). Critical co-constructed autoethnography. *Cultural Studies-Critical Methodologies*, 12(2), 146–158.

Chang, H. (1992). *Adolescent life and ethos: An ethnography of a US high school.* London: Falmer Press.

Chang, H. (2008). *Autoethnography as method.* Walnut Creek, CA: Left Coast Press, Inc.

Chang, H. (2011). Autoethnography as method for spirituality research in the academy. In H. Chang & D. Boyd (Eds.), *Spirituality in higher education: Autoethnographies* (pp. 11–29). Walnut Creek, CA: Left Coast Press, Inc.

Chang, H. (2013). Individual and collaborative autoethnography as method: A social scientist's perspective. In T. Adams, C. Ellis, & S. Holman-Jones (Eds.), *Handbook of autoethnography.* Walnut Creek, CA: Left Coast Press, Inc.

Chang, H., & Boyd, D. (Eds.). (2011). *Spirituality in higher education: Autoethnographies.* Walnut Creek, CA: Left Coast Press, Inc.

Chang, H., McCartha, C., Stiles, C., & Tadesse, G. (2007). Multicultural gendered lives of educators: Ethnography of autoethnographies. Paper presented at the PAC-TE conference, Grantsville, Pennslyvania.

Chapman, V., & Sork, T. J. (2001). Confessing regulation or telling secrets? Opening up the conversation on graduate supervision. *Adult Education Quarterly*, 51(2), 94–107.

Charmaz, K. (2006). *Constructing grounded theory: A practical guide through qualitative analysis.* Thousand Oaks, CA: Sage.

Chatham-Carpenter, A. (2010). "Do thyself no harm": Protecting ourselves as autoethnographers. *Journal of Research Practice*, 6(1), Article M1. http://jrp.icaap.org/index.php/ jrp/article/view/213/183 (accessed January 10, 2012).

Chawla, D., & Rawlins, W. K. (2004). Enabling reflexivity in a mentoring relationship. *Qualitative Inquiry*, 10(6), 963–978.

Cohen, L., Duberley, J., & Musson, G. (2009). Work—life balance? *Journal of Management Inquiry*, 18(3), 229–241.

Coia, L., & Taylor, M. (2006, July 30–August 3). Moving closer: Approaching educational research through a co/autoethnographic lens. Paper presented at the 6th International Conference on Self Study of Teacher Education, Herstmonceux Castle, East Sussex, England.

Coia, L., & Taylor, M. (2009). Co/autoethnography: Exploring our teaching selves collaboratively. In L. Fitzgerald, M. Heston, & D. Tidwell (Eds.), *Research methods for the self-study of practice* (Vol. 9, pp. 3–16). Rotterdam, the Netherlands: Springer.

Creamer, E. G. (2004). Collaborators' attitudes about differences of opinions. *Journal of Higher Education*, 75(5), 556–571.

Creswell, J. W. (2006). *Qualitative inquiry and research design: Choosing among five approaches.* Thousand Oaks, CA: Sage.

Creswell, J. W. (2012). *Educational research: Planning, conducting, and evaluating quantitative and qualitative research* (4th ed.). Boston: Pearson.

Cuthbert, D., & Spark, C. (2008). Getting a GRiP: Examining the outcomes of a pilot program to support graduate research students in writing for publication. *Studies in Higher Education*, 33(1), 77–88.

Defrancisco, V. P., Kuderer, J., & Chatham-Carpenter, A. (2007). Autoethnography and women's self-esteem: Learning through a "living" method. *Feminism & Psychology*, 17(2), 237–243.

DeLyser, D. (2003). Teaching graduate students to write: A seminar for thesis and dissertation writers. *Journal of Geography in Higher Education*, 27(2), 169–181.

Denzin, N. (1997). *Interpretive ethnography: Ethnographic practices for the 21ˢᵗ century*. Thousand Oaks, CA: Sage.

Denzin, N. (2004). The art and politics of interpretation. In S. N. Hesse-Biber & P. Leavy (Eds.), *Approaches to qualitative research: A reader on theory and practice* (pp. 447–472). New York: Oxford University Press.

Denzin, N. K., & Lincoln, Y. S. (2000). *Handbook of qualitative research* (2nd ed.). Thousand Oaks, CA: Sage.

Dillard, A. (1987). *An American childhood*. New York: Harper & Row.

Duarte, F. (2007). Using autoethnography in the scholarship of teaching and learning: Reflective practice from "the other side of the mirror." *International Journal for the Scholarship of Teaching and Learning*, *1*(2). http://www.georgiasouthern.edu/ijsotl (accessed January 12, 2012).

DuFrene, D. D., & Nelson, B. H. (1990). Effective co-authoring for business communication academicians. *Bulletin of the Association for Business Communication*, *53*, 68–71.

Easterby-Smith, M., & Malina, D. (1999). Cross-cultural collaborative research: Towards reflexivity. *Academy of Management Journal*, *42*(1), 76–86.

Ede, L., & Lunsford, A. (1990). *Singular texts/plural authors: Perspectives on collaborative writing*. Carbondale: Southern Illinois University Press.

Ellingson, L. L. (2009). *Engaging crystallization in qualitative research: An introduction*. Thousand Oaks, CA: Sage.

Ellis, C. (1995). *Final negotiations: A story of love, and chronic illness*. Philadelphia: Temple University Press.

Ellis, C. (1996). Maternal connections. In C. Ellis & A. Bochner (Eds.), *Composing ethnography: Alternative forms of qualitative writing* (pp. 240–243). Walnut Creek, CA: AltaMira.

Ellis, C. (1997). Evocative autoethnography: Writing emotionally about our lives. In W. Tierney & Y. S. Lincoln (Eds.), *Representation and the text: Re-framing the narrative voice* (pp. 116–139). Albany: State University of New York Press.

Ellis, C. (1999). Heartfelt autoethnography. *Qualitative Health Research*, *9*(5), 669–683.

Ellis, C. (2004). *The ethnographic I: A methodological novel about autoethnography*. Walnut Creek, CA: AltaMira.

Ellis, C. (2007). Telling secrets, revealing lives: Relational ethics in research with intimate others. *Qualitative Inquiry*, *13*(1), 3–29.

Ellis, C. (2009). *Revision: Autoethnographic reflections on life and work*. Walnut Creek, CA: Left Coast Press, Inc.

Ellis, C., & Bochner, A. P. (1992). Telling and performing personal stories: The constraints of choice in abortion. In C. Ellis & M. G. Flaherty (Eds.), *Investigating subjectivity: Research on lived experience* (pp. 79–101). Newbury Park, CA: Sage.

Ellis, C., & Bochner, A. P. (2000). Autoethnography, personal narrative, and personal reflexivity. In N. K. Denzin & Y. S. Lincoln (Eds.), *Handbook of qualitative research* (2nd ed., pp. 733–768). Thousand Oaks, CA: Sage.

Ellis, C., Kiesinger, C., & Tillmann-Healy, L. M. (1997). Interactive interviewing: Talking about emotional experience. In R. Hertz (Ed.), *Reflexivity and voice* (pp. 119–149). Thousand Oaks, CA: Sage.

Ellis, C. A., Gibbs, S. J., & Rein, G. L. (1991). Groupware: Some issues and experiences. *Communications of the ACM*, *34*(1), 39–58.

Espino, M. M., Muñoz, S. M., & Kiyama, J. M. (2010). Transitioning from doctoral study to the academy: Theorizing trenzas of identity for Latina sister scholars. *Qualitative Inquiry*, *16*(10), 804–818.

Ettorre, E. (2005). Gender, older female bodies and medical uncertainty: Finding my feminist voice by telling my illness story. *Women's Studies International Forum*, *28*(6), 535–546.

Ferguson, T. (2009). The "write" skills and more: A thesis writing group for doctoral students. *Journal of Geography in Higher Education*, *33*(2), 285–297.

Fetterman, D. M. (2010). *Ethnography: Step-by-step* (3rd ed.). Thousand Oaks, CA: Sage.

Finley, S. (2005). Arts-based inquiry: Performing revolutionary pedagogy. In N. K. Denzin & Y. S. Lincoln (Eds.), *The handbook of qualitative research* (3rd ed., pp. 681–694). Thousand Oaks, CA: Sage.

Foley, D. (1997). The heartland chronicles. Philadelphia: University of Pennsylvania Press.

Foster, K., McAllister, M., & O'Brien, L. (2005). Coming to autoethnography: A mental health nurse's experience. *International Journal of Qualitative Methods*, *4*(4), Article 1. http://www.ualberta.ca/~iiqm/backissues/4_4/html/foster.htm (accessed January 5, 2012).

Foster, K., McAllister, M., & O'Brien, L. (2006). Extending the boundaries: Autoethnography as an emergent method in mental health nursing research. *International Journal of Mental Health Nursing*, *15*(1), 44–53.

Fox, K. V. (1996). Silent voices: A subversive reading of child sexual abuse. In C. Ellis & A. Bochner (Eds.), *Composing ethnography: Alternative forms of qualitative writing* (pp. 330–356). Walnut Creek, CA: AltaMira.

Gale, K., Speedy, J., & Wyatt, J. (2010). Gatecrashing the oasis? A joint doctoral dissertation play. *Qualitative Inquiry*, *16*(1), 21–28.

Gallardo, H. L., Furman, R., & Kulkami, S. (2009). Explorations of depression: Poetry and narrative in autoethnographic qualitative research. *Qualitative Social Work*, *8*(3), 287–304.

Galligan, L., Cretchley, P., George, L., McDonald, K., McDonald, J., & Rankin, J. (2003). Evolution and emerging trends of university writing groups. *Queensland Journal of Educational Research*, *19*(1), 28–41.

Galman, S. (2011). "Now you see her, now you don't": The integration of mothering, spirituality, and work. In H. Chang & D. Boyd (Eds.), *Spirituality in higher education: Autoethnographies* (pp. 33–49). Walnut Creek, CA: Left Coast Press, Inc.

Gardner, L. D., & Lane, H. (2010). Exploring the personal tutor-student relationship: An autoethnographic approach. *Journal of Psychiatric & Mental Health Nursing*, *17*(4), 342–347.

Geertz, C. (1973). *The interpretation of cultures*. New York: Basic Books.

Geist-Martin, P., Gates, L., Wiering, L., Kirby, E., Houston, R., Lilly, A., & Moreno, J. (2010). Exemplifying collaborative autoethnographic practice via shared stories of mothering. *Journal of Research Practice*, *6*(1), Article M8. http://jrp.icaap.org/index.php/jrp/article/view/209/187 (accessed January 5, 2012).

Gershon, W. S. (2009). *The collaborative turn working together in qualitative research*. Rotterdam, the Netherlands: Sense Publishers.

Glesne, C. (2011). *Becoming qualitative researchers: An introduction* (4th ed.). Boston: Pearson.

González, K. P., Marin, P., Figueroa, M. A., Moreno, J. F., & Navia, C. N. (2002). Inside doctoral education in America: Voices of Latinas/os in pursuit of the PhD. *Journal of College Student Development*, *43*(4), 540–557.

Guillemin, M., & Gillam, L. (2004). Ethics, reflexivity, and "ethically important moments" in research. *Qualitative Inquiry*, *10*(2), 261–280.

Gurvitch, R., Carson, R. L., & Beale, A. (2008). Being a protege: An autoethnographic view of three teacher education doctoral programs. *Mentoring & Tutoring: Partnership in Learning*, *16*(3), 246–262.

Gust, S. W., & Warren, J. T. (2008). Naming our sexual and sexualized bodies in the classroom: And the important stuff that comes after the colon. *Qualitative Inquiry*, *14*(1), 114–134.

Hale, S. L., & Pruitt, R. H. (1989). Enhancing publication success. *Nursing Connections*, *2*(1), 59–61.

Hansen, H., Barry, B., Boje, D. M., & Hatch, M. J. (2007). Truth or consequences: An improvised collective story construction. *Journal of Management Inquiry, 16*(2), 112–126.

Hernández, F., Sancho, J. M., Creus, A., & Montané, A. (2010). Becoming university scholars: Inside professional autoethnographies. *Journal of Research Practice, 6*(1), Article M7. http://jrp.icaap.org/index.php/jrp/article/view/204/188 (accessed January 12, 2012).

Hernandez, K. C. (2005). Motivation in context: An examination of factors that foster engagement and achievement among African American and African Caribbean high school students (Doctoral dissertation, Temple University). *Dissertation Abstracts International, 65* (10-A), 3690 (UMI. No. 3151006).

Hernandez, K. C. (2006). Under the Afro tree: Perceptions of the school related experiences of British Virgin Islands high school students. In K. Mutua & C. Sunal (Eds.), *Crosscurrents and cross-cutting themes: Research on education in Africa, the Caribbean, and the Middle East* (Volume III, pp. 147–169). Greenwich CT: Info Age Press.

Hernandez, K. C. (2011). Spiritual introspection and praxis in teaching and assessment. In H. Chang & D. Boyd (Eds.), *Spirituality in higher education: Autoethnographies* (pp. 163–179). Walnut Creek, CA: Left Coast Press, Inc.

Hernandez, K. C., & Ngunjiri, F. W. (2013). Relationships and communities. In T. Adams, C. Ellis, & S. Holman-Jones (Eds.), *Handbook of autoethnography*. Walnut Creek, CA: Left Coast Press, Inc.

Hernandez, K. C., Ngunjiri, F. W., & Chang, H. (2011, April 8–12). Exploiting the margins: Women of color advancing in the academy. Paper presented at the American Educational Research Association, New Orleans, Louisiana.

Hunter, A., Murphy, K., Grealish, A., Casey, D., & Keady, J. (2011). Navigating the grounded theory terrain (Part 2). *Nurse Researcher, 19*(1), 6–11.

Jago, B. J. (2002). Chronicling an academic depression. *Journal of Contemporary Ethnography, 31*(6), 729–757.

Kalmbach Phillips, D., Harris, G., Legard Larson, M., & Higgins, K. (2009). Trying on—being in—becoming: Four women's journey(s) in feminist poststructural theory. *Qualitative Inquiry, 15*(9), 1455–1479.

Katz, N., Lazer, D., Arrow, H., & Contractor, N. (2004). Network theory and small groups. *Small Group Research, 35*(3), 307–332.

Kelley, H., & Betsalel, K. (2004). Mind's fire: Language, power, and representations of stroke. *Anthropology and Humanism, 29*(2), 104–116.

Kinnucan-Welsch, K., Seery, M. E., Adams, S. M., Bowman, C. L., Joseph, L. M., & Davis, W. (2000). Write(ing) (ers') support group: Stories of facing "publish or perish." *Teacher Education Quarterly, 27*(2), 105–118.

Klinker, J. F., & Todd, R. H. (2007). Two autoethnographies: A search for understanding of gender and age. *The Qualitative Report, 12*(2), 166–183.

Krathwohl, D. R. (2002). A revision of Bloom's taxonomy: An overview. *Theory into Practice, 41*(4), 212–218.

Lapadat, J. (2009). Writing our way into shared understanding. *Qualitative Inquiry, 15*(6), 955–979.

Lapadat, J., Black, N., Clark, P., Gremm, R., Karanja, L., Mieke, M., & Quinlan, L. (2010). Life challenge memory work: Using collaborative autobiography to understand ourselves. *International Journal of Qualitative Methods, 9*(1), 77–104.

Lapadat, J., Bryant, L., Burrows, M., Greenlees, S., Hill, A., Alexander, J., Marcil, N., Nelson, L., Ormerod, L., & Rendell, D. (2009). An identity montage using collaborative autobiography: Eighteen ways to bend the light. *International Review of Qualitative Research, 1*(4), 515–540.

Lapadat, J., Mothus, T., & Fisher, H. (2005). Role relationships in research: Noticing an elephant. *International Journal of Qualitative Methods, 4*(2), 1–19.

Larcombe, W., McCosker, A., & O'Loughlin, K. (2007). Supporting education PhD and DEd students to become confident academic writers: An evaluation of thesis writers' circles. *Journal of University Teaching and Learning Practice, 4*(1), 54–63.

Lashua, B., & Fox, K. (2006). Rec needs a new rhythm cuz rap is where we're livin.' *Leisure Sciences, 28*(3), 267–283.

Lawrence-Lightfoot, S., & Davis, J. H. (2002). *Art and science of portraiture.* Hoboken, NJ: John Wiley and Sons.

Lee, A., & Boud, D. (2003). Writing groups, change and academic identity: Research development as local practice. *Studies in Higher Education, 28*(2), 187–200.

Lewins, A., & Silver, C. (2007). *Using software for qualitative data analysis: A step-by-step guide.* London: Sage.

Lewins, A., & Silver, C. (2009). Choosing a CAQDAS package: A working paper by Ann Lewins and Christina Silver (6th ed.). CAQDAS Networking Project and Qualitative Innovations in CAQDAS Project. http://eprints.ncrm.ac.uz/791/1/2009ChoosingaCAQDASPackage.pdf (accessed June 1, 2010).

Lietz, C. A., Langer, C. L., & Furman, R. (2006). Establishing trustworthiness in qualitative research in social work: Implications from a study regarding spirituality. *Qualitative Social Work, 5*(4), 441–458.

Lowry, P. B., Curtis, A., & Lowry, M. R. (2004). Building a taxonomy and nomenclature of collaborative writing to improve interdisciplinary research. *Journal of Business Communication, 41*(1), 66–99.

Lund, D. E., & Nabavi, M. (2008a). A duo-ethnographic conversation on social justice activism: Exploring issues of identity, racism, and activism with young people. *Multicultural Education, 15*(4), 27–32.

Lund, D. E., & Nabavi, M. (2008b). Understanding student anti-racism activism to foster social justice in schools. *International Journal of Multicultural Education, 10*(1), 1–20. http://ijme-journal.org/index.php/ijme/article/view/22/152 (accessed February 5, 2010).

Maher, D., Seaton, L., McMullen, C., Fitzgerald, T., Otsuji, E., & Lee, A. (2008). "Becoming and being writers": The experiences of doctoral students in writing groups. *Studies in Continuing Education, 30*(3), 263–275.

Marshall, Y., Rosen Eil, S., & Armstrong, K. (2009). Situating the Greenham archaeology: An autoethnography of a feminist project. *Public Archaelogy, 8*(2), 225–245.

Maxwell, J. A. (2004). *Qualitative research design: An interactive approach* (2nd ed.). Thousand Oaks, CA: Sage.

Maydell, E. (2010). Methodological and analytical dilemmas in autoethnographic research. *Journal of Research Practice, 6*(1), Article M5. http://jrp.icaap.org/index.php/jrp/article/view/223/190 (accessed January 12, 2012).

McMillan, S., & Price, M. A. (2010). Through the looking glass: Our autoethnographic journey through research mind-fields. *Qualitative Inquiry, 16*(2), 140–147.

Meader, E. (2012, March 24). Developing cross-cultural business leaders through mentoring. Paper presented at the Mid-Atlantic Leadership Conference, Newport News, Virginia.

Mills, G. E. (2010). *Action research: A guide for the teacher researchers* (4th ed.). Upper Saddle River, NJ: Pearson.

Morse, J. (2002). Editorial: Writing my own experience. *Qualitative Health Research, 12*(9), 1159–1160.

Morss, K., & Murray, R. (2001). Researching academic writing within a structured programme: Insights and outcomes. *Studies in Higher Education, 26*(1), 35–52.

Moustakas, C. (1994). *Phenomenological research methods.* Thousand Oaks, CA: Sage.

Mullen, C. A. (2001). The need for a curricular writing model for graduate students. *Journal of Further and Higher Education, 25*(1), 117–126.

Muncey, T. (2005). Doing autoethnography. *International Journal of Qualitative Methods*, 4(3), Article 5. http://www.ualberta.ca/~iiqm/backissues/4_1/html/muncey.htm (accessed January 12, 2012).

Muncey, T. (2010). *Creating autoethnographies*. Thousand Oaks, CA: Sage.

Muncey, T., & Robinson, R. (2007). Extinguishing the voices: Living with the ghost of the disenfranchised. *Journal of Psychiatric and Mental Health Nursing*, 14(1), 79–84.

Murakami-Ramalho, E., Piert, J., & Militello, M. (2008). The wanderer, the chameleon, and the warrior. *Qualitative Inquiry*, 14(5), 806–834.

Murray, R., & Newton, M. (2008). Facilitating writing for publication. *Physiotherapy*, 94(1), 29–34.

Nabavi, M., & Lund, D. E. (2010). Youth and social justice: A conversation on collaborative activism. In W. Linds, L. Goulet, & A. Sammel (Eds.), *Emancipatory practices: Adult/youth engagement for social and environmental justice* (pp. 3–13). Rotterdam, the Netherlands: Sense.

Neville-Jan, A. (2003). Encounters in a world of pain. *American Journal of Occupational Therapy*, 57(1), 88–98.

Ngunjiri, F. W. (2007). Painting a counter-narrative of African womanhood: Reflections on how my research transformed me. *Journal of Research Practice*, 3(1), Article m4. http://jrp.icaap.org/index.php/jrp/article/view/53/76 (accessed January 5, 2012).

Ngunjiri, F. W. (2010). Lessons in spiritual leadership from Kenyan women. *Journal of Educational Administration*, 48(6), 755–768.

Ngunjiri, F. W. (2011). Studying spirituality and leadership: A personal journey. In H. Chang & D. Boyd (Eds.), *Spirituality in higher education: Autoethnographies* (pp. 183–197). Walnut Creek, CA: Left Coast Press, Inc.

Ngunjiri, F. W., Hernandez, K. C., & Chang, H. (2010). Living autoethnography: Connecting life and research [Editorial]. *Journal of Research Practice*, 6(1), Article E1. http://jrp.icaap.org/index.php/jrp/article/view/241/186 (accessed January 12, 2012).

Nippert-Eng, C. E. (1995). *Home and work*. Chicago: University of Chicago Press.

Norris, J., Sawyer, R., & Lund, D. E. (Eds.). (2011). *Duoethnography: Dialogic methods for social, health, and educational research*. Walnut Creek, CA: Left Coast Press, Inc.

Nuñez, A., Murakami-Ramalho, E., & Cuero, K. (2010). Pedagogy for equity: Teaching in a Hispanic-serving institution. *Innovative Higher Education*, 35(3), 177–190.

Nussbaum, K. (2012, March 24). Developing cross-cultural non-profit leaders through mentoring. Paper presented at the Mid-Atlantic Leadership Conference, Newport News, Virginia.

O'Shea, E. R., Torosyan, R., Robert, T., Haug, I., Wills, M., & Bowen, B. A. (2011). Spirituality and professional collegiality: Esprit de "Core." In H. Chang & D. Boyd (Eds.), *Spirituality in higher education: Autoethnographies* (pp. 87–107). Walnut Creek, CA: Left Coast Press, Inc.

Olson, L. N. (2004). The role of voice in the (re)construction of a battered woman's identity: An autoethnography of one woman's experience of abuse. *Women's Studies in Communication*, 27(1), 1–33.

Page-Adams, D., Cheng, L. C., Gogineni, A., & Shen, C. Y. (1995). Establishing a group to encourage writing for publication among doctoral students. *Journal of Social Work Education*, 31(3), 402–407.

Palmer, P. J., & Zajonc, A. (2010). *The heart of higher education: A call to renewal*. San Francisco: Jossey-Bass.

Patton, M. Q. (2002). *Qualitative research & evaluation methods*. Thousand Oaks, CA: Sage.

Paulus, T. M., Woodside, M., & Ziegler, M. F. (2008). Extending the conversation: Qualitative research as dialogic collaborative process. *The Qualitative Report*, 13(2), 226–243.

Paulus, T. M., Woodside, M., & Ziegler, M. F. (2010). "I tell you, it's a journey, isn't it?" Understanding collaborative meaning making in qualitative research. *Qualitative Inquiry*, 16(10), 852–862.

Pearce, C. (2010). The crises and freedoms of researching your own life. *Journal of Research Practice*, 6(1), Article M2. http://jrp.icaap.org/index.php/jrp/article/view/219/184 (accessed on January 5, 2012).

Pelias, R. (2002). For father and son: An ethnodrama with no catharsis. In A. Bochner & C. Ellis (Eds.), *Ethnographically speaking: Autoethnography, literature and aesthetics* (pp. 35–43). Walnut Creek, CA: AltaMira.

Pololi, L., Knight, S., & Dunn, K. (2004). Facilitating scholarly writing in academic medicine: Lessons learned from a collaborative peer mentoring program. *Journal of General Internal Medicine*, 19(1), 64–68.

Pompper, D. (2010). Researcher-researched difference: Adapting an autoethnographic approach for addressing the racial matching issue. *Journal of Research Practice*, 6(1), Article M6. http://jrp.icaap.org/index.php/jrp/article/view/187/181 (accessed on January 5, 2012).

Poplin, M. (2011). Finding Calcutta: Confronting the secular imperative. In H. Chang & D. Boyd (Eds.), *Spirituality in higher education: Autoethnographies* (pp. 51–67). Walnut Creek, CA: Left Coast Press, Inc.

Randolph, A. W., & Weems, M. E. (2010). Speak truth and shame the devil: An ethnodrama in response to racism in the academy. *Qualitative Inquiry*, 16(5), 310–313.

Reed-Danahay, D. (1997). *Auto/ethnography: Rewriting the self and the social*. Oxford, UK: Berg.

Reyes Cruz, M., Moreira, C., & Yomtoob, D. (2009). Transgressive borders: A performative diaspora in three movements. *Qualitative Inquiry*, 15(5), 787–805.

Ricci, R. J. (2003). Autoethnographic verse: Nicky's boy: A life in two worlds. *The Qualitative Report*, 8(4), 591–596. http://www.nova.edu/ssss/QR/QR8-4/ricci.pdf (accessed on January 5, 2012).

Richardson, L. (2000). My left hand: Socialization and the interrupted life. *Qualitative Inquiry*, 6(4), 467–473.

Robinson, C. C., & Clardy, P. (2010). *Tedious journeys: Autoethnography by women of color in academe*. New York: Peter Lang.

Rodriguez, N. M., & Ryave, A. L. (2002). *Systematic self-observation*. Thousand Oaks, CA: Sage.

Romo, J. J. (2004). Experience and context in the making of a Chicano activist. *The High School Journal*, 87(4), 95–111.

Ronai, C. (1995). Multiple reflections of child sex abuse. *Journal of Contemporary Ethnography*, 23(4), 395–426.

Ronai, C. (1996). My mother is mentally retarded. In C. Ellis and A. Bochner (Eds.), *Composing ethnography: Alternative forms of qualitative writing* (pp. 109–131). Walnut Creek, CA: AltaMira.

Rose, M. (2008). Creating a learning community through a PE teacher's exploration of inquiry: A collaborative autoethnographic study. Masters thesis, University of Victoria, British Columbia, Canada. http://hdl.handle.net/1828/1034 (accessed January 15, 2012).

Rose, M., & McClafferty, K. A. (2001). A call for the teaching of writing in graduate education. *Educational Researcher*, 30(2), 27–33.

Saldaña, J. (2009). *The coding manual for qualitative researchers*. Thousand Oaks, CA: Sage.

Sawyer, R. D., & Norris, J. (2004). Null and hidden curricula of sexual orientation: A dialogue on the curreres of the absent present and the present absent. In C. Lesley, M. Birch, N. Brooks, E. Heilman, S. Mayer, A. Mountain & P. Pritchard (Eds.),

Democratic responses to an era of standardization (pp. 139–159). Troy, NY: Educator's International Press.

Sawyer, R. D., & Norris, J. (2009). Duoethnography: Articulations/(re)creations of meaning in the making. In W. S. Gershon (Ed.), *The collaborative turn: Working together in qualitative research* (pp. 127–140). Rotterdam, the Netherlands: Sense.

Schneider, B. (2005). Mothers talk about their children with schizophrenia: A performance autoethnography. *Journal of Psychiatric and Mental Health Nursing, 12*(3), 333–340.

Shank, G. D. (2002). *Qualitative research: A personal skills approach.* Upper Saddle River, NJ: Merrill Prentice Hall.

Smith, B. (1999). The abyss: Exploring depression through a narrative of the self. *Qualitative Inquiry, 5*(2), 264–279.

Smith, C. (2005). Epistemological intimacy: A move to autoethnography. *International Journal of Qualitative Methods, 4*(2), Article 6. http://www.ualberta.ca/~iiqm/backissues/4_2/HTML/smith.htm (accessed January 20, 2012).

Smith, J. A., Flowers, P., & Larkin, M. (2009). *Interpretive phenomenological analysis: Theory, method and research.* Thousand Oaks, CA: Sage.

Stephens, N., & Delamont, S. (2006). Balancing the Berimbau: Embodied ethnographic understanding. *Qualitative Inquiry, 12*(2), 316–339.

Stratton, C. R. (1989). Collaborative writing in the workplace. *IEEE Transactions on Professional Communication, 32*(3), 178–182.

Strauss, A. L., & Corbin, J. K. (2008). *Basic of qualitative research: Techniques and procedures for developing grounded theory.* Thousand Oaks, CA: Sage.

Strauss, A. L., & Glaser, B. G. (1967). *The discovery of grounded theory: Strategies for qualitative research.* Piscataway, NJ: Transaction.

Stringer, E. T., Agnello, M. R., Baldwin, S. C., Christensen, L. M., & Henry, D. L. P. (1997). *Community-based ethnography: Breaking traditional boundaries of research, teaching, and learning.* Mahwah, NJ: Lawrence Erlbaum Associates.

Subedi, B., & Rhee, J. (2008). Negotiating collaboration across differences. *Qualitative Inquiry, 14*(6), 1070–1092.

Thorne, S. (2008). *Interpretive description.* Walnut Creek, CA: Left Coast Press, Inc.

Tillmann, L. M. (2009). Body and bulimia revisited: Reflections on "A Secret Life." *Journal of Applied Communication Research, 37*(1), 98–112.

Tillmann-Healy, L. M. (1996). A secret life in a culture of thinness: Reflections on body, food, and bulimia. In C. Ellis & A. P. Bochner (Eds.), *Composing ethnography: Alternative forms of qualitative writing* (pp. 76–108). Walnut Creek, CA: AltaMira.

Tolich, M. (2010). A critique of current practice: Ten foundational guidelines for autoethnographers. *Qualitative Health Research, 20*(12), 1599–1610.

Toor, R. (2010, February). The habit of writing. *Chronicle of Higher Education.* http://chronicle.com/article/The-Habit-of-Writing/64001/ (accessed June 5, 2012).

Toyosaki, S., Pensoneau-Conway, S. L., Wendt, N. A., & Leathers, K. (2009). Community autoethnography: Compiling the personal and resituating whiteness. *Cultural Studies↔Critical Methodologies, 9*(1), 56–83.

Van Maanen, J. (1988). *Tales of the field: On the writing of ethnography.* Chicago: University of Chicago Press.

Vryan, K. D. (2006). Expanding analytic autoethnography and enhancing its potential. *Journal of Contemporary Ethnography, 35*(4), 405–409.

Walford, G. (2008). Finding the limits: Autoethnography and being an Oxford University proctor. In P. Atkinson & S. Delamont (Eds.), *Representing ethnography* (pp. 147–162). London: Sage.

Waterson, A., & Kukaj, A. (2007). Reflections on teaching social violence in an age of genocide and a time of war. *American Anthropologist, 109*(3), 509–518.

Waterston, A., & Rylko-Bauer, B. (2006). Out of the shadows of history and memory: Personal family memories and ethnographies of rediscovery. *American Ethnologist, 33*(3), 397–412.

Weems, M. E., White, C. J., Alvarez McHatton, P., Shelley, C., Bond, T., Brown, R. N., & Wyatt, J. (2009). Heartbeats: Exploring the power of qualitative research expressed as autoethnographic performance texts. *Qualitative Inquiry, 15*(5), 843–858.

Wikipedia (n.d.). Computer assisted qualitative data analysis software. http://en.wikipedia.org/wiki/Computer_assisted_qualitative_data_analysis_software (accessed June 1, 2012).

William-White, L. (2011). Dare I write about oppression on sacred ground [Emphasis mine]. *Cultural Studies↔Critical Methodologies, 11*(3), 236–242.

Wolcott, H. F. (1994). *Transforming qualitative data: Description, analysis, and interpretation.* Thousand Oaks, CA: Sage.

Wolcott, H. F. (2004). The ethnographic autobiography. *Auto/Biography, 12,* 93–106.

Wolcott, H. F. (2010). *Ethnography lessons: A primer.* Walnut Creek, CA: Left Coast Press, Inc.

Wolf, D., & Ober, D. (2010, October 27–30). The mentoring experiences of entrepreneurs. Poster presented at the International Leadership Association, Boston, Massachusetts.

Woodside, M., Ziegler, M., & Paulus, T. M. (2009). Understanding school counselor internships from a communities of practice framework. *Counselor Education and Development, 49*(1), 20–38.

Wray, K. B. (2002). The epistemic significance of qualitative research. *Philosophy of Science, 69*(1), 150–168.

Wyatt, J. (2008). No longer loss: Autoethnographic stammering. *Qualitative Inquiry, 14*(6), 955–967.

Yin, R. K. (2009). *Case study research: Design and methods* (4th ed.). Thousand Oaks, CA: Sage.

APPENDIX A

Writing Prompts Used for Individualized Data Collection

OD7-1: The List of Mentors

Share the list of mentors that you created during Heewon's mentoring presentation at the M-E LDI. What did your analysis of your mentor list reveal about your mentoring relationship in terms of the types of mentors, demographics of mentors, and the present and past relationships? Is there any other insight you gained about your past and present mentoring relationships?

OD7-2: Mentoring Relationships

Select one mentor out of the list you created during Heewon's mentoring presentation at the M-E LDI. Describe your mentoring relationship with the person, including who the person is (do not name the person); how your relationship developed; what you learned, particularly about leadership, if any; and how this relationship affected your character development, professional development, and/or career advancement.

OD8-1: Your Current Role on Campus

Tell us about your current role on campus. If you thought about "defining moments" that contributed to you becoming a professional in higher education and assuming your current role, please describe what comes to mind. Is there any one instrumental in helping you reach the current role and/or function effectively in your role?

OD8-2: Culture of Your Campus

How would you describe the leadership "culture" on your campus? What factors do you perceive to contribute to that culture? Do you have colleagues in your institution, who support the culture with you, if you agree with it, or who may work with you to transform it, if you disagree with it? Describe your professional relationship with the person (no name, please).

OD8-3: Heavy-Handed Versus Light-Handed Mentors

(Note: This question grew out of one of our July Wimba sessions. You're welcome to respond to it as one of your August writings.) In your mentoring experiences, have you had mentors who were more heavy handed (i.e., they felt they knew what you should be doing) or light handed (i.e., listening to your requests, etc.)? How did you respond to their input? What do you think is an appropriate posture for mentors to take?

OD9-1: Learning from Cedar Springs

As you think back on the content of our sessions at Cedar Springs and our interactions there, what new insights did you gain about what is needed for you to be a more effective leader in your current or future role? What kind of developmental relationship would you need to achieve the goal?

OD9-2: Future Goals

Since you've returned to your campus, are you intentionally trying to be (or to do something) new or different because of what you have learned at the M-E LDI? If so, please elaborate. What specific goals have you set for yourself this year based on what you've learned at the institute? What kind of developmental relationship would you need to accomplish your goal?

OD10-1: Interview Your Mentors

Interview your mentor (senior or peer) or coach about their perceptions about your strengths and areas needing improvement. Discuss new insights and affirmation you gained from the interview. How would you apply this learning to your leadership development?

OD10-2: Agreement with Mentor Assessment of You

Interview your mentor about their perceptions of your strengths and areas needing improvement. Do you agree or disagree with your mentor's assessment of your strengths and weaknesses? If you disagree, what do you think contribute to discrepancy between your mentor's perceptions of you and your self-perception?

OD11-1: Interaction with Other People

Keep a log of your interactions with different people (how much time you spend with each person including self and how you interact with each person) for a week (The relationship log worksheet is available inside this forum.). After a week of keeping the log, analyze whom you spent most time with, how you mostly interact with different people, how enjoyable your relationships with these people are, what kind of insights and new learning you have gained, etc. Tell us simply what you have learned from this logging exercise. If you want to share your log with us, it would be great. But it's not a requirement.

OD11-2: Constellation of Relationships

This chart will allow you to plot people in your constellation of relationships. Add to your inner circle (the second closest circle to self) those who inspire you, nourish you, mentor you, care about your growth, like to be with you, and/or provide you with developmental opportunities; add to your middle circle (the mid-sized circle) those who work with you well but are not emotionally close to you; add to your distant circle (the largest circle) those who have working relationship with you but with whom you have difficulty. How are those in your inner circle qualitatively different from those in the middle or distant circles? What have you learned from those in the inner circle, in the middle circle, and in the distant circle respectively? What have you learned about self from this exercise?

OD11-3: Critical Moments for Leadership

Tell us critical moments when you were encouraged to step up to take a leadership role in your life. Who encouraged you and how did the person directly or indirectly prepare you for the role or provided you with support when you carry out leadership responsibilities?

OD12-1: Shadowing Experience

If you had completed your shadowing assignment, share your experience. How has shadowing helped you understand the role you observed? Any surprises and confirmation of your expectations? What leadership lessons did you take away from the shadowing experience?

OD12-2: Expectation of Shadowing

If you have not done your shadowing assignment, what do you plan to learn from the experience? Do you plan to focus your observation on particular aspects of the leader or leadership functioning? Share your reason for your interest.

APPENDIX B

Exemplifying Collaborative Autoethnographic Practice via Shared Stories of Mothering

Patricia Geist-Martin, Lisa Gates, Liesbeth Wiering, Erika Kirby, Renee Houston, Anne Lilly, Juan Moreno

This article originally appeared in the *Journal of Research Practice*, Volume 6, Issue 1, Article M8, 2010. It is reproduced here with permission.

Abstract

In this piece, we articulate the collaborative autoethnographic practice we utilized to illustrate the complexities of mothering that involved: (a) individually writing autoethnographic narratives on mothering; (b) sharing these autoethnographic narratives in a public forum; (c) publicly discussing the heuristic commonalities across these autoethnographic narratives; (d) tying those commonalities back to the literature; and (e) revisiting the autoethnographic narratives for aspects of social critique where our autoethnographic narratives (intentionally or unintentionally) hegemonically reproduced cultural scripts. We argue that presenting knowledge of mothering in this way, through collaborative autoethnographic practice, creates a myriad of opportunities for growth and self-reflexivity, and our stories illuminate a part of our existence that often remains unexamined in other methodologies.

Keywords: mothering; autoethnography; everyday moments; identity; cultural script

Suggested Citation: Geist-Martin, P., Gates, L., Wiering, L., Kirby, E., Houston, R., Lilly, A., & Moreno, J. (2010). Exemplifying collaborative autoethnographic practice via shared stories of mothering. *Journal of Research Practice*, 6(1), Article M8. Retrieved [date of access], from http://jrp.icaap.org/index.php/jrp/article/view/209/187

1. INTRODUCTION

"I would like to put together a panel . . . on mothers and mothering. Let me know what you think" (Patricia Geist-Martin, personal communication, May 2009).

Over a year ago, we joined together as co-authors via this simple e-mail soliciting participants for a panel for the October annual meeting of the Organization for the Study of Communication, Language, and Gender (OSCLG). Thus began the process that would later lead to our writing this article recounting our experience and method, because Patricia wanted to use autoethnographic practice and have the seven of us "offer short stories of our own experience of motherhood, either in our relationship with our own mothers or in our relationship with our children." Accordingly, the original impetus for the present project is mothering and the mother-child relationship; we view autoethnography as an opportunity to explore the selves we become through our mother/ing and so the lived experience of mothering permeates our essay.

Yet mothering is not the focus of this essay—instead, we utilize mothering as an exemplar context for accomplishing autoethnography as research practice via a nontraditional approach. Specifically, we articulate how we utilized "collaborative autoethnographic practice" to illustrate the complexities of mothering by (a) writing sole-authored autoethnographic tales on mothering; (b) sharing these tales in a public forum; (c) discussing collaboratively the heuristic commonalities across these tales; (d) tying those commonalities back to the literature on the topic of mothering; and (e) revisiting the tales for aspects of social critique when we (unwittingly) hegemonically reproduced *cultural scripts* of mothering. Key to this piece on collaborative autoethnographic practice is that we assert this process is not unique to mothering, but instead that sharing narratives around a multiplicity of lived experiences is possible and desirable.

We begin with our scholarly stance on autoethnography as research practice, and offer the procedures we utilized to engage in a collaborative autoethnographic practice of (re)presenting these complicated, rewarding, and challenging relationships. We then share excerpts from our seven autoethnographic tales of mothering. The stories reveal the value of autoethnography as research practice in articulating—even reveling in—what may be lost if not honored, and the value of collaborative autoethnographic practice in "crystallizing" (see Ellingson, 2009) motherhood from many facets. We then revisit the stories via the lens of the literature to illustrate how shared autoethnographies can be knowledge-building and critique our own stories of motherhood. In combination, we hope to illustrate the opportunities and challenges of collaborative autoethnographic practice.

2. UTILIZING COLLABORATIVE AUTOETHNOGRAPHIC PRACTICE TO STUDY THE COMPLEXITIES OF MOTHERING

According to Ellis, the move toward impressionist and artistic aspects of qualitative work in (auto)ethnography means blending:

> the practices and emphases of social science with the aesthetic sensibility and expressive forms of art, [telling stories] that show bodily, cognitive, emotional, and spiritual experience. The goal is to practice an artful, poetic, and empathic social science in which readers can keep in their minds and feel in their bodies the complexities of concrete moments of lived experience. (Ellis, 2004, p. 30)

Autoethnography as research practice offers stories that are:

> drawn from the shadowy, liminal spaces of human life—between dreams and daylight, between memory and action, between secret and story—and then placed within a framework . . . of contemporary everyday life among friends, in the family, and in the broader community. (Poulos, 2009, p. 17)

Writing autoethnography as research practice is a way to engage our "narrative inheritance" (Goodall, 1995), a way to "discover—in the eruption of a story, the soft reminiscent light of accidental talk, in a burst of memory overstepping forgetting—a world of hope" (Poulos, 2009, p. 15).

Our "burst(s) of memory" about (our) mothers sprung forth after responding to Patricia's e-mail that we would like to be involved. In narrating our own experiences of motherhood, we "resist[ed] the disembodied voice that characterizes traditional academic prose" (Ellingson, 2009, p. 34) in recognition that traditional forms of scientific writing may be limited in what they can offer about the complexities of mothering as a meaningful, subjective whole (Denzin, 1997). Embracing autoethnography as an artistic, evocative, research practice allowed us to represent the whole of a meaningful moment of motherhood and illuminate some of the complexities of mothering that often remain in the dark in other methodologies. While such situated stories are inherently "partial, incomplete, and full of silences" (Ellis, 2009, p. 13), concomitantly our written stories can also reveal what we desire in mother-child relationships, what we fear about these relationships, and even the disappointments routinely present in mother-child relationships.

Then, since autoethnography is a knowledge-building practice beyond storytelling, we engaged in a collaborative discussion of the issues that surrounded the mother-child relationships in our stories. Our goal was to create a meta-narrative of sorts about mothering centered in lived experience via sharing our autoethnographies. Questions we created to guide this process included:

a. How does a mother's love help guide us through emotional distress?
b. In what way is a mother's unconditional love reciprocated?
c. Are there limits to a mother's unconditional love?
d. How is mother-love reflected in every-day life?
e. In what ways do we tend to practice the forms of mother-love we have (or have not) previously experienced in our relationships with our own children?

And of course, other questions could be written for diverse arenas of lived experience to produce a similar discussion of heuristic commonality.

Given that this special issue is about methodological practice versus the autoethnographic data, by necessity we offer 220-word excerpted versions of our autoethnographic narratives that we presented at OSCLG in October 2009, using the data as a means to exemplify method. We felt the "cut" of shortening these stories quite deeply; every time we shortened the narratives, our (once rich and descriptive) autoethnographic narratives felt more shallow . . . and of course the question also emerged on a seven-person author team of "Who decides what to cut?" We see this as a compromise between highlighting theory/context and method; we contemplated removing some stories and highlighting others, but this led to the question of "Whose autoethnographies are most valuable?" Thus, to be as inclusive as possible, we highlight excerpts from all seven narratives to provide a glimpse into the rich discourse that prompted us to push forward our collaborative autoethnographic practice past the original panel discussion in the first place. We hope these highlights provide enough background to illustrate how this practice of collaborating across autoethnographic narratives provided unique insights on mothering—and concomitantly led to a meta-narrative that enabled us to critique our stories.

3. (Re)Presenting Our Autoethnographic Tales of the Complexities of Mothering

We begin with Patricia and Renee's stories because they both offer an enduring view of mothering where an activity becomes ritualized. Doing puzzles and making cakes represent communal, yet personal and emotional expressions of time invested for and with a child. We see nurturing in both activities as suspended, yet ephemeral moments. Patricia's tale, *Pieces of Puzzles*, weaves a narrative between present (with her daughter) and past (with her mother), attempting to capture those moments of mothering that can be represented in seemingly mundane activities such as putting together puzzles.

I want to go back, before my mom died of cancer. I want to bend over a card table searching for just the right piece. I can feel her at my side, our elbows a whisper away from each other, "the red flag, I just need a few more pieces with red," she would say, encouraging us to keep her needs in mind as we focused on our own segment of the complicated scene. Slowly but surely, the scene expanded from shades of colors to become black iron chairs, hand built stone walls, multi-colored pansy-lined garden paths, and deep blue skies. With a cry of "I found it!" I lift one small puzzle piece and pass it from my fingertips to my mom's fingertips and watch as she scans her corner to find just the right spot, turning it between her fingers, pressing it down, lifting it up, turning it once more, and then snapping it in place. We pooled our resources to magically transform this inanimate box of cardboard pieces into a place somewhere in time that we could go together. Everyone wanted the joy of hearing that last piece click into place. I remember that suspended moment of just being in that scene. You are there, but you know you are not really there. (Excerpts from *Pieces of Puzzles*, Patricia's autoethnographic tale, September 2009)

Renee's tale, *Baking Values*, illustrates how the meanings of baking a "homemade" birthday cake run deep, and how the quest for the perfect cake can create a communal mothering experience and represent values far beyond the food itself.

By Josh's fourth birthday, which had to be about dinosaurs, my mom insisted on purchasing and mailing a dinosaur cake mold. Somehow I thought using a mold was cheating, but I caved. Problem! I couldn't find the right green frosting. I called mom: "Help!" She had some suggestions, yet the frosting dilemma continued. I couldn't cover the cake without smearing bits of cake into the frosting. Another call: "What now?" "Call your aunt." One phone call empowered me to successfully cover the cake and enjoy a new connection with my aunt, who became a member of the cake debacle brigade. After a decade, I look back and wonder why making cakes is so important to me. Of course, it's a central moment of joy and celebration, but somehow producing those cakes meant more. For a while I was convinced that I was enacting the mothering I experienced, yet in a recent conversation with mom she remembered having made only one of my birthday cakes! In spite of what may seem to be my inaccurate impression of my mother I've come to understand mothering as a community value—a value that means family is connected not only by creation and celebration, but also by the site of discourse that emerges in multiple spaces with spouses, aunts, moms, or even the intended celebrants, our children. (Excerpts from *Baking Values*, Renee's autoethnographic tale, September 2009)

Next we move to the stories offered by Liesbeth, Lisa, and Erika because they extend the notion of responsibility both in terms of what a mother offers her child and what a child hopes for in a mother. But in addition, we see in these stories mothers needing mothering, mothers not being there or not being able or willing to talk, and going on, moving forward despite these tensions. For Liesbeth, her tale, *Pull My Socks* combined joy and pain in her description of going home to take care of her mother who was recovering from a broken hip, and the role her own daughter played in that visit.

"The doctor told me a daughter's care is the best there is for a mother. The best," my mom repeats this several times during the weeks I am with her as she recovers . . . After her shower, as I kneel down in front of her to help her into her briefs and insert a pantyliner, she is muttering apologies, for what she needs me to do, for how she looks, her nudity, her wrinkles, her bruises, her helplessness. I slide socks on her feet. "Pull my socks," she snaps. I recognize that tone from my childhood, but also from my daughter who wants me to do the same thing every morning. "You sound like your granddaughter," I snap back as I pull her socks. We start laughing. We laugh so we don't cry. . . . Three weeks later I am crying my guts out . . . it feels so wrong to leave. Once in the airplane, I lean back and think . . . I will talk with my mom on the phone every week . . . but I can't share my pain about her decline with her. A tear escapes and rolls down my cheek. "Don't cry mama," my daughter says, as she grabs my hand. "I am with you! I will always be with you!" *A daughter's care is the best care there is.* What else can I do but smile? (Excerpts from *Pull My Socks*, Liesbeth's autoethnographic tale, September 2009)

Lisa's tale, *Just Like Her*, recounted her memories of her mother in several life stages; this excerpt highlights the end of life when she was dying of colon cancer.

Despite the fact that cancer—like brown eyes and olive skin—runs in our family, my mother appeared shocked after years of diarrhea added up to the colon cancer that killed her. I was well versed in her cancer treatment options . . . yet our conversations addressed current events, family matters, and where to have lunch. Speaking the truth about her cancer felt like a form of violence against her. So as I walked the sterile, yet homey hospital corridors I wrestled with how to convince her to have chemo after her cancer surgery. . . . "The doctor said if you were his mother he'd give you chemo to kill any cancer cells that might be floating around in there." I gestured toward her abdomen. She replied, "I'll think about it. I *don't* want to lose my hair. It is my decision, Lisa Rose." It came as no real surprise when she decided against chemo. There would be no dramatic deathbed goodbyes. She would die on her terms. I learned from my mom that, just like her, I should do life, and eventually death, on my terms. . . . This new view, this re-birthing, is something that I am thankful to her even now for providing. I don't recall the beginning of my mother's love—it was just always there. And now I realize it has no end. (Excerpts from *Just Like Her*, Lisa's autoethnographic tale, September 2009)

For Erika, her *Unanswered Question* is a pained narrative of the loss of an idealized image of her mother; she recounts a letter from her father to her and her sisters that (in her mind) communicated only one message—"that there was a time when my mother didn't want me."

"When your mother and I originally split up, she was going to leave with him [stepdad] and leave you with me. She was going to leave you, but then decided she was unable to leave her children behind . . . you see he [stepdad] was important enough that she was willing to do that, and so I want you to see how my feeling that she [stepmom] comes before you is justified by knowing that your mother felt that way too . . ." My mom is my best friend. We talk nearly every day. I admire her in so many ways—for the way she raised us on her own, for her love and support, and for her dedication to others in the community. So I wonder, "How could my mother have wanted to leave me? Who IS this person my dad is describing? Are you a 'mother' if you choose to leave your children?" My heart told me I would never be able to leave my kids . . . and honestly, that they come first, not my husband, at least until they are adults. The next day, I tearfully talked to both of my sisters about it, and we all decided not to tell our mom. We have lived for more than a decade not knowing if it is true—and honestly, not wanting to know. (Excerpts from *Unanswered Question*, Erika's autoethnographic tale, September 2009)

Finally, the stories presented by Juan and Anne take us to redemptive moments in crisis, healing moments with our mothers, moments when we savor time with our mothers, not knowing for sure how long they will be a part of our lives. Juan's mothering tale, *A Million Little Pieces* was a journey into the dark parts of his past that were changed by his mother's love.

Mom did everything she could to protect us from Dad's abuse, including bearing the brunt of his fury. I hated myself for not being able to stop his fist from landing on her body. When I was 16, I could take no more. . . . My heart pounded loudly as I walked up to him and said "Don't you ever touch her again!" I closed my eyes really tight, clenched my fist, wound my arm back and swung. I came up short. Before I could open my eyes, I felt that familiar heavy-handed sting on my face. He yelled, "Get the hell out of my house! You are no longer my son." Those words nearly knocked me out. Walking away, I could hear Mom begging me to come back. I turned and saw her heart breaking into a million little pieces. . . . At 16, I was without a family, without a place to truly call home, and was not attending school. One night, several years later, when I felt like giving up, I opened to a knock at the door, and standing there was Mom. Without words she simply hugged me tighter than ever, like she was afraid that I would disappear if she let go. Immediately, I felt the pain and anger washing away with my tears. It was as if that hug was putting all my broken pieces back together. (Excerpts from A Million Little Pieces, Juan's autoethnographic tale, September 2009)

Our final tale, narrated by Anne, is of her annual *Road Trip* to South Lake Tahoe with her mother and the special moments this has created in their relationship—and indeed in her desire to live her life.

Ten years ago, I started our trip to Tahoe alone in the hotel room drinking my sorrows away . . . in a drunken, emotional state with a broken heart, mind, and soul and ready to give up on life. Yet, Mom never gave up on me. She nurtured, consoled, counseled, prayed for, and loved me through every stumble with unconditional love, and I am a sober woman today . . . In a sense, I've had an extended childhood through our Tahoe trips. Extended time with my mom to observe her, laugh with her, heed her advice, and experience her love. No one will ever love me the way that she does, how could they? She carried me for nine months, nurtured, fed, and created me. . . . I am part of her. . . . We walk hand in hand along the beach path as the sun beats down on our laughter. I stop our tracks and gaze in Mom's eyes, "I love you mom." She responds, "Thank you! I love you too darlin'" and we hug ever so tightly for a few precious moments. She seems small and fragile, having that special mom scent of Passion perfume mixed with her sweetness. As we walk on, the smells of warm pine and wood from the Sierras fill the air. Every year I wonder if this will be our last trip. . . . I will always equate Tahoe to time with mom. (Excerpts from *Road Trip*, Anne's autoethnographic tale, September 2009)

All seven stories take us full circle, remembering who we were/who we are with our mothers and who we are becoming as we nurture our children and our own mothers. In all of our stories, mothering is clearly represented in "quality time" mothers and children spend together. The quintessence of mothering is what is valued in that time together—what is known and considered precious but does not need to be spoken as mothers and children luxuriate in suspended moments of caring, supporting, appreciating, and learning from one another.

4. Discerning the Complexities of Mothering through Collaborative Autoethnographic Practice

[Mothering is] an atmosphere . . . the bedrock of existence . . . a foundation . . . a way of life. (Quindlen, 2005, p. 227)

In the moments of performativity, these narratives (especially in their longer form) were powerful, and sharing them in the panel session was emotion-laden for each autoethnographer. The process produced an interesting tension between how writing solo (as in autoethnography) can be a lonely practice, and how there was communality in hearing our stories in chorus. For us, collaborating on these autoethnographic tales in a public forum provided insights into mothering that no one narrative (and certainly no traditional form of social scientific writing) could have provided in isolation. Perhaps the most meaningful point in our collaborative autoethnographic practice was in those moments of sharing, when we were all deeply feeling, understanding, and connecting with each others' experiences. Each mothering story—a time of struggle, a time of recognition, a time of change or transformation, a time of presence—offered an insight that could only be offered in this evocative, narrative form. Autoethnographic writing was discovery, an opportunity to break out of and away from "traditional generic constraints" (Ellingson, 2009, p. 3).

Once the tales had all been shared, our collaborative efforts took the form of discerning what these autoethnographies illustrated about the complexities of mothering. In the resulting discussion after the panel (and interactions after the conference), we discovered that all of the stories could be linked one to the other in a myriad of ways (e.g., stories told about a ritual, a life-changing event, an every-day activity, or a moment never to be forgotten). The autoethnographic stories presented offered an opportunity to understand the sense making that all of us engaged in as we reflected on our mothers, being mothered, and our own process of mothering our children or our mothers. What we realized through these stories is the inclination to write what we desire: We wanted to return to a place, even if it was not ideal.

We deify the mother role, often glorifying the mundane. We learn through reading these stories that mothering goes far beyond performing a particular role almost to a divine appointment; mothering encompasses far more than the day-to-day mundane work that must be performed, although such work is a significant part of mothering (see Rothman, 1989). We learn that we make sense of the mother-child relationship in mundane moments and critical turning points through role-switching, transcendence, suffering, symbolic acts, sacrifice, and even silence. These stories present opportunities for learning through empathy, for validating lived experience, and for understanding the self in the everyday life of mother-child relationships. They also illustrate forms of maternal healing and care; we recognized Glass-Coffin's (2006) heuristic frame of five centralities of maternal care—"sacrifice, empathy, discipline and right action, forgiveness, and surrender/letting go" (p. 896)—exemplified in our stories.

One of the most selfless acts for mothers is to sacrifice for the well-being of their child. This responsibility may fall to mothers as illustrated in Juan's story of his mother offering the ultimate sacrifice of bodily harm to protect him from abuse and Erika's story of her mother's decision to (potentially) sacrifice romantic love for mother-love. Empathy, or the ability to feel the pain of another, is also intuitively maternal as mothers often will care for their child's pain as though it is their own. Still, the nature of empathy as reciprocal is illustrated in Liesbeth and Lisa's stories of the mutuality of pain; in their mother's experience of pain they experience pain. Mothers can both experience and encourage discipline and right action as they accept responsibility for their own mothering experiences as well as encourage discipline and right action in their children. This is exemplified in Renee's story of enacting the narrative of making birthday cakes as carrying forward her own mother's (right) actions, later revealed as her own sense of what mothers "should do."

In mothering, children often experience a "pass" on making mistakes; mothers focus on the innocence of the child and perhaps see children's mistakes as failings of their own teaching (Glass-Coffin, 2006). With our own children, we may be able to forgive, yet do we extend that forgiveness to our mothers in the face of their alleged or actual mistakes? An understanding of the forgiving nature of mothering enables Erika to focus on her mother's decision to stay with her children, thereby offering her forgiveness.

Finally, the metaphor of motherhood involves surrender; mothers surrender a part of themselves when birthing a child and then later surrender control over the child to allow them to grow into their own person (Glass-Coffin, 2006), as illustrated in the story of Anne whose mother's enduring love allowed her to focus on the importance of spending time with her rather than on her daughter's destructive sense of self. Lisa's story highlights another aspect of the power surrender offers us to let go of our own mothers. In letting go she understands that her mother's choices are ultimately hers and recognizes her lack of control in the situation.

Much of the work of mothering is invisible. Perhaps this explains why the value of mothering is most clearly realized when a child, regardless of age, loses it (as described through the stories of Patricia and Lisa, and Liesbeth's impending sense of loss); daughters, in particular, are likely to stay connected to the lost parent (Edelman, 2006). This is true even when mothers were viewed as abusive, addicted, punitive, and/or overly critical because "Your mother is the mirror. Whether you elect to gaze at the reflection with equanimity, to tilt the glass or crack it outright, it is the point from which you always begin. It is *who you are*" (Quindlen, 2005, p. 227, emphasis added).

5. CRITIQUING OUR AUTOETHNOGRAPHIC TALES OF THE COMPLEXITIES OF MOTHERING

> [Mother-love is] universally desired, yet paradoxically [under]valued . . . the supreme archetype of one-way giving. Ideals of the "good mother" dictate a woman who always stands by her offspring, whatever they do, bathing them in the warm glow of unconditional love. (Langford, 1994, p. 98)

After examining our stories in light of the common heuristic of mothering as maternal care and sacrifice, empathy, discipline and right action, forgiveness, and surrender/letting go, Lisa suggested a final step in our collaborative autoethnographic practice—(re)approaching our tales via feminist critique. In telling an isolated autoethnographic tale, none of us may have been self-reflexive enough to recognize our role in (re)producing the cultural institution of motherhood via the story we chose to tell about mothering. Yet in combination, this (re)production across our stories cannot be denied, which illustrates a value-added component of collaborative autoethnographic practice. When (re)approaching our own stories through the lens of feminist/cultural critic, we recognize the perpetual, altruistic nature of mothering, as presented in our stories, may be detrimental to women, including ourselves.

In taking a critical approach to these autoethnographic narratives, we do see an expectation that the mother be more than she is—or at least it is hoped that she will be more than she is—within some of the contexts described in the writings. The ever-present challenge for mothers to be the empathic, smiling encourager of their children is next to impossible. Yet mediated and real-life notions of maternal love challenge mothers to do the work required to be just that and such expectations of the mother have been met with criticism by feminist scholars who argue there may be significant assaults to the self when the emotional work of the mother is romanticized (Hochschild, 2003; Langford, 1994; McQuillan et al., 2008; Walzer, 2004). A feminist critique of our narratives reveals an assumption, expectation, or desire for mothers to meet the needs of their children. Yet when emotional support flows one way, a mother's needs go unmet, challenging her well-being. And, apart from Liesbeth's tale of caring for her mother, the implicit idea of the mother meeting the needs of her child remains unchallenged. If mothering means determining and then meeting needs, we must also ask: What about the mother's needs? This question points to the culturally perceived selflessness involved in mothering.

Connecting the virtue of selflessness with motherhood suggests a great focus on caring for children and offers an explanation for the uniquely valued maternal role. And yet such lofty expectations for altruistic endurance can force mothers to keep a particular narrative going that may wear thin without structures of significant support in place. Well into adulthood, we may be unable to let go of motherhood as the "place" or "space" that embodies the favored story of who we are. At the same time, a collaborative autoethnographic practice reveals spaces in these stories that release individual mothers from such responsibility. Renee relieves herself from having sole responsibility for the cakes by attributing the reason for making them to her mother's practice and then including her mother and her aunt in mothering as a communal activity. Lisa's mother, in an epic decision, refuses the possibly life-saving treatment her daughter desperately wants her to receive. And Erika's mother's contemplation of possibly leaving challenges the conception of mother as the one who not only is always there, but as the one whose primary desire is to always be there.

6. Final Thoughts on Collaborative Autoethnographic Practice

In summary, our collaborative autoethnographic practice involved a series of elements. We started with individually writing autoethnographic narratives on a shared topic of lived experience (in this case, mothering). We then performed these narratives in a public forum, sharing our stories with each other and the audience. In and after the panel discussion, we discussed the heuristic commonalities across these autoethnographic narratives and tied those commonalities back to the literature on the topic of the lived experience of mothering. In our discussion of commonalities, we realized that we had (un)intentionally reproduced cultural scripts of mothering and therefore revisited the autoethnographic narratives through the lens of social critique. Presenting knowledge (of mothering) in this way, through collaborative autoethnographic practice, creates a myriad of opportunities for growth and learning, yet also involves some challenges.

In many ways, our collaborative ethnographic process is an excellent example of the social construction of reality and knowledge. While each person's story offers insights about the facets of mothering, the concept of mothering becomes not just an additive accumulation of these insights but instead the juxtapositioning of these facets creates something new in terms of a conceptualization of mothering. Concomitantly, we have wondered how the combining of multiple stories in a dialogic/collaborative approach might modify the initially perceived reality as lived by the original writer. Stated another way, in this collaborative process, as we seek to delve deeper and perhaps broaden the application, is there something lost in the original point of view of the story? Or, do multiple views allow readers to get something out of the situation they would not have otherwise? How does the notion of the "revision of reality" come into play in collaborative autoethnographic practice and whose reality matters most? What implications does this question have for how and if people will utilize and build upon this method in the future?

Furthermore, these stories have presented us with opportunities to witness moments that reveal the complexity of mothering, yet they also uncover some challenges in bringing these stories to the public arena. These have to do with making public what is inherently private, and implicating and exposing significant others by sharing their intimate information with strangers for the sake of research. Sharing intimate moments brings finality to what used to be an ephemeral, evolving reality. A shared secret is no longer a secret. Our narrated experiences have now become openly accessible, public knowledge. The suspended moments that lingered in our heads have become stories that are, in a way, now out of our control. For some, the release of the story may be a cathartic experience. For others, seeing their story in writing may be an unwelcome form of finality to those cherished suspended moments. It is not unthinkable that letting go of the story is much like opening the proverbial can of worms, as it presents a new form of uncertainty: "Where to go from here? Who am I now?"

Another challenge that comes with collaborating on these stories is found in the exposure of significant others as pivotal characters in our accounts. Many of the stories told in this piece reveal fears of communicating certain messages with our mothers. Does Anne's mother mind that everyone now knows that her daughter thinks every trip with her may be the last? What if Erika's mother finds out about the letter through this publication? How would Liesbeth's mother feel if she learned that her sock habits and use of pantyliners are now public knowledge? Is it ethical to share these stories that implicate them, to an extent, without their consent? Is it fair to discuss, in the name of social science, what we are able to explain in detail here, yet unable to communicate one-on-one to the person we have revealed to be so crucial to our existence?

Ellis (2007) describes these as "situational ethics, the kind that deal with the unpredictable, often subtle, yet ethically important moments that come up in the field" and suggests that "relational ethics requires researchers to act from our hearts and minds, to acknowledge our interpersonal bonds to others" (p. 4). Bochner and Ellis (2006) suggest that autoethnography is an ethical practice, that "shows people in the process of figuring out what to do, how to live, and what their struggle means" (p. 111). Clearly, the autoethnographies presented here shed light on the dialectic tensions of mothering, both through the gifts we give and receive and through the challenges that complicate the mother-child relationship. Autoethnography as collaborative practice is as Ellis (2007) writes "a reflexive attempt to construct meaning in our lives and heal or grow from our pain" (p. 26). The seven autoethnographers remain engaged in the process of figuring out what these stories mean, what secrets to keep, and how this collaborative autoethnographic practice may offer new understandings not only of mothering, but of a multiplicity of life experiences.

REFERENCES

Bochner, A. P., & Ellis, C. (2006). Communication as autoethnography. In G. J. Shepherd, J. St. John, & T. Striphas (Eds.), *Communication as . . . : Perspectives on theory* (pp. 110–122). Thousand Oaks, CA: Sage.

Denzin, N. K. (1997). *Interpretive ethnography: Ethnographic practices for the 21st century.* Thousand Oaks, CA: Sage.

Edelman, H. (2006). *Motherless daughters: The legacy of loss.* Cambridge, MA: DaCapo Lifelong.

Ellingson, L. (2009). *Engaging crystallization in qualitative research: An introduction.* Thousand Oaks, CA: Sage.

Ellis, C. (2004). *The ethnographic I: A methodological novel about autoethnography.* Walnut Creek, CA: AltaMira.

Ellis, C. (2007). Telling secrets, revealing lives: Relational ethics in research with intimate others. *Qualitative Inquiry, 13*, 3–29.

Ellis, C. (2009). *Revision: The autoethnographic reflections of life and work.* Walnut Creek, CA: Left Coast Press, Inc.

Glass-Coffin, B. (2006). A mother's love: Gender, altruism, and spiritual transformation. *Journal of Religion & Science, 41*, 893–902.

Goodall, H. L., Jr. (2005). Narrative inheritance: A nuclear family with toxic secrets. *Qualitative Inquiry, 11*, 492–513.

Goodall, H. L., Jr. (2008). *Writing qualitative inquiry: Self, stories, and academic life.* Walnut Creek, CA: Left Coast Press, Inc.

Hochschild, A. R. (2003). *The second shift.* New York: Penguin.

Langford, W. (1994). Gender, power and self-esteem: Women's poverty in the economy of love. *Feminist Theology, 3*, 94–115.

McQuillan, J., Greil, A. L., Shreffler, K. M., & Tichenor, V. (2008). The importance of motherhood among women in the contemporary United States. *Gender and Society, 22*, 477–495.

Poulos, C. N. (2009). *Accidental ethnography: An inquiry into family secrets.* Walnut Creek, CA: Left Coast Press, Inc.

Quindlen, A. (2005). *Loud and clear.* New York: Ballantine.

Richardson, L. (2000). Writing: A method of inquiry. In N. K. Denzin & Y. S. Lincoln (Eds.), *Handbook of qualitative research* (pp. 923–948). Thousand Oaks, CA: Sage.

Rothman, B. (1989). *Recreating motherhood: Ideology and technology in a patriarchal society.* New York: Norton.

Walzer, S. (2004). Encountering oppositions: A review of scholarship about motherhood. In M. Coleman & L. H. Ganong (Eds.), *Handbook of contemporary families* (pp. 209–223). Thousand Oaks, CA: Sage.

Received 2 March 2010
Accepted 13 July 2010

Index

A

academe 126, 145, 162, 168
academics 39, 65–66, 70
academy 11, 34, 65–66, 115–116, 138
    U.S. 11, 63, 84
    women 27, 116, 130
        of color 141, 146, 151
activism 144–146, 148, 166
    research 13
actors, researcher as 25, 81
Adams, T. 162, 165
administrators 20, 105, 145, 147–149
advocating for change 145
AE
    comparison with CAE 21–22, 24,
        33–35, 89, 110, 156
    data 71, 89, 138, 178
    data types 7, 74
    definition 17–18, 23, 187
    evocative 19
    individual 42, 53, 76, 148
    limitations 21
    method 88, 133
    narratives 128, 175, 178, 185–186
    purpose and scope 22
    stories 66, 183
    tales 176, 182
    value of 176
    writing styles 20, 146
AE approaches
    analytic 20, 32, 169
    co-constructed 140
    collective 37, 56
    dialogical 46
    evocative 65, 163
    performance 52, 169
African American 64–65, 126, 129, 134
age 107, 165, 169, 184
American Educational Research
    Association 71, 161

analysis
    collaborative 33, 48, 65
    ethnohistorical 56
    layer of 102
analytical-interpretive *see* writing,
    analytical-interpretive
Anderson, L. 18, 20, 22–23, 32, 161
assumptions 50, 59, 98, 185
ATLAS.ti 109–110
audio recordings 97–98, 102
authorship 33, 43, 70, 74, 118, 121–123
autobiographical 17–19, 21, 23,
    53, 140
    collecting data 44–45, 68, 86
    data 24, 37, 44–45, 70, 86
    experiences 125
    stories 56, 99
autobiography 17–19, 139
autoethnographers 18–20, 58, 72–73
autoethnographic research 18, 21,
    71, 75, 126, 137
    methods 18, 78
    process 23, 48, 59–60
autoethnography *see* AE

B

balance, work-life 15, 65
Barry, B. 62, 161, 165
Black women clergy 142
Bleil, P. 63, 139, 161
Bochner, A. 18–19, 38, 87, 164,
    168, 187
Boud, D. 116–117
Boyd, D. 144, 162, 167
bulimia 20, 35, 42, 59, 65, 169

C

CAE
    applications 140–141, 146
    activism 13

class project 43, 64, 140, 143, 159
  community building 145, 147
  pedagogy 139–140
  reflexive teaching 139
benefits 12, 25
challenges 30
community building 25, 29–30, 49, 129, 143
data collection 100
definition 11–13, 17, 21, 23
dialogic 22–23, 52, 167, 186
of doctoral experiences 77
focus 83–84
iterative process 24
labels 21, 46
limitations 12
published 29, 40, 148
research method 11, 18, 36
research process 53, 134
researcher 62
team 26, 37, 82, 118, 154
  ideal 58–59
  members 120
team size
  larger 37
  smaller 37
  two-person 37–38
typology 5
Cann, C. N. 162
CAQDAS (computer-assisted qualitative data analysis software) 13, 95, 109–110, 120
categories 7, 102–107
cathartic experience 186
celebrate 131–132, 153, 156, 179
Chang, H. 26, 63, 78–79, 82, 111
Chatham-Carpenter, A. 29, 65, 108
class, social 80, 112
co/autoethnographic 21, 139
co-ethnography 21, 37
co-participants 43, 48
co-researcher relationship 144
co-researchers 44, 48–53
  experience 145
  protection 34

unfamiliar 64
coauthors 131, 134
codes 7, 104–106
  initial 104
  new 104
  preconstructed 104–105
coding 98, 103–104
  micro 104–105
cognitive processing 79
Cohen, L. 39, 67, 86, 93
Coia, L. 44, 139–140
collaboration
  definition 11
  extent 11–12
    full 41, 68, 123–124, 153, 155
    partial 52
  mode 12, 37, 45, 52
    concurrent 13, 44–45, 49, 51, 69, 90–92
    sequential 44–45, 68–69, 88, 90
  model 55, 71, 138
  process 41, 61
  situation 45, 69
collaborative
  data 56, 73
  discussion 49, 177
  process 58–59, 129, 133, 186
  self-analysis 55
  self-exploration 55
  writing, process 130, 134, 155
collaborative autoethnographers 23, 37, 56, 89–90
collaborative autoethnographic approaches 46–47
collaborative autoethnographic practice 41, 146–147, 175–177, 182, 185
collaborative autoethnography see CAE
collaborative research
  circle 121
  meaning-making 110
  steps 42
collection 87
collective voice 70, 146

color
    faculty of 26, 39, 84, 88
    leaders of 76, 89
    researchers of 40
    students of 48
    women of 11, 31
commonalities 17, 21, 23, 41, 83–84, 95, 129, 176
    heuristic 41, 175–176, 178, 186
communal 13, 29, 51, 137, 178
communication 30, 119, 132, 154
community autoethnography 49–50, 58, 144
community ethnography 49, 144
computer-assisted qualitative data analysis software *see* CAQDAS
conceptual frameworks 67
confidentiality 29–30, 33–34, 70–72
consensus 61, 63–64, 145
    building 30, 32
consent 33, 70, 72, 78, 187
constellation of relationships 173
contexts 11, 23, 178
    shared 119
    sociocultural 17–19, 53, 98, 113
continuum 18, 20, 124, 153
Corbin, J. K. 103, 169
core strengths 154
Creswell, J. W. 101, 162
critique
    feminist 184–185
    social 41, 175–176, 186
cross-gender mentoring 107
cultural groups 17, 83
culture 146, 164, 169, 171
culturegram 7, 79–80, 99
Curtis, A. 118, 123–124, 154, 166

D
data
    archival 5, 12, 74–75, 77–78, 102
    audio 96–98
    documents 73
    excerpts 107–108
    fragments 21, 93, 98, 104, 107
    labeling 104

    personal 21, 87
    personal memory 75, 103
    pool 26–27, 42, 45, 76, 89
    segments 103–104, 179
    self-analytical 5, 78–79, 83
    set 45, 96, 98, 102
    shared 101
    sources 23, 27, 77, 86, 92
        external 73
        text 50, 74, 95, 97
        visual 96–97
data analysis
    autoethnographic 59
    collaborative 109
    direction 85
    goal 101
    macro-review 102–105
    micro-review 103–104
    qualitative 101–102, 110, 138
    segmenting 98, 102, 104–105
data analysis and interpretation, stage of 27, 98
data collection
    activities 78, 88
    collaborative 86, 89, 92
    group 89–90
    individual 87, 89, 99, 147
    model 46, 90
        concurrent 99
        sequential 90
    process 44–45, 87–88, 100
    qualitative 12
    self-analytical 79, 83
    sessions 27, 87–88
    topics 88, 140
data interpretation 6, 66, 95, 98, 110–113
data management 5, 95–96
data organization 13, 95–96, 98
Davis, W. 165–166
deadlines 31
decision-making 32, 40, 45, 119, 121, 153
Delamont, S. 38
DeLyser, D. 116
DeMeulenaere, E. 162

Denzin, N. 111
depression 33–34, 127, 129–130
descriptive-realistic *see* writing,
    descriptive-realistic
design, flexibility 67
differences 23, 48, 51, 61, 83–84, 144
    community of 144
    negotiating 92
Dillman, D. 139, 159
disagreements 56–58, 90, 156
discourse, academic 19–20
discovery 110, 142, 144
discrimination, racial 29
doctoral
    dissertation advisor 76–77
    dissertations 15, 142
    experiences 77, 127
    program 63, 117, 127
doctoral students
    CAE 14, 39–40, 64, 77, 87
    of color 48, 127
dual roles 18, 22
Duberley, J. 67, 86, 92–93
duoethnography 46

E
e-mail exchanges 31, 86, 92,
    119–120, 142
Easterby-Smith, M. 57, 61
educational research 139
Ellingson, L. L. 176–177
Ellis, C. 18–19, 23, 38, 49, 85
emotional experiences 44, 163
empathy 183–184
empowerment 148
    co-researchers 145
    personal 147
    students 147
Espino 129
ethical standards 71–72
ethics 30, 72, 122, 140
    practical 72
    procedural 131
    relational 72, 131, 187
ethnicity 25–26, 64–65, 80, 107, 112
ethnographic 18, 20, 53

ethnography, definition 17
evocative 13, 19, 21–22, 124
experiences, shared 11, 129, 134

F
faculty learning community 147–148
faith 15, 130
family 11, 73, 79, 177, 179–180
    member 138
    relationships 71, 81
father 180
Ferguson, T. 117
fiction 71, 125
Finley, S. 52
flexibility 70, 87–88, 110
focus group 148, 152
forgiveness 183–184
Fornicola, G. 63, 139, 143, 161
forum, public 41, 175–176, 182, 186
Furman, R. 42, 59, 129

G
Galligan, L. 117
Geertz, C. 93
Geist-Martin, P. 57, 119
gender 65, 80, 84, 107
Glass-Coffin, B. 184
Glesne, C. 98, 101
Goodall, Jr., H. L. 177
grounded theory 102–103,
    161–162, 169
group
    member
        roles 121
        tasks 7, 122
    process 33, 66, 69, 88, 131–132
    supportive 129
    writing 117, 151
grouping, topical 104
guidelines, ethical 33–34, 70–71,
    78, 141

H
Hernández, F. 40, 42, 57
Hernandez, K. C. 39, 79,
    146, 159

higher education 38, 65, 107, 130, 147
  institutions 39, 56
  leaders of color 97, 107
HyperRESEARCH 109–110

I
identities 48, 57, 80, 99, 144
identity
  construction 26, 48, 57
  doctoral student 127
  researcher 48, 127
  scholar 57
  teacher educator 140
  the unemployed 79
illness 19–20
immigrant faculty 56
  women of color 97, 159
individual stories 28, 42, 60, 69, 108
  sharing 60, 120
  writing 129
informed consent 71–72, 131
Institutional Review Board *see* IRB
instrument 22, 24, 117
interactive interview 59, 78, 85–87, 98
interests, common 30, 56, 58, 61–63
interpretation
  autoethnographic 19
  cultural 23
interpretive narration 19
interpretive paradigms 111–112
intersubjectivity 18
interview 74, 138, 152, 172
  data 85, 91, 138
inventorying exercises 76
IRB (Institutional Review Board) 33, 71, 131, 140
IRB approval 71–72, 131
iterative process 24, 93

J
Jago, B. J. 33–34
Jew 59
journal, personal 41, 74, 77
journey, doctoral 127
justice, social 56, 166–167

K
Kalmbach Phillips, D. 40–41, 65
Kiesinger, C. 42, 49, 85
kinsgram 7, 81–82
Kiyama, J. M. 129
knowledge 43, 49, 52, 97
  construction 141, 146–147, 186
  prior 56–57
  public 186–187

L
Langer, C. L. 42, 59, 87
Langford, W. 184
Lapadat, J. 75, 78, 132, 140
Larcombe, W. 117
layoff, women executives 63, 100, 142
leadership 76, 105, 145
  mentoring 138
  position 105
learning 142–143, 148, 161
  collaborative 13, 137
  holistic 108
  from others 12
Lee, A. 161, 166
lens 22, 28, 139
  feminist/cultural critic 185
  social critique 186
Lewins, A. 109–110
Lietz, C. A. 42, 59, 65, 87
Lincoln, Y. S. 163
lived experiences 42, 45, 50, 53, 56, 58
log, written 172–173
logistical challenges 30–31, 39
long-term colleagues 57
Lowry, M. R. 118, 120, 123
Lowry, P. B. 118, 120, 123
Lund, D. E. 50–51, 144

M
MAXQDA 109–110
Maxwell, J. A. 99, 101
McAllister, M. 71
McClafferty 117, 168
McDonald 164

McMillan, S. 125, 145, 147
meaning-making 23, 28, 110–111
    group 24, 33, 118
    individual 24, 147
    interpretive 113
members, non-autoethnographer 58
membership 63, 80, 121
memory
    data 75, 77, 79
    personal 12, 74–75, 77,
        96–97, 138
memory work 75, 95, 165
memos 74, 103, 105
    writing 103
mentoring
    experiences 64, 89, 107
    professional 107
    relationships 39, 77
mentors 107, 138, 171
Militello, M. 48
Mills, G. 102
Moreno, J. 175
Morse, J. 71
Morss, K. 117
mother, love 180–181
mother-child 179, 183–185
motherhood 20, 27, 184
mothering 40, 49
    complexities of 175, 177
    shared stories of 125, 164, 175
    topic of 41, 48, 176
mothering experiences 120, 183
mothers, teen 39, 83
multivocality 130, 144
Muncey, T. 83, 126
Muñoz, S. M. 129
Murakami-Ramalho, E. 65, 83
Murray, R. 117
Musson, G. 39, 46, 67

N
Nabavi 51, 144, 147
narrative
    interpretation 19–20, 25
    reflection 129
narratives 43, 65, 129

negotiation among researchers 39–40,
    57, 60
Ngunjiri, F. W. 15, 26, 39, 133
nodes 81
Norris, J. 50–51, 133
NVivo 97–98, 109

O
O'Brien, L. 71
observation 99, 173
online discussion 97, 148
O'Shea, E. R. 40, 65
others
    of difference 83
    of opposition 83
    of similarity 82–83
ownership, of data 34

P
paradigm 35, 112
    traditional 25–26, 116
participants 24–25, 29, 70, 121, 134,
    159
    female 107
    involuntary 33, 72
partnerships 148–149, 164
    university-community 148
patterns 98, 153
Paulus, T. M. 62, 69, 113
peace 127
performance 52–53
performative 51–52, 146
phases, pre-writing 123
phenomena, sociocultural 19, 24, 26, 94
photos 74, 97
Piert, J. 39, 48
pilot studies 138, 141–142
place 78, 96, 179, 185
plática 129
poetry 99, 108, 125
Position Statement on Qualitative
    Research and IRBs 34
Poulos, C. N. 177
power
    differential 26, 34, 43, 66, 140
    sharing 12, 101

predetermined schema 74
Price, M. A. 125, 145, 147, 166
probing
      questions 58–59, 68–69, 86
      sessions 86
professional development 148
proximity 30–31, 119
publication pipeline 152–153

Q
QDA Miner 109–110
qualitative, inquiry 17, 67, 131
qualitative research
      process 109, 138
      textbooks 101
      traditions 101, 103
qualitative research method 12,
      17, 102

R
racism 126, 166, 168
Rawlins, W. K. 38, 77
recollection 74, 77, 79
recording, audio 78–79, 98
redirect, research focus 92
reflexivity 79, 140, 162–164
regrouping data 98, 102, 104, 108
relational diagrams 79, 81
relationships
      co-researcher 140
      collegial 56, 143
      developmental 172
      student-mentor 79
report, final 32–33, 118
representation 25, 43, 111, 163
research
      agendas 151
      direction 58, 66–67
      focus 55, 62–63, 67, 92, 99
      participants 26, 33, 43, 67
      questions 125, 152, 155
      social science 27, 43, 71–72
      topic 62, 75, 99
research design, flexibility 67
research team
      collaborative 26, 58, 97, 148

effective 56, 60
manageable 62
ready-made 131
size 5, 52
research teammates 111–112
researcher
      backgrounds 57, 63, 112, 138
      boundaries 55, 69–71
      educational 127, 161, 168
      roles 132
      self 21
researcher-participants 18, 21–22,
      25–26, 112, 138, 146
researcher subjectivity 25, 100
responsibilities
      defining 69, 119–121, 131
      dividing 70
      shared 15, 40–41
reviewers 116, 128, 155
Rhee, J. 38, 66
rights 33–34, 70
Robinson, R. 83
roles, defining 55, 69, 71
Ronai, C. 49

S
sacrifice 183–184
Saldaña, J. 96, 103
Sawyer, R. 50–51, 133
scope 22, 148, 154
secrets 134
self-analysis 55, 78
self-observation 5, 77–78, 85, 97
self-reflection 78–79, 85
self-reflexivity 17, 26, 79, 175
shadowing 173
Silver, C. 109–110
similarities 83–85
Smith, B. 92, 169
Smith, C. 20, 169
Smith, J. A. 102, 169
social
      context 30, 34, 119
      network 30, 81, 129
      phenomena 24–25, 35, 112
sociogram 7, 81–83

solidarity 142–144
spirituality 144, 148, 162
stained-glass ceiling 142
standpoint 112
Stephens, N. 38, 169
stories
    abortion 39
    coherent 49
    cohesive 98, 128
    collective 129, 161
    competing 128
    evocative 19
    favored 185
    good 98
    individuals' 45
    interpretive 18
    intimate 60
    life 18, 26, 29, 72, 142
    mothers 179
    multiple 109, 186
    participant 43
    personal 18, 26
    self-esteem 108
    sensitive 61
    sharing 129, 175
    short 99, 176
    situated 177
    written 177
strategies, storing 96
Strauss, A. L. 103
Stringer, E. T. 49
students, hands-on experiences of 138
Subedi, B. 38, 66
subjectivity 18, 25–26, 41, 100
subjects
    human 33, 43, 71
    of investigation 18, 26, 33, 65, 72
subtopic 66, 90
support
    emotional 117, 134
    graduate research 162
synthesize 79–80

T
Taylor, M. 44, 139–140
teachers, pre-service 139

team 154
    conflict 34, 57, 61, 69
    conflict resolution 61
    formation 118, 120
    leader 121
    model 27
    recruit 63, 89
    seven-person 128, 178
    two-person 60
teamwork 23, 161
tenure 12, 105, 152
text 111, 141, 144
themes 7, 98, 107, 155
    analysis of 108
    definition 106
    finding 102, 106, 110
theming 106–107
Thorne, S. 2, 95, 111–112, 169
Tolich, M. 33–34, 131
topics
    professional 20, 65
    recurring 103–104
    selected 44, 69, 90
    sensitive 29, 86
Toyosaki, S. 45, 49, 58, 63, 86
Transana 109–110
transcription, audio data 97–98
trust 30, 50–51, 61
trustworthiness 30
tutor-student relationship 66
typology 46, 123–125, 128

U
unanswered question 180–181
understanding, deeper 23, 25, 28, 103, 144
university 146–149, 164
utterances 74–75

V
values 83
Venn diagram 7, 83–85
voices
    composite 29, 60
    different 27, 113
    dominant 32

multiple 25, 32, 123, 128–130
silencing 32
stifled 32
vulnerability 30, 48, 108, 129,
143, 145

W
wanderer 125, 127, 167
war 39, 66, 127, 169
warrior 125, 127, 167
White privilege 29, 40, 57–58
whiteness 50, 65, 144
wives 27–28
women
business leaders 161
of color 11, 31, 39, 121,
141, 145
of faith 130
in higher education 31
identity 28
immigrant 11, 130, 151
faculty 97
minority 145
shared experience 11
women executives

layoff 63, 88, 100, 142, 159
mentoring 142
Woodside, M. 62, 69–70, 110, 113
Wray, K. B. 62, 170
writing
collaborative 60, 118, 124, 151
collaborative autoethnographic
117, 120
pre-CAE 13, 115, 118
writing prompts 88–90, 99, 148
writing styles 124, 126–127,
146, 156
analytical-interpretive 102,
124–125, 127, 153
confessional-emotive 102,
124–127, 129
descriptive-realistic 124–125, 127
imaginative-creative 124
Wyatt, J. 19

Y
youth activist 147

Z
Ziegler, M. F. 69–70, 155

About the Authors

Heewon Chang, Ph.D., is a professor of multicultural education and organizational leadership at Eastern University in Philadelphia, Pennsylvania. After completing a bachelor's degree in education at Yonsei University in South Korea, she came to the University of Oregon to pursue a Master's and Ph. D. in educational anthropology under the tutelage of Dr. Harry Wolcott. She has authored/edited three books: *Adolescent Life and Ethos: An Ethnography of a US High School* (1992), *Autoethnography as Method* (2008), and *Spirituality in Higher Education: Autoethnographies* (2011, edited with Drick Boyd). "Her writings, in particular on autoethnography," have appeared in various journals and books including *Handbook of Autoethnography* (2013). Her research agenda includes qualitative research methods including autoethnography, leadership mentoring, educational equity and justice, multicultural education, and anthropology of education. She founded two open-access scholarly journals and currently serves the *International Journal of Multicultural Education* (www.ijme-journal. org) as editor-in-chief.

Faith Wambura Ngunjiri, Ed.D., is an associate professor of leadership studies and research methods at Eastern University, where she also serves as Director of Research at the graduate college. She has a doctorate in leadership studies and master's degree in organization development from Bowling Green State University, Bowling Green, Ohio; a master's degree in mission studies from Nairobi Evangelical Graduate School of Theology; and a bachelor's degree in education (language and literature) from Kenyatta University in Kenya. Her research interests revolve around women and leadership, particularly studies on African women, servant leadership, spirituality, and tempered radicalism. She also teaches and writes about culturally responsive research approaches. Her work has been published in *Journal of Research Practice, International and Intercultural Communication Annual, Journal of Business Communication, Journal of Educational Administration, UCEA Review, Gendered Perspectives on International Development,* and *Journal of Pan African Studies.* She is the author of *Women's Spiritual Leadership in Africa: Tempered Radicals and Critical Servant Leaders* (State University of New York Press, 2010). Faith is president and coach at Global Leadership Development, LLC, a company focused on coaching, mentoring, training, educating, and developing authentic leaders.

Kathy-Ann C. Hernandez, Ph.D. is an associate professor of educational psychology and research methods and Director of Research for the Loeb School of Education at Eastern University. She is also CEO of Nexe Consulting in Philadelphia. She earned a bachelor's degree in English literature and behavioral science and a master's degree in educational administration and supervision from Andrews University, and a Ph.D. in educational psychology from Temple University. A regular presenter at academic conferences, she researches and writes on the Black Diaspora, the role of cultural ethnicity, gender, spirituality, and class in identity formation, and research methods. She is author of several book chapters and journal articles. Her work has been published in the *Journal of Research Practice*, the *Journal of Black Masculinity*, and *Callaloo*. As a scholar-practitioner, she regularly consults with the School District of Philadelphia, and has conducted work for the Center for Research in Human Development and Education at Temple University, the Government of the British Virgin Islands, and the University of the Virgin Islands. She is author of *Black Masculinities and Spirituality* (Information Age, 2014).